Stylin' with CSS:
A Designer's Guide

CHARLES WYKE-SMITH

New
Riders

Stylin' with CSS: A Designer's Guide
Charles Wyke-Smith

New Riders
1249 Eighth Street
Berkeley, CA 94710
510/524-2178
800/283-9444
510/524-2221 (fax)

Find us on the World Wide Web at: www.peachpit.com
To report errors, please send a note to errata@peachpit.com
New Riders is an imprint of Peachpit, a division of Pearson Education

Project Editor: Cheryl England
Production Editor: Andrei Pasternak
Copyeditor: Rebecca C. Rider
Tech Editor: Shaun Inman
Compositor: Owen Wolfson
Indexer: Julie Bess
Cover design: Aren Howell
Cover Image: Veer
Interior design: Mimi Heft

ISBN 0-321-30525-6

9 8 7 6 5 4 3 2

Printed and bound in the United States of America

For Jemma and Lucy

Acknowledgements

First, my most heartfelt thanks go to my delightful and beautiful wife Beth and our two lovely daughters, who have endured nine months of me shutting myself in my home office virtually every evening and weekend. I love you all and I promise to make up to you the parties I missed, the movies I did not go to, and the housework I avoided (well, maybe not that).

Next, I'll thank Michael Nolan of New Riders, longtime friend, business associate, and New Riders acquisitions editor, for advocating my book and calling frequently during the writing process to ask me when I was going to be finished. Next is Cheryl England of Peachpit Press who has been the most supportive, enthusiastic, and conscientious editor I could hope for and who has improved this book immeasurably.

Also at Peachpit, I have to thank managing editor Marjorie Baer, production coordinator Andrei Pasternak, designer Mimi Heft, cover designer Aren Howell, and marketing maven Kim Lombardi for helping to bring *Stylin'* to life. A special thanks goes to one of the smartest people in the world of Web, Shaun Inman, for being *Stylin'*'s technical editor and making sure that my mistakes were caught and the finer nuances of CSS were accurately explained.

At Nacio, where I work, I'll sincerely thank Stephen King, Thom Kennon, and Murray Goldenberg for giving me the time and support I needed to write this book. And thanks to Adam London, Eddie Colmanares, Arkardy Kaminski, Demetrio Cuzzocrea, Kris Fragmeni, and Herb Gottlieb, for making my work day fun.

Next, I'll bow down while repeating "Unworthy, unworthy", before Jeffrey Zeldman, Molly Holzschlag, Eric Meyer, and Doug Bowman, the Web gurus whose work has changed the face of the Web for the better, thoroughly influenced my work, and, who, through their writing and seminars have taught me, and thousands of others, so much; it was a great experience to meet and spend time with them at the South by Southwest interactive conference in Austin, TX this year.

Closer to home, special thanks to Russ, Elizabeth, Devin and Shannon Mayhew, and Robert, Bonnie and Dakota Mitchell for always being there for our family and for helping out in numerous ways while I was writing this book. And, Russ, yes, it's actually finished.

I'll thank Ken Ruotolo of ANTS software, inc. for being a true friend, business associate, and client and Dave Kleinberg, my long-time business mentor who turned out to be an absolutely incredible musician too! Thanks for everything, guys.

A sad mention for Flash whiz Rob Meyer, who died recently, far too young.

And a tip of the hat to some true friends and creative forces: Chuck Berg, Steve Haney, Frank Ruotolo, Judy Dang, Jim Hollenbeck, Austin Markus, Donna Casey, Paul Markun, Debbie Torgan, Raphael Olivas, and Russ Volkmann.

I am fortunate to know everyone mentioned here.

—*Charles Wyke-Smith, March 28th 2005*

About the Author

Photo – Lowell Downey,
Art and Clarity, Napa, CA

Charles Wyke-Smith has been creating Web sites since 1994 and is currently Director of Production at Nacio (www.nacio.com), a corporate hosting and development company in Novato, CA. In 1986, Charles started PRINTZ Electronic Design, which was the first all-computerized design house in San Francisco. The former vice-president of Web development for eStar.com, a celebrity information site, Charles has worked as a Web design consultant for such companies as Wells Fargo, ESPN Videogames, and the University of San Francisco. An accomplished speaker and instructor, he has also taught multimedia and interface design and spoken at many industry conferences. Charles lives in Napa Valley, CA with his wife Beth and two daughters. In his spare time, he composes and records music in his home studio. Charles has also written one screenplay and is busily working on a second one.

Contents

INTRODUCTION • X

CHAPTER 1 : XHTML: GIVING STRUCTURE TO CONTENT • 2

Sorry, IDWIMIE • 4

The Times They Are A-Changing • 7
A Legacy of Kluges • 7
Let's Play Spot the Content! • 8
The Future Will Be Here Soon • 9

XHTML and How to Write It • 10
XHTML Markup Rules • 11
Understanding Markup • 17
Document Hierarchy: Meet the XHTML Family • 25

CHAPTER 2 : HOW CSS WORKS • 28

The Three Ways to Style Your Document • 30
Inline Styles • 30
Embedded Styles • 32
Linked Styles • 33

Anatomy of a CSS Rule • 35

Writing CSS Rules • 35

Targeting Tags Within the Document Hierarchy • 36
Using Contextual Selectors • 37
Working with Child Selectors • 40
Adding Classes and IDs • 41
Simple Use of a Class • 42
Contextual Class Selectors • 43
Introducing IDs • 46
The Difference Between IDs and Classes • 46
The Universal Selector • 47
The Adjacent Sibling Selector • 48
Attribute Selectors • 48
Summary of Selectors • 50

Pseudo-Classes • 50
Anchor Link Pseudo-Classes • 50
Other Useful Pseudo-Classes • 52

Pseudo-elements • **53**

Inheritance • **54**

The Cascade • **55**
Sources of Styles • 55
The Cascade Rules • 57

Rule Declarations • **60**
Numerical Values • 61
Color Values • 63

CHAPTER 3 : STYLIN' FONTS AND TEXT • 66

Specifying Fonts in CSS • **69**
Introducing Font Collections • 69

Exploring Font Families • **72**
Using Embedded Styles (for Now) • 74
Setting the Font Family for the Entire Page • 75

Sizing Fonts • **76**
Inherited styles in nested tags • 81

Font Properties • **83**
Font-Style Property • 83
Font-Weight Property • 84
Font-Variant Property • 85
The Font Property Shorthand • 85

Text Properties • **86**
Text-Indent Property • 88
Letter-Spacing Property • 90
Word-Spacing Property • 91
Text-Decoration Property • 91
Text-Align Property • 92
Line-Height Property • 92
Text-Transform Property • 94
Vertical-Align Property • 95

Using Font and Text Styles • **97**

CHAPTER 4 : POSITIONING ELEMENTS • 100

Understanding the Box Model • **102**
The Box Border • 103
The Box Padding • 106
The Box Margins • 106
Collapsing Margins • *108*

How Big Is a Box? • **109**

The Position Property • **112**
Static Positioning • 112
Relative Positioning • 113
Absolute Positioning • 114
Fixed Positioning • 115
Positioning Context • 116

Floating and Clearing • **117**
The Float Property • 117
The Clear Property • 119

The Display Property • **122**

CHAPTER 5 : BASIC PAGE LAYOUT • **124**

A Simple Two-Column Layout • **126**

Three-Column Layout • **130**

Three-Column Layout with Header • **135**

Three-Column Layouts with Float and Clear • **139**
The Alsett Clearing Method • 144

CHAPTER 6 : ADVANCED PAGE LAYOUT • **148**

A Digression on Backgrounds • **150**
Background Basics • 151

Building Full-Length Columns • **153**
Faux-Column Technique • 154
Columns for Fluid Center Layouts • 160

A Robust Fluid Layout • **162**

A Template With Negative Margins • **167**

CHAPTER 7 : CREATING INTERFACE COMPONENTS • **172**

Understanding Lists • **174**
Styling Lists • 176
Basic Link Styling • 184

Creating CSS-Based Menus • **186**
Horizontal Navigation Components • 186
The Hover Behavior for Internet Explorer • 193

Creating Drop-Down Menus • **195**
Marking Up Drop-Down Menus • 195

Making Multiple Level Drop-Downs • **203**
Rollovers with Graphical Backgrounds • 205

Developing Forms • **208**
Understanding the Form Element • 208
Adding Radio Buttons and Check Boxes • 213
Creating a Form Select • 215
Two Final Touches • *216*

Implementing Search • **217**

CHAPTER 8 : BUILDING WEB SITES • **220**

Getting Started With the Snergs Site • **222**
Setting Up the Folder Structure • 223
Creating the Site Architecture • 226

Modifying the Markup • **227**
Creating the Header • 230
Creating the Left Navigation • 232
Styling the Right Column • 234
Styling the News Links • 238
Creating the Content Area • 241
Creating a Caption for the Main Image • *241*
Styling the Footer • 243

Cleanup Time • **246**
Constraining Min and Max Widths • 251

In Closing . . . • **252**

APPENDIX : CSS PROPERTIES AND VALUES • **254**

INDEX • **266**

Introduction

Stylin' was inspired by my friend Dan Reich, who called me back in spring of 2004 with a CSS question. After I provided a lengthy explanation about what he needed to do, he said, "You should put this all in a book—I'd buy it." So I jotted down a few ideas about what I would put into a CSS book and thought no more about it until a month later when my former business partner Michael Nolan, who is now an acquisitions editor for New Riders, called me to ask if I had any names of potential authors for Web related books. Fatefully, I uttered the word "Me?" and after a brief discussion of my ideas, sent him my outline. Within two weeks, *Stylin'* was scheduled for publication. All I had to do then was write it.

I have discovered that writing a book is no trivial task. Before I started, I asked another New Riders author, Jesse James Garrett, if he liked writing, and he replied: "I like having written." Now I know what he means. Part of the reason that *Stylin'* has been a nine-month labor-of-love (besides having two small children and full-time job) is that I have tried to make it both in-depth and easy to understand. If you want to use CSS to design Web sites you can't do it in a half-baked way. You are in or you're not in.

Web design has changed in the last few years, and CSS is at the center of that change. The focus is now on structure first, rather than presentation, so that content is clean and free of the mass of presentation tags such as FONT and table tags that ten years of presentation driven "killer Web sites" have left us with. Today, we want to present our content on a number of different user agents, such as the new generation of standards-compliant Web browsers, cell phones, and handhelds. The problem is that our Web sites are covered in presentational "chocolate sauce" written to make content display on obsolete Web browsers; some serious remedial work must be undertaken to separate the content from its presentation.

The pay-offs of are great though; using CSS, we can take clean, structural markup, and using style sheets, present it in a variety of layouts for a variety of user agents. Sites like CNN have already bitten this bullet and converted their pages to Web standards by cleaning all the presentational elements out of their content, and using CSS to lay it out onscreen; they can now look forward to the future of delivering their content easily and economically on a myriad of current and yet-to-come devices. We will examine the practical issues around this new approach to Web design in greater depth throughout this book.

Stylin' is also a very practical book, from which it is very easy to take ideas and code for your own work. I take you step-by-step from using simple typographical CSS styles through to building complex layouts created entirely from simple XHTML with all aspects of presentation controlled by CSS. Each example is designed to take your CSS skills to the next level, from basic beginner concepts to the techniques used in professional site development.

You can copy the examples, either from the book, or as code from the *Stylin'* Web site (www.bbd.com/stylin), and drop them into your designs to rapidly create numerous useful elements such as navigation links, drop-down menus, and graphical links. On the Web site, you'll find page templates for all of the layouts in the book, organized by chapter.

Also, I will show you numerous "hacks"; the term given to using CSS in ways that it was not intended, to enable consistent display of your pages across both newer, standards-compliant browsers and also the older, "legacy" browsers, still used by many, that cannot correctly interpret CSS. As long as Microsoft holds out on joining the Web standards party, the hacks must continue.

Most, of all, I hope this book will help you successfully realize your creative ideas. This is not a book about design, per se, but it *is* a book for designers, and contains key techniques you need to make standards-based Web design a reality. If you have been thinking about adopting CSS as a design tool, or want to move entirely to CSS-based presentation for your Web pages, this book is for you.

CHAPTER 1

XHTML:
Giving Structure to Content

Using different size text headers

Using basic image tags

How to separate content from presentation

How and why to validate code

Ordered vs. unordered lists

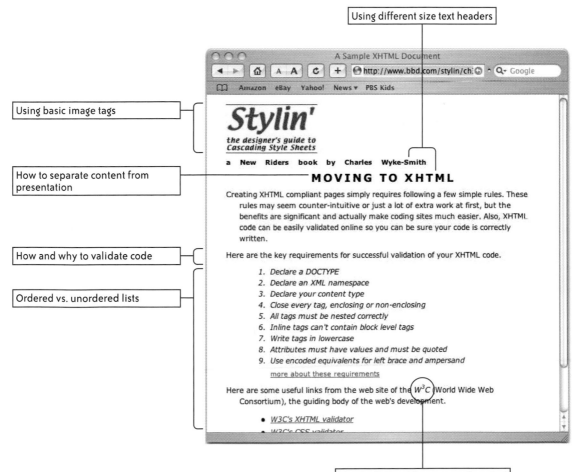

A Sample XHTML Document

http://www.bbd.com/stylin/ch...   Q▾ Google

Amazon   eBay   Yahoo!   News ▾   PBS Kids

Stylin'
the designer's guide to
Cascading Style Sheets

a   New   Riders   book   by   Charles   Wyke-Smith

MOVING TO XHTML

Creating XHTML compliant pages simply requires following a few simple rules. These rules may seem counter-intuitive or just a lot of extra work at first, but the benefits are significant and actually make coding sites much easier. Also, XHTML code can be easily validated online so you can be sure your code is correctly written.

Here are the key requirements for successful validation of your XHTML code.

1. *Declare a DOCTYPE*
2. *Declare an XML namespace*
3. *Declare your content type*
4. *Close every tag, enclosing or non-enclosing*
5. *All tags must be nested correctly*
6. *Inline tags can't contain block level tags*
7. *Write tags in lowercase*
8. *Attributes must have values and must be quoted*
9. *Use encoded equivalents for left brace and ampersand*
   more about these requirements

Here are some useful links from the web site of the W^3C (World Wide Web Consortium), the guiding body of the web's development.

* *W3C's XHTML validator*
* *W3C's CSS validator*

How to distinguish acronyms from text

Stylin' with CSS is all about designing and building Web pages that look stylish and professional, that are intuitive for visitors to use, that work across a wide variety of user agents (browsers, handhelds, cell phones, and so on) and whose content can be easily updated and distributed for other purposes.

Like any artist, your ability to achieve your creative vision is governed by your technical abilities. In this book, I'm not going to wade into all the excruciating details that underpin the workings of the Web, but I will say that without a certain degree of technical knowledge, you will never achieve your Web design goals. So this book is intended to give you the core technical information you need to realize your creative vision, and hopefully to give you the confidence to "go in" further as you build your skills. But most of all, we will focus on design; by this I mean design in its broadest sense, not just aesthetics (visual appearance), but also ergonomics (logical organization) and functionality (useful capabilities).

Everything in this book is based on *Web standards*, the rules of browser behavior defined in the recommendations of W3C (the World Wide Web Consortium), which all the major browser developers have agreed to follow. As you will see, browsers based on the Gecko engine—the current versions Mozilla/Firefox and Netscape—and those based on the Konquerer engine—including the excellent browser Safari for Mac—do a much better job delivering standards-based performance than the once-ubiquitous Microsoft Internet Explorer, which fails to implement many CSS specifications.

Every so often I'll mention CSS2 or CSS3. These terms simply refer to a specific version of the CSS standard. Just as with any technology, CSS continues to be refined.

Sorry, IDWIMIE

You might expect Internet Explorer to be the best browser, but, despite its current dominance, that is far from true. Frequently in this book, I mention a CCS feature and tell you IDWIMIE—It Doesn't Work In Microsoft Internet Explorer. Internet Explorer is frozen in a non-standards past and, as a consequence, is losing market share rapidly. For some of Internet Explorer's shortcomings, there are workarounds known as *hacks*—the non-standard use of CSS to fool particular browsers into seeing or ignoring certain styles. It's tedious and time-consuming to create hacks; Internet Explorer must get with the program or continue to lose ground to its more compliant fellow browsers.

For us Web site designers and the visitors to the sites we create, Web standards offer the prospect of sites displaying and behaving consistently in every browser, on every platform. We're not there yet, but the days of every browser supporting a different feature set, with all the resultant technical inconsistencies that can make cross-browser/cross-platform Web development slow and frustrating, are it seems, almost over.

So, following the rules of Web standards, *Stylin'* shows you how to publish *content* by defining its structure with *XHTML* and then defining its presentation with *CSS*.

Remember, XHTML defines a document's structure while CSS defines a documents presentation.

1. **Content** is the collective term for all the text, images, videos, sounds, animations, and files (such as PDF documents) that you want to deliver to your audience.

2. **XHTML** (e**X**tensible **H**yper**T**ext **M**arkup **L**anguage) enables you to define *what* each element of your content is. Is it a heading or a paragraph? Is it a list of items, a hyperlink, or an image? You determine this by adding XHTML *markup* to your content. Markup comprises tags (the tag name is enclosed in angle brackets < >) that identify each element of your content. You create an *XHTML element* (hereafter just called an element) by either surrounding a piece of content with an opening and a closing tag like this

    ```
    <p>This text content is defined by the tag as a
    paragraph</p>
    ```

    or, for content that is not text (an image, in this example), by using a single tag

    ```
    <img src="images/fido.gif" alt="a picture of my dog" />
    ```

    This chapter focuses on XHTML and how to use it, but the most important thing to know right now is this:

    XHTML defines a document's *structure*.

3. **CSS** (**C**ascading **S**tyle **S**heets) enable you to define *how* each marked-up element of your content is presented on the page. Is that paragraph's typeface Helvetica or Times, is it bold or italicized? Is it indented or flush with the edge of the page? CSS controls the formatting and positioning of each of the content elements. To format the size of the text in a paragraph, I might write

    ```
    p {font-size: 12px;}
    ```

    which would make it 12 pixels high. Almost this entire book is dedicated to teaching you CSS, but the most important thing to know right now is this:

    CSS defines a document's *presentation*.

Providing a means of separating a document's structure from its presentation was the core objective in the development of Web standards, and it is key to development of content that is both portable (can be displayed on multiple devices) and durable (ready for the future).

The Top 10 Benefits of Standards-Based Coding

You may be wondering "Why should I bother to change the way I have been marking up pages for years?" Here are ten great reasons to adopt standards-based coding practices.

1. **Deliver to multiple user agents.** The same piece of marked-up content is readily deliverable in a wide variety of browsers and other devices (or user agents, to use the official term), such as browsers, personal digital assistants (PDAs), cell phones, and devices that read text for the sight impaired. Just create a different style sheet for each use.

2. **Improve performance.** Pages are much lighter (smaller in size) and therefore download faster, because your content only needs minimal structural markup. We can now replace all of the presentational markup we used to load onto the tags in every page of a site with a single style sheet. As you will see, a single style sheet can define the presentation of an entire site and the user only needs to download it once.

3. **Serve all browsers.** With a little effort, you can have your pages degrade nicely in older browsers, so all users get the best experience possible with their available technology.

4. **Separate content and presentation.** You can modify, or entirely change, either the content or the presentation (read: design) of your site without affecting the other.

5. **Build fluid pages.** It's easier to code for varying quantities of dynamic content within your pages. For example, it's much easier to create pages that can accommodate however many items appear in a given listing or menu of your e-commerce store.

6. **Confirm your code is good.** Validation services for XHTML and CSS can be used during development to report instantly on errors in your coding. This provides faster debugging, and the assurance that a page is truly completed when it both displays correctly on screen and passes validation.

7. **Streamline production.** Production is more efficient. It's too easy for you (the designer) to be side-tracked into content management, because you are the only person who knows where the content goes in the mass of presentational markup, and so you end up being the one to add it—a tedious job and probably not what you were hired to do. By adopting standards-based practices, you can provide simple markup rules to the content team and work in parallel on the presentational aspects, knowing their content and your design will marry seamlessly down the line.

8. **Distribute content more easily.** Distributing your content for third-party use is much easier because the content is separate from any specific presentation rules, and in many cases, simply not feasible otherwise.

9. **Make it accessible.** It's easier to make your site accessible and meet legal requirements such as the Americans with Disabilities Act, Section 506, known colloquially as ADA 506.

10. **Do less work.** You write less code and it's a whole lot quicker and easier to get the results you want and modify your work over time.

The Times They Are A-Changing

To get a sense of how far from standards compliance most of today's Web sites are, we need to take a quick look back at HTML's development and examine the difficulties most sites face today.

As of early 2005, the typical Web site's markup is loaded with masses of presentational markup aimed at the capabilities of the browser for which it was written (such as Internet Explorer 5 for Windows, or the utterly obsolete Netscape 4.0). In today's world of information delivery, where you want to get your content out on not just today's standards-compliant browsers, but on cell phones, PDAs, and even the door of your viewers' refrigerators, you may be unpleasantly surprised to find that your Web site's content is tightly locked in a million yards of old presentational code.

A Legacy of Kluges

HTML was originally intended to be used to lay out pages of text containing hyperlinks to other pages of text. It was not intended to enable complex brochure-like layouts. But as soon as the Web broke out of academia and into the mainstream, that's exactly what designers wanted to do with it. And the kluges abounded.

For example, if a photographic image was considered too close to the edge of the page, a designer might use a 1-pixel-square transparent GIF image, "force-sized" with a width attribute to be much larger so that it could invisibly shove the image out into the page.

Tables were also used in creative ways. Tables are an HTML element designed for laying out grids of data (like an Excel spreadsheet), but if you need to divide a page into say, a header, navigation, and content areas, then you might use a table to divide up the page, and you would drop each piece of content into a different cell of the table. Basically, it got to the point where table-based design was almost a standard in itself and was taught as good practice in untold numbers of Web books.

When it comes to (ab)using HTML, I know of what I speak; I did these things for years myself, along with the rest of the world's Web developers—there was no other way.

Although the end justified the means, there was an unforeseen, or simply ignored, consequence that now affects almost every Web site: the content of the world's Web pages is crammed with markup that is only there to achieve the desired presentation on a small group of soon-to-be obsolete Web browsers; it provides no actual information at all. It's safe to say that most Web pages are over 60 percent presentational markup, and the result is that the actual content is almost impossible to extract for other uses.

And while we are on this sad subject . . .

Let's Play Spot the Content!

Take this snippet of markup from the Microsoft home page, July 1, 2004.

```
<table cellpadding="0" cellspacing="0" width="100%"
height="19" border="0" ID="Table5">

<tr>

<td nowrap="true" id="homePageLink"><></td>

<td><span class="ltsep">|</span></td>

<td class="lt0" nowrap="true" onmouseenter="mhHover('loca
lToolbar', 0*2+2, 'lt1')" onmouseleave="mhHover('localTo
olbar', 0*2+2, 'lt0')"><a href="http://go.microsoft.com/
?LinkID=508110">MSN Home</a></td>

<td><span class="ltsep">|</span></td>

<td class="lt0" nowrap="true" onmouseenter="mhHover('loca
lToolbar', 1*2+2, 'lt1')" onmouseleave="mhHover('localTo
olbar', 1*2+2, 'lt0')"><a href="http://go.microsoft.com/
?linkid=317769">Subscribe</a></td>

<td><span class="ltsep">|</span></td>

<td class="lt0" nowrap="true" onmouseenter="mhHover('loca
lToolbar', 2*2+2, 'lt1')" onmouseleave="mhHover('localTo
olbar', 2*2+2, 'lt0')"><a href="http://go.microsoft.com/
?linkid=317027">Manage Your Profile</a></td>

<td width="100%"></td>

</tr>

</table>
```

All of this code produces just one row of buttons on this page (**Figure 1.1**):

FIGURE 1.1 All of the code on the previous page generates just the four links seen in the row below the Microsoft logo.

The four links

The total *content* of the code you just saw is in orange—247 characters out of 956, or less than 26 percent. The remaining 74 percent is just gooey chocolate sauce. Except for the href attributes, everything inside the tags is *presentation* and could all be ripped out and converted into a few brief definitions in a style sheet. The table is not used to display data; its purpose is solely to line everything up. The rest of the code is mostly concerned with making rollovers work. Each link requires a class to identify it to JavaScript, a forced nowrap attribute to keep the words on the link together, and two JavaScript function calls—yeah, on *every* link. (As an aside, rollovers are easy to create with CSS and require two simple CSS styles.) Note also that a table cell that contains a nested span with a class is required to display each tiny vertical line between the links.

Please don't think I'm picking on Microsoft—almost any site you might choose is equally challenged.

Today, with browsers and many other devices standardizing around XHTML and CSS, non-compliant Web sites are finding that it is difficult to deliver their existing content on these newer devices and browsers. Have you seen your home page on a handheld computer lately?

The Future Will Be Here Soon

So let's leave our past, redolent with bloated markup and nested tables, far behind, and look forward. Although bringing your current Web site into the modern age may take a substantial amount of work, you can console yourself that by following the new Web standards, you can do it once and do it right. If you are starting a new site, you can do it right first time.

In *Stylin',* you learn to future-proof your site by separating the content from the presentation; you do this by creating pages of XHTML markup with only content in them, and then, using a single line of code, you link these pages to a separate file called a *style sheet,* which contains the presentation rules that define how the markup should be displayed.

The power of this church-and-state separation is this—you can have different style sheets for browsers, for PDAs, for cell phones, for printing, for screen readers for the visually impaired, and so on; each style sheet causes the content to be presented in the best possible way for that use, but you only ever need *one* version of the XHTML content markup. As you will see, an XHTML page can automatically select the correct style sheet for each environment in which it finds itself. In this way, your write-once, use-many content becomes truly portable, flexible, and ready for whatever presentational requirements the future may bring its way. Note, however, that like any great vision of the future, there are still some current realities that we need to deal with.

XHTML and How to Write It

Because CSS is a mechanism for styling XHTML, you can't start using CSS until you have a solid grounding in XHTML. And what, exactly, is XHTML? XHTML is a reformulation of HTML as XML—didja get that? Put (very) simply, XHTML is based on the free-form structure of XML, where tags can be named to actually describe the content they contain; for example, `<starname>`Cher`</starname>`. This very powerful capability of XML means that when you develop your set of custom tags for your XML content, you also must create a second document, known as a *DTD* (document type definition) or a similarly formatted XML schema, to explain to the device that is interpreting the XML for how to handle those tags.

XML has been almost universally adopted in business, and the fact that the same X (for eXtensible) is now in XHTML emphasizes the unstoppable movement toward the separation of presentation and content.

The rest of this chapter is dedicated to the latest, completely reformulated, totally-modern, and altogether more flexible version of HTML. Ladies and gentlemen, please welcome … XHTML!

If you want more than this rather simplistic description of XML, check out the XML tutorial at the SpiderPro Web site (www.spiderpro.com/bu/buxmlm001.html).

XHTML Markup Rules

Correctly written XHTML markup gives you the best chance that your pages will display correctly in a broad variety of devices for years to come. The clean, easy-to-write, and flexible nature of XHTML produces code that loads fast, is easy to understand when editing, and prepares your content for use in a variety of applications.

You can easily determine if your site complies with Web standards—if your markup is *well-formed and valid XHTML,* and your style sheet is *valid CSS,* then it will comply. (Whether it's well designed or not is a rather more subjective matter, but we will consider that as we go along.)

Well formed means that the XHTML is structured correctly, according to the markup rules described in this chapter. *Valid* means the markup contains only XHTML, with no meaningless tags, tags that are not closed properly, or *deprecated* (phased out, but still operational) HTML tags. You can check to see if your page meets these criteria by uploading the page onto a server and then going to http://validator.w3.org and entering the page's URL. Press Submit, and in a few seconds you are presented with either a detailed list of the page's errors or the very satisfying "This Page Is Valid XHTML!" message (**Figure 1.2**). CSS can be validated in the same way at http://jigsaw.w3.org/css-validator.

FIGURE 1.2 If your site complies with Web standards, you'll get the ever-gratifying This Page Is Valid XHTML message from the W3C validator.

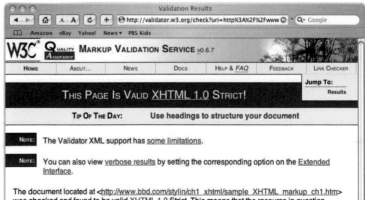

For a list of deprecated tags that you should abandon and replace with their CSS equivalents, refer to the About.com Web site (http://Webdesign.about.com/library/tags/bltags-deprecatedtags.htm).

Here's the complete (and mercifully, short) list of the coding requirements for XHTML compliance:

1. **Declare a DOCTYPE**. The DOCTYPE goes before the opening `html` tag at the top of the page and tells the browser whether the page contains HTML, XHTML, or a mix of both, so that it can correctly interpret the markup. There are three main DOCTYPEs that let the browser know what kind of markup it is dealing with:

    Strict: All markup is XHTML compliant.

    ```
    <!DOCTYPE html PUBLIC "-//W3C//DTD XHTML 1.0 Strict//EN"

        "http://www.w3.org/TR/xhtml1/DTD/xhtml1-strict.dtd">
    ```

    Transitional: This states that markup is a mix of XHTML and deprecated HTML. Many sites are currently using this one, so their old HTML code works as well (in this context, "as well" means "also" rather than "equally well") as the XHTML they are now adding.

    ```
    <!DOCTYPE HTML PUBLIC "-//W3C//DTD HTML 4.01
    Transitional//EN"

    "http://www.w3.org/TR/html4/loose.dtd">
    ```

    Frameset: This is the same as transitional but in this case frames, which are deprecated under XHTML, are OK too.

    ```
    <!DOCTYPE HTML PUBLIC "-//W3C//DTD HTML 4.01 Frameset//EN"

    "http://www.w3.org/TR/html4/frameset.dtd">
    ```

    It is important to specify a DOCTYPE. Browsers that don't see a DOCTYPE in the markup assume that the site page was coded for browsers developed long before Web standards.

You can learn more about Quirks mode at the Dive Into Mark Web site (http://diveintomark.org/archives/2002/05/29/quirks_mode).

    Without a DOCTYPE, many browsers go into what is known as *Quirks mode,* a backwards-compatibilty feature supported by Mozilla, Internet Explorer 6 for Windows, and Internet Explorer 5 for Macintosh. In Quirks mode, the browser functions as if it has no knowledge of the modern DOM (document object model), and pretends it has never heard of Web standards. This ability to switch modes depending on the DOCTYPE, or lack thereof, enables browsers to do the best possible job of interpreting the code of both standards-compliant and non-compliant sites.

    Note that for some weird reason, the `DOCTYPE` tag does not need to be closed with a backslash and DOCTYPE is always in caps. This entirely contradicts XHTML rules 4 and 7 below. Go figure.

2. **Declare an XML namespace.** Note this line is your new html tag. Here's an example:

```
<html xmlns="http://www.w3.org/1999/xhtml" lang="en" xml:
lang="en">
```

When a browser is handling an XHTML page and wants to know what's in the DTD, which lists and defines all the valid XHTML tags, here's where it can find it—buried away on the servers of the WC3.

In short, the DOCTYPE and namespace declarations ensure that the browser interprets your XHTML code as you intended.

3. **Declare your content type.** The content type declaration goes in the head of your document, along with any other meta tags you may add. The most common is

```
<meta http-equiv="Content-type" content="text/html;
charset=iso-8859-1" />
```

This simply states what character coding was used for the document. ISO-8859-1 is the Latin character set, used by all standard flavors of English, so if you are coding for an audience who uses the alphabet instead of, for example, Chinese or Farsi characters, this is the one you need. If your next site is going to be in Cyrillic or Hebrew, you can find the appropriate content types on Microsoft's site (http://msdn.microsoft.com/workshop/author/dhtml/reference/charsets/charset4.asp).

4. **Close every tag, whether enclosing or nonenclosing.**

Enclosing tags have content within them, like this

```
<p>This is a paragraph of text inside paragraph tags. To
be XHTML compliant, it must, and in this case does, have
a closing tag.</p>
```

Non-enclosing tags do not go around content but still must be closed, using space-slash at the end, like this

```
<img scr="images/siamese.jpg" alt="My cat" />
```

5. **All tags must be nested correctly.** If a tag opens before a preceding one closes, it must be closed before that preceding one closes. For example

```
<p>It's <strong>very important</strong> to nest tags
correctly.</p>
```

Here, the strong tag is correctly placed inside the <p>; it closes before the containing p tag is closed. A tag enclosed inside another in this way is said to be *nested.*

This is wrongly nested

```
<p>The nesting of these tags is <strong>wrong<p></strong>
```

Multiple elements can be nested inside a containing element; a list nests multiple `li` elements inside a single `ul` or `ol` element, like this

```
<ul>

    <li>Item 1</li>

    <li>Item 2</li>

    <li>Item 3</li>

</ul>
```

Because CSS relies on proper nesting in order to target styles to elements, you have to get this right or your code won't validate.

6. **Inline tags can't contain block level tags.** Block-level tags are tags that provide visual structure to your document, such as `p` (paragraph) and `div` (division). Block-level elements stack on top of one another on the page—if you have two paragraphs, the second paragraph appears by default under the previous one; no line breaks are required. By contrast, inline tags, such as `a` (anchor, a hyperlink) and `em` (emphasis, usually displayed as italics) occur in the normal flow of text, and don't force a new line.

   We discuss block and inline elements in detail later in Chapter 4, but for now, just remember that if you nest a block element, such as a paragraph `p`, inside an inline element, such as a link `a`, your code won't validate.

   Also, some block-level elements can't contain other block-level elements either; for instance, a `h1-6` (heading) tag can't contain a paragraph. Besides using validation, you can let common sense be your guide to avoid these problems; you wouldn't put an entire paragraph inside a paragraph heading when you were writing on paper or in Word, so don't do illogical things like that in your XHTML either, and you won't go far wrong.

7. **Write tags entirely in lowercase.** Self-explanatory—no capital letters at all. I've always done this myself, but if you haven't, the days of `P` are over; now it has to be `p`. Sorry.

8. **Attributes must have values and must be quoted.** Some tags' attributes don't need values in HTML, but in XHTML, all attributes must have values. For example, if you previously used the `select` tag to create a drop-down menu in HTML and wanted to choose which item showed by default when the page loaded, you might have written something like this

```
<SELECT NAME=ANIMALS>

<OPTION VALUE=Cats>Cats</OPTION>

<OPTION VALUE=Dogs SELECTED>Dogs</OPTION>

</SELECT>
```

which would have given you a drop-down menu with Dogs displayed by default.

The equivalent valid XHTML is this

```
<select name="animals">

<option value="cats"></option>

<option value="dogs" selected="selected">Dogs</option>

</select>
```

Note that in this revised version, all the attribute names are in lowercase and all the values are in quotes.

Quoted attribute values don't have to be lowercase, but it's good practice to write everything lower case; then you can't go wrong.

What Are Attributes?

Attributes can be added to a tag and can help further define that tag. Each attribute comprises two pieces: the *attribute name* and the *attribute value*, in the format `name="value"`. For example, this image tag

```
<img src="images/myPicture.jpg" alt="my favorite picture">
```

has two attributes: the image source (its relative location on the server), which has the value `"images/myPicture.jpg"`, and an alternative text description whose value is a string of text that appears onscreen if the image fails to load, or could be read by a screen reader.

Before Web standards, it was common practice to load up tags with presentational attributes. Now we can move all presentational information into the style sheet and thereby greatly reduce the complexity of our markup.

9.   **Use the encoded equivalents for a left angle bracket and ampersand within content.** When XHTML encounters a left angle bracket, < (also known as the less-than symbol), it quite reasonably assumes you are starting a tag. But what if you actually want that symbol to appear in your content? The answer is to encode it using an entity. An *entity* is a short string of characters that represents a single character; when used, this string causes XHTML to interpret and display the character correctly and not to confuse it with markup. The entity for the left angle-bracket/less-than symbol is <—remember LT stands for less than.

Entities not only help avoid parsing errors like the one just mentioned, but they also enable certain symbols to be displayed at all, such as © for the copyright symbol (©). Every symbolic entity begins with an ampersand (&) and ends with a semicolon (;). Because of this, you probably aren't surprised to find out that XHTML regards ampersands in your code as the start of entities, and so you must also encode ampersands as entities when you want them to appear in your content; the ampersand entity is &.

Various tools take your old HTML markup and convert it to XHTML. Of these, HTML Tidy is considered the best. The Infohound site (http:// infohound.net/tidy) has an online version of HTML Tidy and links to downloadable versions and documentation. After the conversion is complete, you always have some final hand cleanup to do, but HTML Tidy and others can save you hours of work.

A good rule of thumb is that if a character you want to use is not printed on the keys of your keyboard (such as é, ®, ©, or £), you need to use an entity in your markup.

There are some 50,000 entities total, which encompass the character sets of most of the world's major languages, but you can find a shorter list of the commonly used entities at the Web Design Group site (www.htmlhelp.com/reference/html40/entities).

And those are the rules of XHTML markup; they are relatively simple, but you must follow them exactly if you want you pages to validate (and you do).

Understanding Markup

Here is a sample unstyled but valid XHTML page that illustrates the rules of XHTML (**Figure 1.3**):

FIGURE 1.3 This unstyled but valid XHTML isn't visually interesting, but it is definitely usable.

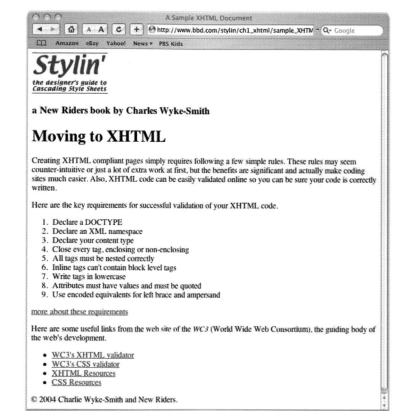

The minimal styling that you do see in the page such as the different sizes of header text, the bulleted lists, links, and so on is due to the fact that the browser has an internal style sheet that styles valid XHTML markup, and the only reason for you to style it differently is if you want it to look different.

The browser's default styles are the baseline design for your markup; if the browser doesn't read your style sheet for some reason, these default styles are your fall back, so it's worth making sure that your marked-up but unstyled page displays meaningfully in the browser before you start on the CSS—if it's valid XHTML, it will.

The page isn't pretty, but it is certainly usable. And, this page's markup is lean and simple. There is no presentational code. and this XHTML passes muster with the WC3 HTML validator. In Chapter 3, I'll begin teaching you how to turn this unstyled markup into a more attractive-looking page using CSS.

Now let's get into more detail on the XHTML rules by taking a look at the markup that created the page shown in Figure 1.3 line by line.

LINES 1 - 2

```
<!DOCTYPE html PUBLIC "-//W3C//DTD XHTML 1.0 Strict//EN"

    "http://www.w3.org/TR/xhtml1/DTD/xhtml1-strict.dtd">
```

Here the DOCTYPE is set to XHTML 1.0 Strict. In this case, you're indicating that code will be interpreted as pure, non-backward-compatible XHTML.

I focus on the strict DOCTYPEs throughout this book, which means I do not use any deprecated HTML. If you need to support deprecated HTML tags such as frames, you need a different DOCTYPE (see "XHTML Markup Rules," #3 earlier in this chapter).

LINE 3

```
<html xmlns="http://www.w3.org/1999/xhtml" lang="en" xml:
lang="en">
```

Next is the opening `html` tag, which did not have attributes in the past. Now it has a URL that points to the *namespace* (the collection of XML declarations and attributes) of this document.

As mentioned earlier in "XHTML Markup Rules", the DOCTYPE and namespace declarations ensure that the browser understands what flavor of (X)HTML you are using, so it interprets your code as you intended.

LINE 4

```
<head>
```

Learn more about metatags by visiting the Webdeveloper.com site (www.webdeveloper.com/html/html_metatags.html).

This tag opens the document head. The head of your document, which is sandwiched between the `head` and `/head` tags), contains information that, with the exception of the title, is not displayed to the viewer. Besides the essential `head` tags I list next (Lines 5–9), optionally there can be others: `meta` tags can contain all kinds of information (page descriptions, keywords, author names, etc.) used by search engines and other indexing software that might visit you site.

There can also be style tags that contain JavaScript and CSS that relate to, and can only be used by, the page they are on.

LINE 5

```
<title>A Sample XHTML Document</title>
```

Technically, you don't *have* to use a `title` tag for your page to validate, but if you don't add it, the validator will encourage you to add it, and after you read the "About Title Tags" sidebar, you always will.

> ### About Title Tags
>
> It's easy to miss the title of a page because it is displayed at the very top of the browser window, but title tags carry tremendous weight with search engines—for example, the pages that get listed on page one of Google's results almost always have some or all of your search terms present in their titles, which are also displayed as the titles of each of the results. So make sure your page title contains keywords that your users might use to search with and is written so it entices clicks when it appears in results. Don't waste your title tag with the useless and all-too common "Welcome to our Home Page."

LINES 6 - 7

```
<meta http-equiv="Content-type" content="text/html;
charset=iso-8859-1" />

<meta http-equiv="Content-Language" content="en-us" />
```

These two required `meta` head tags provide information that helps the browser and server properly manage and display the page.

XHTML insists that you provide character encoding information, which ensures that the browser is displaying the pages with an appropriate character set. Here, in the first `meta` tag, 8859-1 is the code for Latin-1, the alphabet and associated symbols used in writing English and some other languages (see "XHTML Markup Rules," #3 earlier in this chapter). Note that as nonenclosing tags, they are both closed with the space-slash-angle bracket construction.

Language information is also required. In the second `meta` tag, I state that the language is U.S. English; a language type such as Chinese causes the browser to display text from right to left.

LINES 8 - 9

```
<link href="demo_styles.css" rel="stylesheet" type="text/css" />

</head>
```

The `link` tag links the XHTML markup to a CSS style sheet, which is a separate file located using the `href`. (I show you how to create a linked CSS style sheet later in this book so in this case the browser does not find the file and simply ignores this line.) The `link` tag isn't required, but linking is how you relate a style sheet to your markup, and by adding the same style sheet link to each page of your site, you can enable the pages to all share the same set of styles. You can also use the `@import` tag to link to a style sheet, and I'll show you both of these linking methods and when you might use one or the other or both, later in the book.

Make sure you close the document head using the /head tag.

LINE 10

```
<body>
```

Start the document body. The body contains the content that displays on your page.

LINE 11

```
<!--header-->
```

This is a comment. It is not displayed; it is just here to make the code more understandable. Note that in XHTML you can only use two dashes, instead of the unlimited number allowed by HTML, at the start and end of each comment.

LINE 12

```
<div id="logo"> <img src="logo_area.jpg" width="150"
height="80" alt="Stylin logo" />
```

Comments on Comments

The browser does not display comments, but the visitor can see them if he views the source code of your page. I comment my code heavily, especially with what I call "start comments" that show me where each section of my document starts. Doing so helps me find my way around long documents and helps others understand my page if they have to edit it later.

Often, I write comments first to get an overview of my page structure; I then start adding the tags between them. Remember, comments are your friend and, while they may add a few minutes to the initial coding, they can save you hours later.

Note in the code samples that I also write a corresponding end comment for each start comment. Sometimes the opening and closing `<div>` tags that are often used to define a content block can be hundreds of lines apart and can have other divs nested close by inside them—it gets confusing fast. If you comment the beginning and end of any div that is likely to have more than a few lines of code in it, you can quickly and confidently make major edits as you organize your markup. If you don't get the value of this yet, keep it in mind as we proceed—I'll show you plenty of examples.

Divs divide the page into rectangular, box-like areas. These areas are invisible unless you turn their borders on or color their backgrounds. This div tag has an id attribute with the value of "logo"; you can use this ID name to target CSS styles at this div to set its position, size, background color, and much more; furthermore, the div allows you to position all the content within it as a group and target styles at each of the tags it contains.

The logo image tag (img) is a nonenclosing element and is therefore closed with a slash before the closing brace. Note the alt tag, which displays if the graphic doesn't load or is spoken by a screen reader. You must use alt tags on every image, even if the value is "" (that is, two quotes with nothing, not even a space, in between). Only do this if the image serves no informational purpose. You can leave the alt tags blank on everything, but such tags will be flagged by an XHTML validator. Also, this isn't very user friendly and does not aid accessibility. Note that all attribute values (such as the 150 and 80 in this example) must now be in quotes. Yes, really.

Naming Classes and IDs

IDs and class attributes are identifiers you can add to your tags. You can add a class or an ID attribute to any tag, although most commonly, you add them to block-level elements. IDs and classes help you accurately target your CSS at a specific element or set of elements. I get into the uses for (and differences between) IDs and classes later, but for now, it's helpful to know that the attribute value must be a single word, although you can make compound words that the browser sees as single words using underscores, such as class="navigation_links".

Because the browser can misinterpret attribute names made of bizarre strings of characters, my advice is to start the word with a letter, not a number or a symbol. Because the only purpose of a class or ID is to give an element a name that you can reference in your style sheet (or JavaScript code), the value can be a word of your own choosing. That said, it's good practice to name classes and IDs something meaningful such as class="navigationbar" rather than class="deadrat". Although the deadrat class might provide a moment of levity during a grueling programming session, the humor may be lost on you when you are editing your code at some point in the future. Don't save time with abbreviated names either; call the class "footer" rather than "fr" or you are apt to waste your time (or someone else's) later trying to figure out what you meant. Do yourself a favor and take the time to give classes and IDs nonambiguous and descriptive names.

LINES 13 - 15

```
  <h3>a New Riders book by Charles Wyke-Smith</h3>

</div>

<!--end header-->
```

A size 3 text heading is a block-level element and therefore it occurs on a new line, or more precisely, under the previous element. No br / tags are required.

```
</div>
```

Remember to close the header division using the /div tag and make a comment that the header ends here.

LINES 16 - 20

```
<!--main content-->

<div class="contentarea">

  <h1>Moving to XHTML</h1>

<p>Creating XHTML compliant pages simply requires following
a few simple rules. These rules may seem counter-intuitive
or just a lot of extra work at first, but the benefits are
significant and actually make coding sites much easier. Also,
XHTML code can be easily validated online, so you can be
sure your code is correctly written.</p>

<p>Here are the key requirements for successful validation of
your XHTML code.</p>
```

Now, the content area starts with a div, which is a block-level element. The main header is size 1 text. Next, are two paragraphs. Paragraph tags, like all enclosing tags, must be closed with a backslash tag; in this case, /p. Note that paragraphs are block-level elements and have a default amount of space around them, top and bottom.

LINES 21 - 31

```
  <ol>

    <li>Declare a DOCTYPE.</li>

    <li>Declare an XML namespace.</li>

    <li>Declare your content type.</li>

    <li>Close every tag, enclosing or non-enclosing.</li>
```

```
    <li>All tags must be nested correctly.</li>

    <li>Inline tags can't contain block-level tags.</li>

    <li>Write tags in lowercase.</li>

    <li>Attributes must have values and must be quoted.</li>

    <li>Use encoded equivalents for left brace and
ampersand.</li>

  </ol>
```

This is an ordered list; each list item has a number by default. (Unordered lists (ul) have bullets by default rather than numbers).

LINE 32

```
  <a href="more.htm">more about these requirements</a>
```

This is a hyperlink to a page named more.htm in the same folder as the current page.

LINES 33 - 34

```
  </div>

  <!--end main content-->
```

This closes the content area div. The comment is, of course, optional.

LINES 35 - 37

```
<!—navigation-->

<div id="navigation">

  <p>Here are some useful links from the web site of the
<acronym title="World Wide Web Consortium">WC3</acronym>
(World Wide Web Consortium), the guiding body of the web's
development.</p>
```

It's good practice to style acronyms in a way that differentiates them from the text around them. Internet Explorer does not provide any default styling for acronyms; Safari will put them in italics (such as in Figure 1.3). If you add a title tag to an acronym, a tool tip containing the text from the title attribute pops up when a user mouses over it. It's also good practice to indicate the tool-tip's availability by underlining the acronym with a dotted line; this is achieved by styling the acronym element with a dotted border-bottom. Don't make the underline solid, which by convention would indicate the text is a link. These same markup techniques can also be applied to the abbr (abbreviation) tag.

LINES 38 - 45

```
<ul>

    <li><a href="http://validator.w3.org">WC3's XHTML
validator</a></li>

    <li><a href="http://jigsaw.w3.org/css-validator/">WC3's
CSS validator</a></li>

    <li><a href="http://www.w3.org/MarkUp/">XHTML Resources</
a></li>

    <li><a href="http://www.w3.org/Style/CSS/">CSS
Resources</a></li>

    </ul>

</div>

<!--end navigation-->
```

This navigation aid is constructed as a list in which each list item is a link. All of this is inside a div block with an ID that enables you to reference it accurately from the style sheet. Note that there is no line break (which, for you purists, is purely presentational markup) at the end of each link; none is needed. By default, links appear in a row because they are inline elements, but here, because they are contained within list items, which are block-level elements, they display stacked.

LINES 46 - 50

```
<!--footer-->

<div id="homepagefooter">

    <p>&copy; 2004 Charlie Wyke-Smith and New Riders.</p>

</div>

<!--end footer-->
```

The last element of the page is a div that contains the footer text inside a paragraph tag.

LINES 51 - 53

```
</body>

</html>

<!--end of sample doc-->
```

Now you just close out the body and the page, and you're done. Any questions? No? Good! Moving right along . . .

Document Hierarchy: Meet the XHTML Family

OK, the *document hierarchy* is one more important concept you need to understand before you can get to CSS. The document hierarchy is like a family tree or an organizational chart based on the nesting of a page's XHTML tags. A good way to learn to understand this concept is to take a snip of the body section of the markup we just discussed and strip out the content so that you can better see the organization of the tags. Here's the stripped-down header

```
<body>

        <!--header - this is just a comment, not code-->

   <div id="logo">

      <img />

      <h3>    </h3>

   </div>

        <!---end header - remaining tags removed here for
clarity-->

  </body>
```

Now you can clearly see the relationships of the tags; for example, in the markup, you can see that the body tag contains (or nests) all the other tags. You can also see that the div tag (with the ID of "logo") contains two tags; an image tag and head 3 tag.

Figure 1.4 shows another way to represent this structure—with a hierarchy diagram.

Figure 1.4 You can clearly see the hierarchical structure in this diagram.

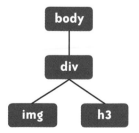

XHTML Starter Kit

If this has whetted your appetite and you want jump right into coding standards-compliant sites, here's the framework of an XHTML page (this example is Strict, meaning it contains no frames or deprecated tags), and you can download this template, or a transitional version, at www.bbd.com/stylin. For more HTML and XHTML templates, see The Web Standards site (www.webstandards.org/learn/templates/index.html).

You just need to change the text in the `title` tag to the title of your page and start adding your own XHTML inside the `body` tag.

```
<!DOCTYPE html PUBLIC "-//W3C//DTD XHTML 1.0 Strict//EN"

    "http://www.w3.org/TR/xhtml1/DTD/xhtml1-strict.dtd">

<html xmlns="http://www.w3.org/1999/xhtml" lang="en" xml:lang="en">

 <head>

  <title>A Sample XHTML Document</title>

  <meta http-equiv="Content-type" content="text/html; charset=iso-8859-1" />

  <meta http-equiv="Content-Language" content="en-us" />

  <link href="demo_styles.css" rel="stylesheet" type="text/css" />

 </head>


 <body>

<!--YOUR XHTML IN HERE-->

</body>

</html>
```

When examining this hierarchical view, we can say that the both the img tag and the h3 tag are the *children* of the div tag, because it is the containing element of both. In turn, the div tag is the *parent* tag of both of them, and the img tag and the h3 tag are *siblings* of one another because they both have the same parent tag. Finally, the body tag is an *ancestor* tag of the img and h3 tags, because they are indirectly descended from it. In the same way, the img and h3 tags (and the div, for that matter) are *descendants* of the body tag. To quote Sly Stone: "It's a family affair . . . "

In CSS, you write a kind of shorthand based on these relationships; for example

```
div#logo img {some CSS styling in here}
```

Such a CCS rule only targets img tags inside of (descended from) the div with the ID of "logo" (the # is the CSS symbol for an ID). This rule means "any image that is descended from the div with an ID of "logo"; other img tags in the page are unaffected by this rule because they aren't contained within the "logo" div. In this way, you can add a border around just this image or set its margin to move it away from surrounding elements.

We will get into learning to write CSS rules like this in great detail in the next chapter, but the important concept to understand is that every element within the body of your document is a descendant of the body tag, and, depending on its location in the markup, the element could be an ancestor, a parent, a child, or a sibling to other tags in the document hierarchy.

By creating rules that use (and often combine) references to IDs, classes, and the hierarchy structure, you have means by which you can accurately dictate which CSS rules affect which XHTML elements, and this is exactly what you will learn to do next.

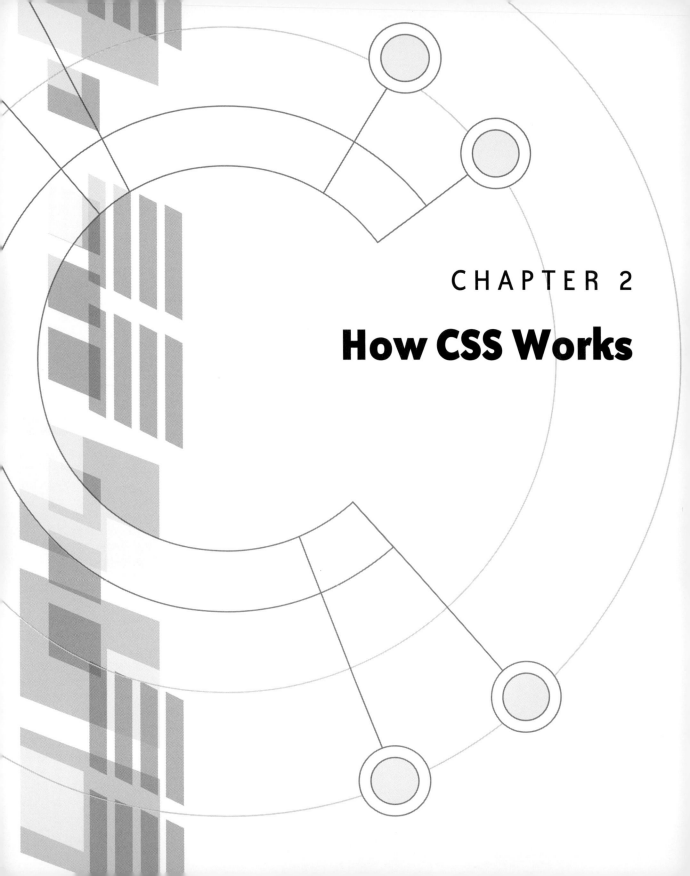

CHAPTER 2

How CSS Works

Learn how the cascade works

Discover how to style specific elements

Inline styles and embedded styles vs. linked styles

Understanding inheritance

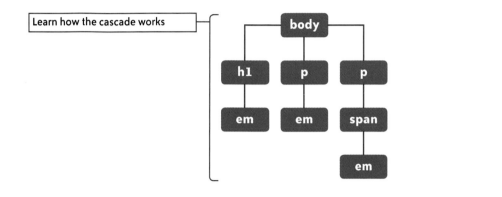

In the previous chapter, I showed you how XHTML markup creates a structural hierarchy of tags. Along the way, I dropped some hints about how you can use CSS to style those tags so that you can precisely control the layout and appearance of the onscreen elements, such as text and graphics. Now it's time to learn about the mechanics of CSS. By the end of this chapter, you'll be ready to create your own styles for the piece of sample XHTML markup we studied in Chapter 1.

The Three Ways to Style Your Document

There are three ways to add CSS to your Web pages, *inline*, *embedded*, and *linked* from a separate CSS style sheet. The only one that really makes any sense in terms of developing Web sites is to link your XHTML pages to a CSS style sheet, but we will examine the other two as well, as they can be useful while developing your pages.

A style sheet is an entirely separate file from your XHTML file, and contains only CSS. A style sheet can be shared by an infinite number of XHTML pages, which helps ensure a consistent look from page to page and allows edits made to a style to be instantly reflected across an entire site.

Inline Styles

Inline styles (also known as local styles) are added to a tag using the XHTML `style` attribute, like this

```
<p>This paragraph simply takes on the browser's default
paragraph style.</p>

<p style="font-size: 25pt; font-weight:bold; font-style:
italic; color:red;">By adding inline CSS styling to this
paragraph, we can override the default styles.</p>

<p>And now we are back to a regular default paragraph without
any inline styles.</p>
```

which looks like this

FIGURE 2.1 Inline styles are only applied to the tag to which they are attached.

Here are some things you need to know about inline styles:

- Their scope is very restricted. An inline style only affects the tag to which it is attached.

- The practice of using inline styles is simply another way of putting presentational markup directly on the tags, as we did in days of yore. Adding inline styles everywhere is as bad for the portability and editability of your markup as adding (X)HTML attributes such as FONT. Inline styles should be generally avoided.

- On those rare occasions when you need to override a style in just one specific instance and there is no better way to do it, you can create an inline style and not feel too guilty about it. That said, you can almost always avoid using inline styles by adding a unique ID or class to the tag in question, and then writing a corresponding style in your style sheet.

- Using an inline style is a good way to try out a style before you move it into the style sheet (see "Linked Styles" on the next page). Just remember to clear out the style attribute entirely once you achieve the effect you want and cut and paste just the style itself into the style sheet. Otherwise that inline style will always trump whatever change you try to make to that particular tag from the style sheet, and you can spend hours trying to fix the style sheet when the problem is hidden in the markup.

- Inline styles win out over styles you define with embedded styles (described next), which win out over global styles you define in style sheets. (See "The Cascade" later in this chapter for details on how style conflicts are resolved).

Embedded Styles

You can place a group of CSS styles in the head of your XHTML document—these are known as embedded styles (or page styles). The terms "embedded styles" and "page styles" are often confused as the former is the official name and the latter is the more commonly used name—but they are synonymous. Embedded styles work like this

The commented CDATA tags (/* <![CDATA[*/ and /*]]> */) are wrapped around the styles. This prevents them from being interpreted as XML which could cause parsing confusion over characters that XML expects to find coded as entities. (Remember, XHTML is XML-based.) For the embedded styles examples in this book, I have not added CDATA tags, and I have never encountered problems that can be attributed to leaving them off. However, you can decide if you want to add them after reading the W3 Schools' explanation of XML CDATA (www.w3schools.com/xml/xml_cdata.asp).

```
<head>

<title>Inline Styles example</title>

<meta http-equiv="Content-type" content="text/html;
charset=iso-8859-1" />

<meta http-equiv="Content-Language" content="en-us" />

<style type="text/css">

/* <![CDATA[ */

h1 { font-size: 16pt; font-weight:bold;}

p {color:blue;}

/* ]]> */

</style>

</head>

a comment */
```

The style tag tells the browser it is about to encounter code other than (X)HTML; the tag's attribute states that the code is CSS. (If you want to include JavaScript in the head of your document instead of CSS, use a `style` tag with the `"text/javascript"` attribute).

Here are some comments on embedded (or page) styles:

- The scope of embedded styles is limited to the page that contains the styles.

- If you are only publishing a single page with these particular styles, you can embed the styles in the head of the document, although you are not truly separating the styles from the content; they are still in the same document. You will become familiar with embedded styles as you follow along with the hands-on single-page examples in this chapter.

- If you are working up multiple styles for a complex layout such as a form, sometimes it's easier to write the styles as embedded styles in the head of the document, so you don't have to constantly switch between the markup and the style sheet. Then, once everything is working, you can move the styles into the main style sheet and replace the styles in the header with a link to the style sheet.

- Page styles win out over style sheets, but they lose out to attributes you define in inline styles. (See "The Cascade" later in this chapter for details on how such style conflicts are resolved).

Linked Styles

You can place styles in a separate document (a style sheet) that links to multiple pages so that the styles have global (site-wide) scope— the styles defined in this style sheet can affect every page of your site, not just a single page or a single tag. This is the only method of the three that truly separates the presentational styles from the structural markup. If you centralize all your CSS styles in a style sheet in this way, Web site design and editing becomes much easier.

For example, if you need to make changes that affect the whole site ("The client wants all the body text to be blue, not black."), doing so is as quick and painless as modifying one CSS style. This is certainly much easier than the pre-CSS task of modifying every font attribute of every paragraph tag in every page of the site.

You can link your style sheet to as many XHTML pages as you wish with a single line of code in the head of each XHTML page:

```
<link href="my_style_sheet.css" media="screen"
rel="stylesheet" type="text/css" />
```

Then the styles are applied to each page's markup as the page loads.

Note that, in the above `link` tag, the `media` attribute is defined as `"screen"`, meaning the style sheet is designed for the screen, which currently means Web browsers. (Certain user agents look for particular media attributes that best suit their display capabilities; possibilities here include: all, projection, handheld, print, aural. See a full list on the W3 Schools site (www.w3schools.com/css/css_mediatypes.asp).

Any browser that loads the page uses the style sheet the `link` tag indicates. But by adding a second `link` tag with the `media` attribute of `"print"`, you can offer a second style sheet that the browser will use when printing. A style sheet for printing might hide navigation and other elements that don't make sense when the content goes to paper.

If you create a second style sheet for printing, its link tag might look like this

```
<link href="my_style_sheet_print.css" media="print"
rel="stylesheet" type="text/css" />
```

So now that you know what style sheets are, let's look at how you write style sheet rules, and how concepts like Inheritance, Specificity, and The Cascade control how these rules affect your markup.

What Are Cascading Style Sheets?

Let's split the question in two: What are style sheets? and How do they cascade? I'll answer the first question right off and, although I've hinted at the answer above, I'll talk about the cascade later in the chapter.

A *style sheet* is simply a text file with the file name extension `.css`.

A style sheet is list of CSS *rules*. Each rule defines a particular style that is applied to your XHTML markup; a rule can define the font-size of the text of paragraphs, the thickness of a border around an image, the position of a headline, the color of a background, and so on. Many of the sophisticated typography and layout features of print-design programs such as Adobe InDesign can now be emulated in Web pages with CSS; Web designers finally have comprehensive control of the layout of their pages, without having to resort to workarounds like tables and spacer GIFs.

Anatomy of a CSS Rule

While a p tag in the XHTML markup is enclosed in angle brackets, in the CSS style, you just write the tag name without the angle brackets.

Let's start learning about how CSS is written by looking at a simple CSS rule. For example, here's a rule that makes all text in all paragraphs of your document red

```
p {color: red}
```

So if you have this XHTML markup

```
<p>This text is very important</p>
```

then it will be red.

A CSS rule is made up of two parts: the *selector,* which states which tag the rule selects, (or, as I like to say, which the rule the selector *targets*)—in this case, a paragraph—and the *declaration,* which states what happens when the rule is applied—in this case, the text displays in red. The declaration itself is made up of two elements: a *property,* which states what is to be affected—here, the color of the text—and a *value,* which states what the property is set to—here, red. It's worth taking a good look at this diagram (**Figure 2.2**) so that you are absolutely clear on these four terms; I'll be using them extensively as we move forward.

FIGURE 2.2 There are two main elements of a CSS rule and two sub-elements.

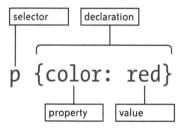

Writing CSS Rules

CSS demands absolute accuracy; a missing semicolon can cause CSS to ignore an entire rule.

This basic structure of the selector and the declaration can be extended in three ways:

Multiple declarations can be contained within a rule.

```
p {color:red; font-size:12px; line-height:15px;}
```

Now our paragraph text is red, 12 points high, and the lines are 15 points apart. (For all practical purposes, a point is the same as a pixel; pixels are the tiny dots that make up your screen display.)

Note that each declaration ends with a semicolon to separate it from the next. The last semicolon before the closing curly bracket is optional, but I always add it so that I can tack on more declarations later without having to remember it.

Multiple selectors can be grouped. If, say, you want text for tags h1 through h6 to be blue and bold, you might laboriously type this

```
h1 {color:blue; font-weight:bold;}

h2 {color:blue; font-weight:bold;}

h3 {color:blue; font-weight:bold;}
```

and so on.

But you don't have to; you can group selectors in a single rule like this

```
h1, h2, h3, h4, h5, h6 {color:blue; font-weight:bold}
```

Much easier! Just be sure to put a comma after each selector except the last. The spaces are optional, but they make the code easier to read.

Multiple rules can be applied to the same selector. If, having written the previous rule, you decide that you also want just the h3 tag to be italicized, you can write a second rule for h3, like this

```
h1, h2, h3, h4, h5, h6 {color:blue; font-weight:bold;}

h3 {font-style: italic;}
```

You may be wondering what other values properties such as font size and color may have. For example, you might want to know if you can specify a color using RGB (red, green, blue) instead of a color name (the answer is yes, you can). For now, just hang in there while I focus on showing you how selectors work. Then, later in this chapter, I'll show you the declaration part of the rules.

Targeting Tags Within the Document Hierarchy

If you have forgotten what the document hierarchy is since the end of the last chapter, you might want to reread "Document Hierarchy: Meet the XHTML Family" in Chapter 1 now so that I can avoid the redundancy of repeating myself repeatedly and redundantly.

To view the code discussed below, you can go to the Stylin' site (www. bbd.com/stylin) and download the template, contextual_selectors _tmpl.htm, and paste the styles between the style *and* /style *tags in the head of the document, as indicated in the template. Then just open the document into your browser to see what those styles do to the markup.*

If you are new to XHTML, note that span *is a neutral container like* div *that has no default attributes: in other words,* span *has no effect on your markup until you explicitly style it. It's useful for marking up elements in your markup that have some meaning to you not defined by XHTML; however, If your document finds itself in an environment where it cannot use your style sheet, the spans will have no effect on the presentation. Unlike* div, *which is a block element and forces a new line,* span *is an inline element, and so it does not force a new line. By default,* strong *results in bold text, and* em *(emphasis) results in italics; but of course, you can use CSS to restyle them if you wish.*

Using Contextual Selectors

If you write a rule where you simply use the tag name as the selector, then every tag of that type is targeted. For example, by writing

```
p {color:red;}
```

every paragraph would have red type.

But what if you only want one particular paragraph to be red? To target tags more selectively, you use contextual selectors. Here's an example

```
div p {color:red;}
```

Now only paragraphs within div tags would be red.

As you can see in example above, contextual selectors use more than one tag name (in this case, div and p) in the selector. The tag closest to the declaration (in this case the p tag) is the tag you are targeting. The other tag or tags state where the target tag must be located in the markup in order for it to be affected. Let's look at this idea in detail.

Take a look at this bit of markup

```
<h1>Contextual selectors are <em>very</em> selective.</h1>

<p>This example shows how to target a <em>specific</em> tag
    using the document hierarchy.</p>

<p>Tags only need to be descendants <span>in the <em>order
stated</em> in the selector</span>; other tags can be in
between and the selector still works.</p>
```

Both of paragraphs in the code above contain em tags, so if you were to write a rule to act on any em tags enclosed within p tags that rule would apply to both paragraphs. However, if you were to write a rule that applied only to the em tags inside of span tags inside of p tags, then the rule would only apply to the second paragraph.

Figure 2.3 shows how this code looks with just the browser's default styling.

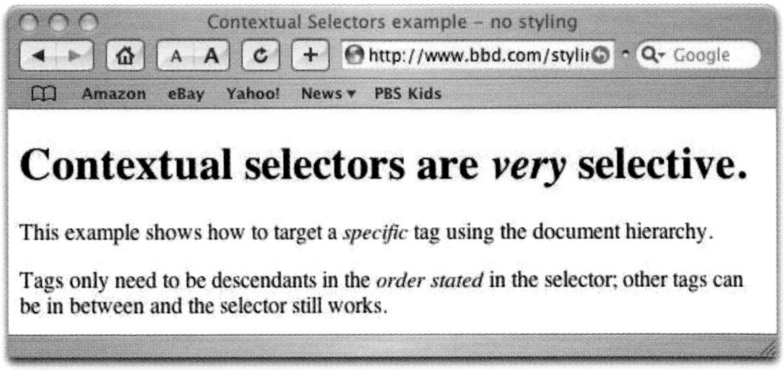

FIGURE 2.3 Here, only the browser's default styles are applied.

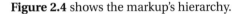

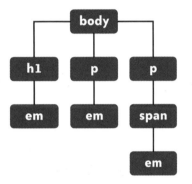

FIGURE 2.3 Here, only the browser's default styles are applied.

Figure 2.4 shows the markup's hierarchy.

FIGURE 2.4 This is the hierarchy for the code on the previous page.

This hierarchy diagrammatically shows which tag is inside which. If you write this style

```
em {color:green}
```

for the markup on the previous page by adding it between the style tags in the head of the template found at www.bbd.com/stylin then, as you learned in the "Writing CSS Rules" earlier in the chapter, all the text in em tags would turn green (**Figure 2.5**).

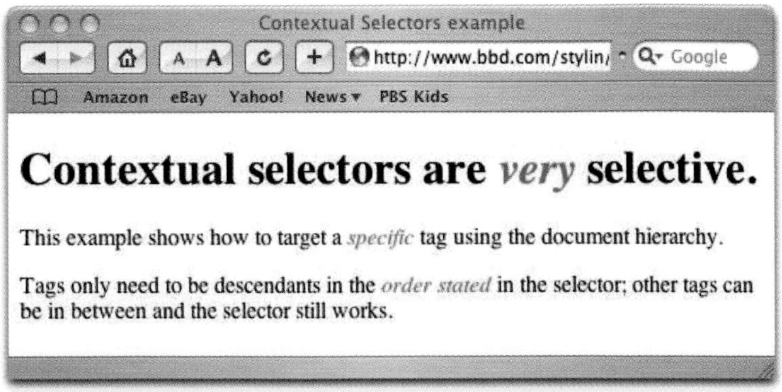

FIGURE 2.5 In this example, all text within em tags is green.

But what if you want to be more selective? Let's say you only want the em text within the paragraphs to be green. If this is the case, you would write a rule like this

```
p em {color:green}
```

which would result in **Figure 2.6**.

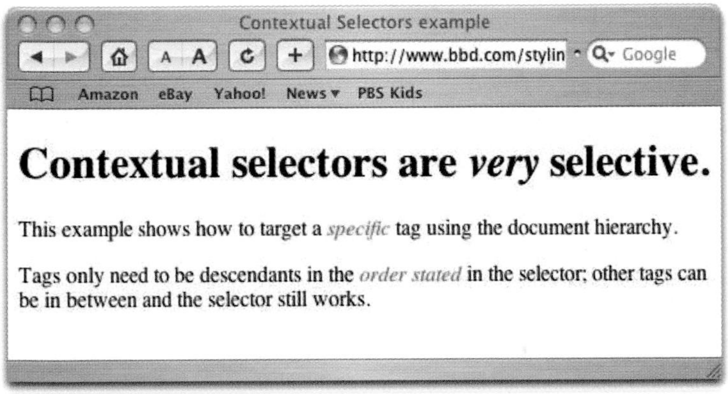

FIGURE 2.6 By adding a contextual selector, you cause the rule to affect only paragraphs, not the heading.

Because you preceded the em with a p in the selector, only em tags within p tags are now targeted by the rule; the em tag in the h2 tag is no longer affected. Note that, unlike the group selectors you saw earlier, contextual selectors have spaces, not commas, between the selectors.

Rules with group selectors cause the rule to be applied to all the tags listed, whereas rules with contextual selectors are applied only to the last tag listed, and then only if the selectors that precede it appear in this same order *somewhere* in the hierarchy above it. It doesn't matter how many tags appear in between.

Because of this, the em tag within the span tag is affected by this rule. Even though it is not a child of the p tag; the rule still applies, because it is a descendant of the p tag. (You may want to read "Document Hierarchy: Meet the XHTML Family" in Chapter 1 again if this does not make sense to you.)

Here's an example of how you can state multiple tags in the selector to make the targeting even more specific

```
p span em {color:green}
```

This results in **Figure 2.7**.

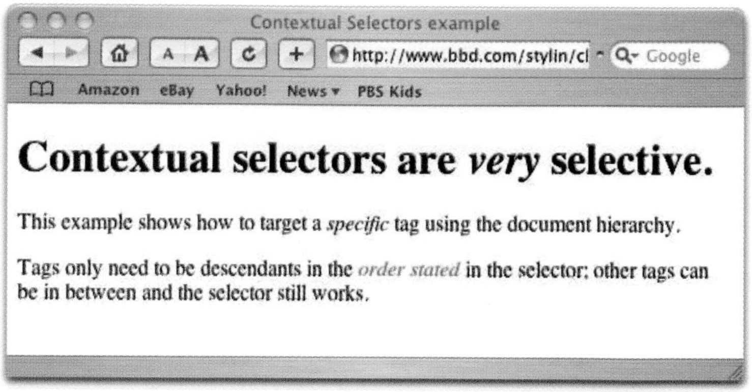

FIGURE 2.7 With three elements in the selector, you can get very specific about which text will be green.

Contextual Selectors example

http://www.bbd.com/stylin/cl Q- Google

Amazon   eBay   Yahoo!   News ▾   PBS Kids

Contextual selectors are *very* selective.

This example shows how to target a *specific* tag using the document hierarchy.

Tags only need to be descendants in the *order stated* in the selector; other tags can be in between and the selector still works.

Your rule now states that only an em within a span within a p tag is selected; you set a very specific context in which the rule works, and only one tag meets this criterion. In a contextual selector like this, you can list as many selectors as you need to ensure that the tag you want to modify is targeted.

However, things get more difficult if you want to target the word "specific" only; as you saw in Figure 2.5, the rule p em {color: green;} selects the em tags inside both the paragraphs and you simply can't target just this particular tag with a standard contextual selector. What you need here is a *child selector*.

Working with Child Selectors

In Chapter 1 I mentioned that a child tag is a direct descendant of an enclosing tag. If you want to write a rule so that the tag you're targeting *has* to be a child of a particular tag, then you can do that too, like this

```
p>em {color:green;}
```

Now you have successfully targeted the word "specific" without affecting the other em text, because "specific" is contained in an em tag that is a child of the p tag, but the words "ordered stated" are not (**Figure 2.8**).

The > symbol is used between the two selectors to mean "child of."

FIGURE 2.8 A child selector provides the required context to select
the word "specific" in this markup.

Before you drop this book in your haste to start using child selectors in your CSS, it's important to know that, at the time of writing,
IDWIMIE, Internet Explorer for Windows simply ignores them
(although Internet Explorer for Macintosh does implement them).
However, there are work-arounds if you find yourself in situations
where only a child selector will do. As you will see shortly, classes
and IDs let you target any individual tag you wish, but to use them,
you'll need a little extra markup.

So until there's a version of Internet Explorer that can understand
child selectors, you'll mainly use child selectors to create variations
in your style sheet to work around Internet Explorer's various
non-standards-compliant quirks. We will use them in this way in
later chapters.

Adding Classes and IDs

So far you've seen that when you have a rule with a selector that
simply states a tag name such as p or h1, the rule is applied to every
instance of that tag. You've also seen that to be more specific in the
selection process, you can use contextual selectors to specify tags
within which target tags must be contained.

However, you can also target specific areas of your document by
adding IDs and classes to the tags in your XHTML markup. IDs and
classes give you a second approach to styling your document—one
that can operate without regard for the document hierarchy.

SIMPLE USE OF A CLASS

Let me use this piece of markup to illustrate how you might use a class

```
<h1 class="specialtext">This is a heading with the <span>same
class</span> as the second paragraph</h1>

<p>This tag has no class.</p>

<p class="specialtext"> When a tag has a class attribute, we
can target it <span>regardless</span> of its position in the
hierarchy.</p>
```

Note that I've added the class attribute specialtext to two of these tags. Let's now apply these styles to this markup where specialtext is formatted as bold (**Figure 2.9**)

```
p {font-family: Helvetica, sans-serif;}

.specialtext {font-weight:bold;}
```

When you write a class selector, start it with a . (period).

FIGURE 2.9 Here I use a class selector to bold two different tags.

These rules result in both paragraphs displaying in the Helvetica font (or the browser's generic sans-serif font if Helvetica is not available) and the paragraph with the specialtext class displaying in Helvetica bold. The text in the h1 tag remains in the browser's default font (usually Times) but it is bold, because it also has the specialtext class. Note that the span, a tag that has no default attributes, does nothing because I didn't explicitly style it.

CONTEXTUAL CLASS SELECTORS

If you only want to target one paragraph with the class, you create a selector that combines the tag name and the class, like this (**Figure 2.10**)

```
p {font-family: Helvetica, sans-serif;}

.specialtext {font-weight:bold;}

p.specialtext {color:red}
```

FIGURE 2.10 By combining a tag name and class name, you make the selector more specific.

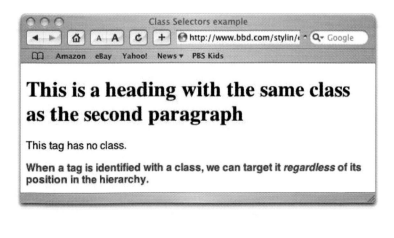

This is another kind of contextual selector because the class must be in the context of a paragraph for the rule to be applied.

You can go one step further and write the following (**Figure 2.11**)

```
p {font-family: Helvetica, sans-serif;}

.specialtext {font-weight:bold;}

p.specialtext {color:red}

p.specialtext span {font-style:italic}
```

FIGURE 2.11 By adding a second selector, you can be very specific about which tag is styled.

Now the word "regardless" is bold *and* italicized because it is in a span tag that is in a paragraph with the specialtext class, as the rule specifies. If you also want this rule to target the span in the h1 tag, you can modify it in one of two ways. The easiest way is to not associate the class with any specific tag (**Figure 2.12**).

```
.specialtext span {font-style:italic}
```

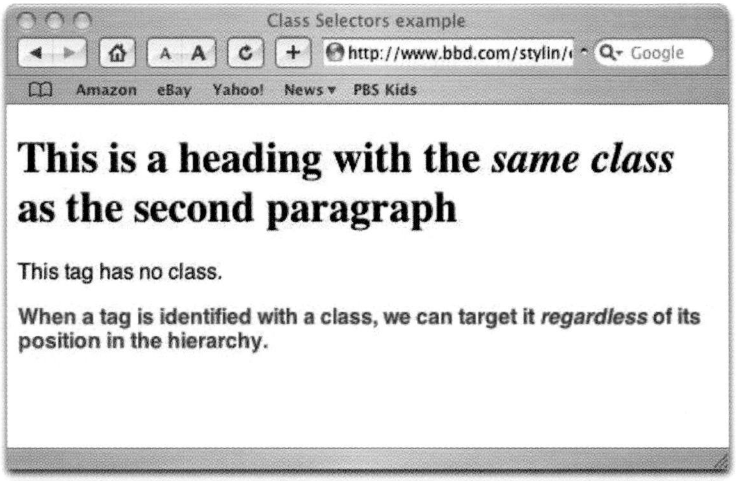

FIGURE 2.12 With a less specific selector, the headline's span text is also selected.

The word "class" in the headline is now also italicized. By deleting the p from the start of the selector, you remove the requirement for the class to be attached to any specific tag, so now both span tags are targeted. The rule states the span tag can be a descendant of *any* tag with the specialtext class because no tag is specified.

The benefit of this approach is that you can use a class without regard for the tag to which it belongs, so you are escaping the inherent constraints of the hierarchy when you do this.

The downside is that other tags that you don't intend to style might also be affected because this modified rule is less specific than it was. So, say you later added a span inside another tag that also had the specialtext class, such as this one

```
<div class="specialtext">In this div, the span tag <span>may
or may not</span> be styled.</div>
```

The text within the span would be italicized also, which may or may not be the desired effect (**Figure 2.13**).

FIGURE 2.13 The less specific the selector, the more likely other tags will be inadvertently targeted.

If you don't want to style this new div's span, you can adopt a second, more focused, group selector approach, like this (**Figure 2.14**)

```
p.specialtext span, h1.specialtext span {font-style:italic}
```

FIGURE 2.14 By using two grouped rules, you focus your targeting to specific tags.

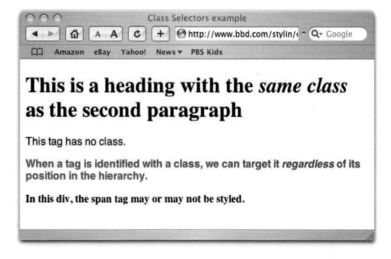

Now only the two tags in question are targeted and your new tag is not affected. Your grouped rules don't target that span because it's descended from a div, whereas if you use the more simple and less specific .specialtext span approach, it is selected.

Although this may seem like a lot to think about when you are styling a four-line example like this, when you are working on a style sheet that might be dozens or hundreds of lines long, you need to keep these considerations in mind, as we do in later chapters.

Introducing IDs

IDs are written in a similar way to classes, except you use a # (hash symbol) to indicate them instead of the class's . (period)

```
#specialtext {font-weight:bold;}
```

If a paragraph is marked up with an ID, like this

```
<p id="uniquetext">This is the special text</p>
```

then the corresponding contextual selector looks like this

```
p#uniquetext {some CCS rules here}
```

Other than this, IDs work in the same way as classes, and everything in our discussion of classes above applies equally to IDs. So what's the difference?

The Difference Between IDs and Classes

So far, I have shown aspects of classes and IDs that might make them seem to be interchangeable—we have used them both to identify a specific tag within our markup. However, an ID is more powerful than a class, rather like the queen is more powerful than a pawn in a game of chess. (You will see just how true this is when you look at the concept of rule specificity in the "The Cascade" section later in this chapter.) To extend this queen/pawn chess analogy, according to the rules of XHTML, only a single instance of a particular ID (such as `id="mainmenu"`) can be in a page, but a class (such as `class="strongparagraph"`) can appear many times.

So, if you want to identify a unique piece of your page's markup, such as the main navigation menu to which you want to target a special set of CSS rules, use an ID. To identify a number of paragraphs in a page that all require the same styling, use a class.

You also use an ID to enable JavaScript to be targeted at a tag (for example, to activate a DHTML animation when the user mouses over a link). You JavaScript jocks might like to know that the `id` attribute replaces the deprecated `name` attribute (which the XHTML validator flags as invalid) that was formerly used for this purpose. It's especially important that you make sure JavaScript-related IDs appear only once in a page, or the JavaScript may behave unpredictably.

> ### Don't Go Crazy with Classes
>
> Generally, you should use IDs and classes sparingly; the right kind of use is putting them on the `divs` that contain the main sections of your markup, and then accessing the tags within them with contextual selectors that begin with the ID or class's name.
>
> What you want to avoid is what Jeffrey Zeldman describes as "classitis—the measles of markup," where you add a unique class or ID to just about every tag in your markup and then write a rule for each one. This is only one step removed from loading up your markup with FONT tags and other extraneous markup. The good doctor Zeldman has cured me and many others of this nasty affliction. If you are already in the habit of slapping classes on every tag, as most of us do when we enthusiastically jump into CSS, take a look at the markup sample in Chapter 1 in light of what you just read in this chapter. You'll see that you can target styles at every tag quite easily without adding any more IDs or classes.
>
> If you use IDs and classes to identify only the main sections of your markup—and those occasional tags that can't be specifically targeted with contextual tag-based selectors—you won't go far wrong. This has the added benefit of making your style sheet simpler too.

To be clear, you can use multiple `id` attributes in a page, but each one must have a unique value (name) to identify it. You can apply a particular class to as many tags as you need to. Let's now take quick look at some other selectors that you may not use as much as contextual selectors, classes, and IDs, but which offer powerful capabilities just the same.

The Universal Selector

The * (asterisk) selector means "anything," so if you use

```
* {color:green;}
```

in your style sheet, all type will be green except where you specify it to be different in other rules. Another interesting use for this selector is as the inverse of the child selector—a not-a-child selector, if you will.

```
p * em {font-weight:bold;}
```

Here, any em tag that is at least a grandchild of the p tag, but not a child, is selected; it doesn't matter what the em's parent tag is.

The Adjacent Sibling Selector

This rule selects a tag that follows a specific sibling tag (sibling tags are at the same level in the markup hierarchy—that is, they share the same parent tag). Here's an example

```
h1 + p {font-variant:small-caps}
```

Applying this rule to this markup

```
<div>

    <h1>All about siblings selectors</h1>

    <p>There must be at least two selectors, with a + sign
before the last one.</p>

    <p>The targeted selector will only be affected if it is a
sibling to, and preceded by, the one before the + sign.</p>

</div>
```

results in what is shown in **Figure 2.15**, because only the first paragraph is preceded by a sibling h1 tag.

FIGURE 2.15 Sibling selectors work based on the preceding tag in the markup, and both must be nested at the same level. This is one of the trickier selectors to understand.

As you can see, the p tag that follows the h1 meets the condition of the rule and so it is in small caps. The second p tag, which is not adjacent to the h1, is unaffected. (This doesn't hold true for Internet Explorer for Windows).

Attribute Selectors

Attribute selectors use the attributes of the tag. They are primarily used in XML but have their uses in XHTML too.

This rule

```
img [title] {border: 2px solid blue;}
```

causes any img with a title tag, like this

```
<img src="images/sunset.jpg" alt="Lahina Sunset"
title="Lahina Sunset">
```

to have a blue, 2-pixel border around it; it doesn't matter what the value of the title attribute is, just that there is one. You might use such a style to indicate to the user that if they point at this image, a tool tip (pop-up text generated by the title attribute) displays. (It's common practice to duplicate the alt and title attribute values—the <alt> tag text displays if the image does not load, or can be read by an audio reader, and the title causes a tool-tip to appear if the user points at the image.

You can also be specific about what the attribute's value should be. For example, the rule

```
img [alt="Stylin logo"] {border: 2px solid blue;}
```

only puts the border around the image if the image's alt attribute is "Stylin logo"; in other words, if the image markup looks something like this

```
<img src=images/stylin_logo" alt="Stylin logo">
```

This rule is made more useful by the fact that it lets you specify just the first characters of the attribute value, but the "common" part of the attribute must be separated from the "different" part of the attribute with a hyphen. So, if you have carefully written your img tags with attributes like these

```
<img src="images/car1.gif" alt="car-toyota_prius">
```

```
<img src="images/car2.gif" alt="car-honda_accord">
```

then you can select them by adding the pipe symbol (usually typed with Shift-/) into your rule, like this

```
img [alt|="car"] {border: 2px solid blue;}
```

By the way, this rule would also select this example

```
<img src="images/car_montage.gif" alt="car">
```

even though this example's alt tag doesn't have the hyphenated extension to the value.

The text of these image alt tag examples are deliberately very brief for the sake of clarity. From an accessibility point of view, however, always write alt text that is meaningful for a user who can't see the image.

Summary of Selectors

So far, you've seen that you can target CSS rules in several ways: by using tag selectors, by using class and ID selectors, by using selectors that are a combination of both, and even by selecting based on the attributes that are attached to the tag.

One common aspect of these selectors is that they all are targeting *something* in the markup—a tag name, a class, an ID, an attribute, or an attribute value. But what happens if you want some kind of styling to happen when *some event* occurs, such as the user pointing at a link? In short, you want a way to apply rules based on events. And of course, after all this build-up, you know I'm going to tell you there's a way to do that.

Pseudo-Classes

Named for the fact that they are classes that aren't actually attached to tags in the markup, pseudo-classes cause rules to be applied when certain events occur. The most common event that occurs is that the user points at or clicks on something. With the newer browsers (sadly, not Internet Explorer; at least not without adding a special JavaScript function), it's easy to make any onscreen object respond to a rollover; the act of moving the pointer over something, also known as hovering. For example, a pseudo-class can cause a border to appear around an image when the pointer rolls over it.

Anchor Link Pseudo-Classes

Pseudo-classes are most commonly used with hyperlinks (a tags), enabling things like a change in their color or causing their underlining to be removed when rolled over.

There are four pseudo-classes for anchor links, since links always are in one of these four states:

Link. The link is just sitting there looking like a link and waiting for someone to click on it.

Visited. The user has clicked on the link at some point in the past.

Hover. The link is currently being pointed at (rolled over).

Active. The link is currently being clicked.

The distinctive : (colon) in the selector screams (well, indicates) "I am pseudo-class!"

Here are the corresponding pseudo-class selectors for these states (using the a selector with some sample declarations):

```
a:link {color:black;}

a:visited {color:gray;}

a:hover {text-decoration:none;}

a:active {color:navy;}
```

First, let's save the debate about appropriate link colors and behavior for later and simply observe that, according to the declarations above, links are initially black (and underlined by default). When the mouse rolls over them (the hover state), the underlining is removed, and they stay black, because no color is defined here for the hover state. When the user holds the mouse down on the link (the active state), it turns navy, and forever after (or more accurately, until the browser's History of the visit to the link's URL expires or is deleted by the user), the link displays in gray. When using these pseudo-class selectors, you have complete control over the look and behavior of the four states of links.

And that's all very nice, but the real power comes when you start using these anchor link pseudo-classes as part of contextual selectors. Then you can create different looks and behaviors for various groups of links in your design—navigation, footers, sidebars, and links in text, for example. We'll explore using these pseudo-classes for styling of links and other things to the point of tedium (or perhaps, ecstasy) later in the book, but for now, let's note the following and then move on:

You don't have to define all four of these states. If you just want to define a link and a hover state, that's fine. Sometimes it doesn't make sense to have links show as having been visited.

A browser may skip some of these rules if you don't state them in the order shown above: link, visited, hover, active. The mnemonic "LoVe-HA!" is an easy, if cynical, way to remember this.

You can use *any* selector with these pseudo-classes, not just a, to create all kinds of rollover effects. For example

```
p:hover {background-color: gray;}
```

This code will, well, I don't think I even need to tell someone as smart as you what is apt to happen to your paragraph at this point.

(As mentioned before, be aware that older browsers don't support rollovers on anything but anchor links and you need to help even current versions of Internet Explorer in this regard, as you will see later in this book).

Other Useful Pseudo-Classes

The purpose of pseudo-classes is to simulate classes being added to your markup when certain conditions occur. We have look at how they get applied in response to user actions such as pointing and clicking, but they can also be applied based on certain conditions being true in your markup.

:FIRST-CHILD

Where x is a tag name — `x:first-child`

This pseudo-class selects the first-child element with the name x. For example, if this rule

```
div.weather strong:first-child {color:red;}
```

is applied to this markup

```
<div class="weather">

It's <strong>very</strong> hot and <strong>incredibly</strong> humid.

</div>
```

then very is red and incredibly is not.

:FOCUS

Where x is a tag name — `x:focus`

An element such as a text field of a form is said to have focus when the user clicks it; that's where the characters appear when the user types. For instance, the code

```
input:focus {border: 1px solid blue;}
```

puts a blue border around such a field when the user clicks it.

Pseudo-elements

Pseudo-elements provide the effect of extra markup elements magically appearing in your document, although you don't actually add any extra markup. Here are some examples.

This pseudo-class

> Where x is a tag name

```
x:first-letter
```

```
p:firstletter {font-size:300%; float:left;}
```

enables you, for example, to create a large drop-cap effect at the start of a paragraph.

This pseudo-class

> Where x is a tag name

```
x:first-line
```

enables you to style the first line of (usually) a paragraph of text. For example,

```
p:first-line{font-varient:small-caps;}
```

results in the first line, not surprisingly, being in small capital letters. If you have a liquid layout where the line length changes as the browser window is sized, words automatically change format as required so that only the first line is styled in this way.

These two pseudo-classes

```
x:before and x:after
```

cause specified text to be added in before and after an element, so this markup

```
<h1 class="age">25</h1>
```

and these styles

```
h1.age:before {content:"Age: "}
```

```
h1.age:after {content:" years old."}
```

result in text that reads "Age: 25 years old." Note that the spaces added inside the quoted content strings ensure proper spacing in the resultant output. These two selectors are especially useful when the tag's content is being generated as a result of a database query; if all the result contains is the number, then these selectors allow you to provide that data point with some meaningful context when you display it for the user.

There are four other pseudo-classes. The first is :lang, *which is applied to elements with a specific language code, and the other three are* :left, :right *and* :first, *which apply to paged media (print) rather than content displayed in browsers. They are little used and unevenly or not at all supported by browsers, so I am not covering them here.*

Because search engines can't pick up pseudo-element content (they don't appear in the markup), don't use these elements to add important content that you want a search engine to index.

Inheritance

Just like the money you hope you'll get from rich Uncle Dick, inheritance in CSS involves passing something down from ancestors to descendants. But, rather than the mountain of green drinking vouchers you hope to get upon the sad, but strangely longed-for, demise of generous old Dickie, in the case of CSS, what is inherited is the values of various CSS properties.

You may remember from our discussion on the document hierarchy in Chapter 1 that the body tag is the great-ancestor of them all—all CSS-targeted tags in your markup descend from it. So, thanks to the power of CSS inheritance, if you style the body tag like this

```
body {font-family: verdana, helvetica, sans-serif; color:
blue}
```

then the text of every text element in your entire document inherits these styles and displays in blue Verdana (or in one of the other choices if Verdana is not available), no matter how far down the hierarchy it is. The efficiency is obvious; rather than specify the desired font for every tag, you set it once in this way as the primary font for the entire site. Then you only need font-family properties for tags that need to be in a different font.

For now, simply remember that styles that relate to text and its color are inherited by the descendant elements. Styles that relate to the appearance of boxes created by styling divs, paragraphs, and other elements, such as borders, padding, margins, and background colors, are not inherited.

Many CSS properties are inherited in this way, most notably text attributes. However, many CSS properties are *not* inherited because inheritance doesn't make sense for them. These properties primarily relate to the positioning and display of box elements, such as borders, margins, and padding. For example, imagine you want to create a sidebar with text in it. You might do this by writing a div (which you can think of as a rectangular box), which has several paragraphs inside it, and styling the div with a border, say a 2-pixel red line. However, it makes no sense for every one of those paragraphs within the div to automatically get a border too. And they won't—border properties are not inherited. When we look at the box model in Chapter 4, we'll look at inheritance in greater detail.

Also, you must be careful when working with relative sizes such as percentages and ems; if you style a tag's text to be 80 percent and it's descended from a tag whose text is also sized at 80 percent, your text will be 64 percent (80 percent of 80 percent), which is probably not the effect you want. In Chapter 3, I discuss the pros and cons of absolute and relative text sizing.

The Cascade

OK, now we have enough information to have a meaningful discussion about one of the toughest aspects of CSS to get your head around—the cascade. If this section gets to be too much, skip ahead and read the "Charlie's Simple Cascade Summary" sidebar later in this chapter. This sidebar is a simplified, if slightly less accurate, version that will serve you until you have done some CCS coding and really need the details.

As its name suggests, the cascade in Cascading Style Sheets involves styles falling down from one level of the hierarchy of your document to the next, and its function is to let the browser decide which of the many possible sources of a particular property for a particular tag is the one to use.

The cascade is a powerful mechanism. Understanding it helps you write CSS in the most economical and easily editable way and enables you to create that documents are viewed as you mean them to be seen, while leaving appropriate control of aspects of the document's display, such as overall font sizes, with users who have special needs.

Sources of Styles

Styles can come from many places. First, it's not hard to accept that there must be a *browser style sheet* (the default style sheet) hidden away inside the browser, because every tag manifests styles without you writing any. For example, h1 tags create large bold type, em tags create italicized type, and lists are indented and have bullets for each item, all automatically. You don't style anything to make this formatting happen.

If you have Firefox installed on your computer, search for the file html.css and you can then see the Firefox default browser style sheet. Modify it at your peril.

Learn more about the browser default style sheet on Eric Meyer's blog (www.meyerweb.com/ eric/thoughts/2004/09/15/ emreallyem-undoing-htmlcss).

Then there is the *user style sheet*. The user can create a style sheet, too, although very few do. This capability is handy, for example, for the visually impaired, since they can increase the baseline size of type or force type to be in colors that they can discern one from another. You can add a user style sheet to Internet Explorer for Windows by selecting Tools > Internet options… and clicking the Accessibility button. This capability, for example, enables visually impaired users to add a style like

```
body {font-size:200%}
```

that doubles the size of all type—inheritance at work again! This is why it is important to specify type in relative sizes such as ems rather than fixed sizes such as points, so you don't over-ride such changes. We will discuss this interesting topic more in Chapter 3.

Then there are *author style sheets*, which are written by you, the author. We have already discussed the sources of these: linked style sheets, embedded styles at the top of pages, and inline styles that are attached to tags.

Here's the order in which the browser looks at, or cascades through, the various locations:

The cascade defines which style sheet is looked at in which order and which style wins out if a style is defined in two or more places.

- Default browser style sheet
- User style sheet
- Author style sheet
- Author embedded styles
- Author inline styles

The browser updates its settings for each tag's property values (if defined) as it encounters them while looking sequentially in each location. They are defined in the default browser style sheet and the browser updates any that are also defined in the other locations. If, for example, the author style sheet style defines the <p> tag's font-family to be Helvetica but the <p> tag is also specified to be Verdana in an embedded (page) style, the paragraph will be displayed in Verdana—the embedded styles are read after the author style sheet. However, if there is no style for paragraphs in the user or author style sheet, they will display in Times, because that's the style defined in all browser default style sheets.

That's the basic idea of how the Cascade works, but in fact, there are several rules that control the Cascade.

The Cascade Rules

Get more info on the cascade at the W3C site (www.w3.org/TR/CSS2/cascade.html).

In addition to the order in which styles are applied, you should know several rules about how the cascade works.

Cascade Rule 1: Find all declarations that apply to each element and property. As it loads each page, the browser looks at every tag in the page to see if a rule matches it.

Cascade Rule 2: Sort by order and weight. The browser sequentially checks each of the five sources, setting any matched properties as it goes. If a matched property is defined again further down the sequence, the browser updates the value and does this repeatedly, if necessary, until all five possible locations of properties for each tag in that page have been checked. Whatever a particular property is set to at the end of this process, that's how it is displayed.

In **Table 2.1**, we look at this process for a page with numerous p tags. Let's assume, for the sake of the example, that two of those p tags have inline styles that define their color as red.

In this case, every p tag text is blue, except for ones with the inline color attribute—these are red.

TABLE 2.1 Cascade Example

LOCATION	TAG	PROPERTY	VALUE
Default style sheet	P	color	black
User style sheet			
Author style sheet	P	color	blue
Author embedded styles			
Author inline styles	P	color	red

Of course, things aren't quite that simple. There is also the *weight* of the declaration. You can define a rule as important, like this

Note the exclamation point

```
p {color:red !important; font-size:12pt}
```

The word !important follows a space after the style you want to make important but before the ; (semicolon) separator.

This style defines the text's red color as important, and therefore, it displays this way, even if it is declared as a different color further down the cascade. Think hard and long before you force a particular style on the user with !important rule definition, because you may be messing up someone's personal style sheet, which may be set that way for a very good reason; be sure that it truly is important for such a style to dominate over any other possible style for that tag.

Charlie's Simple Cascade Summary

You need to remember just three things in this simplified version of the cascade rules. These are true for virtually every case.

Rule 1: Selectors with IDs win out over selectors with classes; these, in turn, win out over selectors with only tags.

Rule 2: If the same property for the same tag is defined in more than one location in the cascade, inline styles win over embedded styles, which win over style sheet styles. Rule 2 loses out to Rule 1 though—if the selector is more specific, it wins, wherever it is.

Rule 3: Defined styles win over inherited styles regardless of specificity.

A little explanation is required for Rule 3. This markup

```
<div id="cascadedemo">

<p id="inheritancefact">Inheritance is <em>weak</em> in the Cascade</p>

</div>
```

and this rule, which has a high specificity,

`2-0-4` ——[`html body div#cascadedemo p#inheritancefact {color:blue:}`

results in all the text, including the word *weak*, being blue because the em inherits the color from its parent, the p tag.

As soon as we add this rule for the em, even though it has very low specificity

`0-0-1` ——[`em {color:red}`

the em text is red. The inherited style is overridden by the defined style for the em, regardless of the high specificity of the rule for the containing paragraph.

There, three simple cascade rules. That was much easier, wasn't it?

Cascade Rule 3: Sort by specificity. Besides being very hard to pronounce, **specificity** determines just how specific a rule is. I tried to get you started on this idea by using the word specific in exactly this way many times while we were discussing selectors. As you saw, if a style sheet contains this rule

```
p {font-size:12px;}
```

and this rule

```
p.largetext {font-size:16px;}
```

then this markup

```
<p class="largetext">A bit of text</p>
```

displays text 16 pixels high because the second rule is more specific—it wins.

This may seem intuitively obvious, but what happens to that bit of markup if you use these styles instead?

```
p {font-size:12px}

.largetext {font-size:16px}
```

Both these rules match the tag, but the class wins out and the text is 16 pixels. Here's why: the numeric specificity of the tag selector is 1, but the class has a specificity of 1-0. Here's how to calculate the specificity of any selector. There is a simple scoring system for each style that you plug into a three-value layout like this:

A - B - C

The dashes are separators, not subtraction signs. Here's how the scoring works:

1. Add one to A for each ID in the selector.

2. Add one to B for each class in the selector.

3. Add one to C for each element name (tag name).

4. Read the result as a three-digit number. (It's not *really* a three-digit number; it's just that in most cases, reading the result as a three-digit number works. Just understand that you can end up with something like 0-1-12, and 0-2-0 is still more specific.)

So, let's look at the specificity of these examples

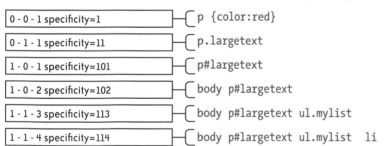

0 - 0 - 1 specificity=1	`p {color:red}`
0 - 1 - 1 specificity=11	`p.largetext`
1 - 0 - 1 specificity=101	`p#largetext`
1 - 0 - 2 specificity=102	`body p#largetext`
1 - 1 - 3 specificity=113	`body p#largetext ul.mylist`
1 - 1 - 4 specificity=114	`body p#largetext ul.mylist  li`

Each example is a higher specificity that the previous one.

Cascade Rule 4: Sort by order. If two rules have exactly the same weight, the one furthest down the cascade wins.

And that, dear reader, is the cascade and, yes, it *is* somewhat hard to understand, especially if you have not yet had much experience with CSS. So I now offer you my simplified version of the Cascade rules, which applies in about 98 percent of cases. If you find that something isn't behaving the way you want when you're using this simplified version, refer to the above rules.

Specificity is more important than order, so a more specific rule high up the cascade wins out over a less specific one further down.

Rule Declarations

So far I've focused on how you use CSS rule selectors to target tags, but you haven't yet looked much at the other half of a CSS rule, the declaration. I've used numerous different declarations to illustrate the selector examples but have only explained them minimally. Now it's time to look at declarations in detail.

The diagram showing the structure of a CSS rule earlier in this chapter (Figure 2.2) shows that a declaration is made of two parts: a property and a value. The *property* states what aspect of the element are affected (its color, its height, and so on) and the *value* states what that property is set to (green, 12px, and so on).

Every element has a number of properties that can be set using CSS; these differ from element to element. You can set the `font-size` property for text, but not for an image, for example. In each subsequent chapter of this book, I use real-world examples to show you the properties you can set for different elements and the values you can set for those properties. Because there are only a few different types of CSS rule values, let's look at them now.

Values fall into three main types:

Words. For example, in `font-weight:bold`, `bold` is a type of value.

Numerical values. Numerical values are usually followed by a unit type. For example, in `font-size:12px`, 12 is the numerical value and `px` is the unit type—pixels in this example.

Color values. Color values are written as `color:#336699` where the color in this example is defined with a hexidecimal value.

There's not much I can tell you about word values that would make sense until you start using them, because they are specific to each element. Numerical and color values, however, can only be expressed in certain ways.

Numerical Values

You use numerical values to describe the length (and I use "length" generically to mean height, width, thickness, and so on) of all kinds of elements. These values fall into two main groups: absolute and relative.

Absolute values (**Table 2.2**) describe a length in the real world (for example, 6 inches), as compared to a relative measurement, which is simply a relationship with some other measurable thing (when you say "twice as long" that's a measure relative to something else).

TABLE 2.2 Absolute Values

ABSOLUTE VALUE	UNIT ABBREVIATION	EXAMPLE	INCH EQUIVALENT
Inches	in	height:6in	
Centimeters	cm	height:40cm	2.54
Millimeters	mm	height:500mm	25.4
Points	pt	height:60pt	72
Picas	pc	height:90pc	6
Pixels	px	height:72px	72

*Examples are not equivalent lengths.

When writing CSS that relates to fixed-sized elements such as images, I use only pixels. It's up to you, but pixels are also the only absolute unit that I use throughout this book, except in print style sheets—because paper is measured in inches, it makes sense to design print layouts with the same units.

Although the absolute units are pretty self-explanatory, the relative units (**Table 2.3**) warrant a little more explanation.

TABLE 2.3 Relative Values

RELATIVE VALUE	UNIT VALUE	EXAMPLE
Em	em	height:1.2em
Ex	ex	height:6ex
Percentage	%	height:120%

Em and ex are both measurements of type size. The em is equal to the height of the character box for a font, so its size varies depending on which font you are using. Ex is the equivalent of the x-height of the given font (so named because it is the height of a lowercase x—

in other words, the center bit without the ascenders and descenders that appear on characters such as p and d.)

Percentages are useful for setting the width of containing elements, such as divs, to the proportion of the browser width, which is the one way to create "liquid" designs that smoothly change size as the user resizes the browser window. Using percentages is also the right way to get proportional *leading* (pronounced like lead, the metal), which is the distance between the baseline of one line of text and the next in a multiple-line text block such as a paragraph. You will learn more about leading in Chapter 3.

Why You Should Use Ems to Specify Type Sizes

There are two important benefits to using a relative sizing method like ems to specify your font sizes:

- You can use inheritance to your advantage by declaring the body element to have a size of 1em, and this becomes a sizing baseline because it causes all other element's text to size relative to it. Because your content text always goes inside other elements, such as p and h4, you then simply write rules that state that the p tag is .8em, and that text links are .7em, for example. In this way, you establish proportional relationships between all the text elements of your design.

  Note that in Internet Explorer, when you set an em size for the body, paragraphs size in proportion automatically, but h1 thru h6 don't; you have to explicitly set some relative size for them (such as 1.1em for h1, .9em for h2, and so on), otherwise they remain fixed at their default sizes.

  If you later decide to increase the overall size of the text in your site, you can go back to the body tag and set its size to, say, 1.2em. Magically, all your text increases in size proportionally by the same amount (a fifth larger, in this case) because all the other tags inherit their size from the body tag.

- If you don't define font sizes with relative units, you effectively disable the font sizing capabilities available in the View menu of Internet Explorer (although other browsers can resize absolute font-size units) , and therefore disenfranchise visually impaired users who rely on that capability to get your content to a size where they can read it. You need to check frequently during development to make sure that upping the font size in this way doesn't break your page's structure.

For these two reasons, I advise you to *set all font sizes in ems* rather than in absolute units such as pixels. If you are designing a row of tabs in a fixed horizontal space, the layout has the potential to break if the text gets resized. If you're careful, however, and design with this possibility in mind, you can develop such components of your design so that they can accommodate larger type when the size is changed by the user.

Color Values

You can use several value types to specify color, use whichever one of the following you prefer.

Hexadecimal (#RRGGBB and #RGB). If you already know languages like C++, PHP, or JavaScript, then you are familiar with hexadecimal (hex) notation for color. The format is this

#RRGGBB

In this value, the first two define red, the next two green, and the next two blue. Computers use units of two to count, rather than base 10 like us mortals, and that's why hex is base 16 (2 to the power of 4), using the 16 numbers/letters 0–9 and A–F. A thru F effectively function as 11 through 16. Because color is represented by a pair of these base 16 numbers, there are 256 (16 × 16) possible values for each color, or 16,777,216 combinations (256 × 256 × 256) of colors. You definitely get the most color options by using hexadecimal, although you can get by with far less. You'd be hard pressed (to say nothing of your monitor) to discern the difference between two immediately adjacent hex colors. Don't forget the # (hash) symbol in front of the value.

So, for example, pure red is #FF0000, pure blue is #00FF00, and pure green is #0000FF.

You can also use the following shorthand hex format

#RGB

If you select a color where each pair has the same two letters, such as #FF3322 (a strong red) you can abbreviate it to #F32.

Percentages RGB (R%, G% B%). This is notation that uses a percentage of each color like this

R%, G%, B%

Acceptable values are 0% to 100%. Although this only yields a piddling one million color combinations (100 x 100 x 100), that's more than enough for most of us. Also, it's much easier to make a guess at the color you want in RGB compared with hex notation.

So, for example, 100%, 0%, 0% is max red, 0%, 100%, 0% is max green, and 46%, 76%, 80% is close to that dusky green-blue color I demonstrated in hex above.

Most colors aren't easy to guess at a glance; for example, #7CA9BE is a dusky green-blue color. But if you just look at the first value in each RGB pair, 7, A, and B in this case, then you can see that red is slightly below half of 16, the maximum value, and green and blue are higher and about the same value. With this information, it's easier to make an informed guess as to what the color is.

Color Name (red). As you have seen from all the preceding color examples in the selector discussions, you can simply specify a color by name, or keyword to use the official term. However there are limitations. There is no W3C specification to say exactly how you should render a color like olive or lime; basically, every browser manufacturer assigns their own (presumably hex) values to each color keyword. Also, only 16 colors are in the W3C spec and, therefore, you can be sure to find only these 16 in every browser. Here they are, in alphabetical order

aqua, black, blue, fuchsia, gray, green, lime, maroon, navy, olive, purple, red, silver, teal, white, yellow

Most modern browsers offer many more colors (usually 140), but if you want to specify colors by name, you can only absolutely rely on these 16.

I usually use hex colors because I program, and that's how you do it in the murky world of coding. To save you from struggling to mix up colors yourself, visit www.webcolors.freeserve.co.uk/, which has color palettes—the Web-safe one (see the sidebar "You Don't Have to Limit Yourself to Web-Safe Colors") and others—as well as a great overview of color.

You Don't Have to Limit Yourself to Web-Safe Colors

If you use Macromedia Dreamweaver or other Web development tools, you are used to picking colors from a Web-safe palette. This is a set of 216 colors that only an engineer would have come up with, comprising mostly bright and saturated colors, with limited choices in dark and pale colors. These colors, you may (not) be interested to know, comprise twin hex pairs like this, #3399CC or #FF99CC, and only use the values 0, 3, 6, 9, C, and F. So any color you can come up with that meets these criteria is Web safe. These colors are a large subset of the 256 colors (40 are reserved for the system) that a monitor driven by an 8-bit VGA card can display (remember 8-bit?), so for years, we were told not to use any others. But today, under 1 percent (source: www.thecounter.com) of the world's surfers still use 8-bit color, so you can confidently use any color in your designs that you can create with the methods listed in this chapter.

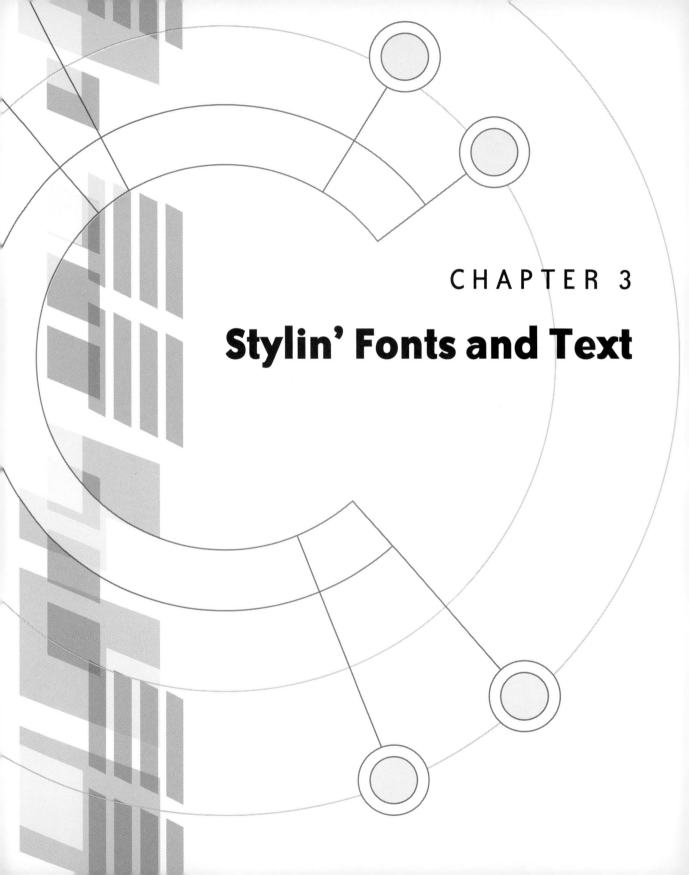

CHAPTER 3

Stylin' Fonts and Text

Learn typography basics

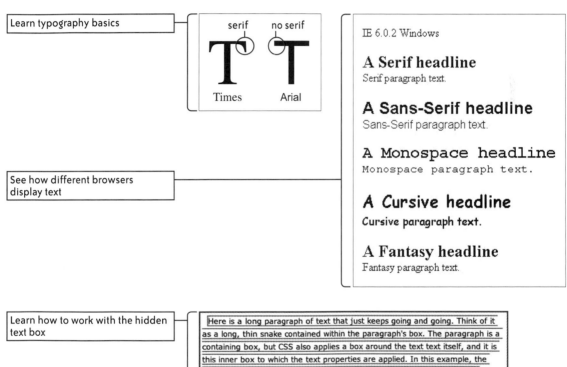

See how different browsers display text

Learn how to work with the hidden text box

Style type like a pro

Much of Web design is dealing with type—in paragraphs, headlines, lists, menus, and forms. As a result, the properties in this chapter are essential to making the difference between a site that looks thrown together and one that looks like it has the professional touch. More than any other factor, type makes the clearest visual statement about the quality of your site's offerings. Graphics are the icing on the cake; typography is where good design begins.

If the chapter title has you wondering "Aren't fonts and text the same thing?" the answer is No, and here's why.

Fonts are the different kinds of typefaces. Each font is a set of letters, numbers, and symbols with a unique visual appearance. All fonts belong to large *collections,* which describe their general look, such as serif, sans-serif, or monospace. Font collections are made up of *families,* such as Times and Helvetica. A font family in turn can be broken down into font *faces,* which are variations on the basic family, such as Times Roman, Times Bold, Helvetica Condensed, Bodoni Italic, and so on.

Text simply describes a block of type, like this sentence or the heading of a chapter, regardless of the font in which it is set.

CSS has a set of properties relating to fonts and a set of properties relating to text. *Font properties* relate to the size and appearance of collections of type. What is its family (Times or Helvetica, for example)? What size is it? Is it bold or italic? *Text properties* relate to the font's treatment—setting its line height and letter spacing, underlining, and so on.

Here's a way I think about this perhaps seemingly subtle distinction. You can apply font styles, such as bold and italic, to a single character, but text properties, such as line height and text indent, only make sense in the context of a block of text such as a headline or a paragraph.

Let's start with fonts.

Specifying Fonts in CSS

In this section, you'll learn how to use CSS to specify fonts. You can use any length units, both absolute and relative, to specify font sizes, but for reasons discussed throughout this chapter, it's best to use a relative measurement such as ems, so the user can easily scale the type to other sizes.

FIGURE 3.1 Serif fonts have noticeable details at the ends of the character strokes. Sans-serif fonts do not have these details.

Introducing Font Collections

Example: body {font-family: sans-serif;}

Values: serif, sans-serif, monospace, fantasy, cursive

The simplest way to specify fonts in CSS is by using the five generic collection names—serif, sans-serif, monospace, fantasy, and cursive. These generic names cause the user agent (browser, PDA, cell phone, and so on) to serve up one of these font types. Generic collection names represent the lowest level of support for font styling, and as you will see in a moment, CSS offers some better options than these:

Serif fonts are so named because of the little details, known as serifs, at the ends of the character strokes. These are particularly noticeable in the uppercase letters. Examples of serif fonts include Times, Bodoni, and Garamond.

Sans-serif fonts do not have any details at the ends of the character strokes. They have a more plain appearance than serif fonts. Examples of sans-serif fonts include Helvetica, Ariel, and Verdana.

Sans-Serif Fonts Are Better for the Web

Look at the big, text-heavy sites on the Web, such as CNN, MSNBC, or Amazon; see how just about all of them use sans-serif fonts? The small details of serif fonts provide useful additional visual information when you're reading print, but the inherently low-resolution world of the screen does not render serifs well, especially at small font sizes.

If you are new to Web design, I recommend using sans-serif fonts, at least while you gain some experience using serif fonts. Sans-serif fonts look crisper and more professional—simply changing from the default Times served up by virtually all browsers to a sans-serif font is the most effective and immediate single thing you can do to make your site look more professional.

Monospace fonts such as Courier and Monotype give equal spacing to every letter ("i" has the same amount of space as "m") and are typically used for code blocks in computer related books (this book is no exception), or to simulate the look of a typewriter, whatever that is.

```
This is some text in a monospaced font, where every
character occupies the same amount of horizontal space.
```

Cursive fonts look like cursive handwriting, although much neater than my own. Examples include Park Lane and Brush Script. Cursive is ideal for wedding invitations and therefore really doesn't get used much on the Web. If you use it, check it in various browsers, because every browser seems to use a different font for cursive.

Here is some cursive text, which isn't used much on the Web.

Fantasy fonts are ones that don't fit in the other categories. The main fantasy here is the hope that this might be a useful way to specify a font. It's almost impossible to predict what font might be served up as a fantasy font from browser to browser, and, therefore, it's best if you avoid fantasy fonts. Also, "fantasy" isn't really an accepted font collection name in the way that cursive and serif are; I have only seen this used as a collection name in CSS, but perhaps I don't get out enough.

Fantasy fonts are not recommended for use on the Web because you can't predict how they will be displayed.

If you want to specify a generic font, you write a declaration like this

```
body {font-family:sans-serif;}
```

In this case, the browser dishes up Helvetica or Arial or whatever sans-serif font is set as its default *and* is also on the viewer's computer (**Figures 3.2–3.5**). It's the most basic way to specify a font. But you can be more specific and declare a font family by name; usually that's what you want to do.

Firefox 0.8.0+

A Serif headline
Serif paragraph text.

A Sans-Serif headline
Sans-Serif paragraph text.

A Monospace headline
Monospace paragraph text.

A Cursive headline
Cursive paragraph text.

A Fantasy headline
Fantasy paragraph text.

FIGURE 3.2 Generic font families as displayed by Firefox for Windows.

IE 5.2.3 Mac

A Serif headline
Serif paragraph text.

A Sans-Serif headline
Sans-Serif paragraph text.

A Monospace headline
Monospace paragraph text.

A Cursive headline
Cursive paragraph text.

A FANTASY HEADLINE
FANTASY PARAGRAPH TEXT.

FIGURE 3.3 Generic font families as displayed by Internet Explorer for Mac OS X.

IE 6.0.2 Windows

A Serif headline
Serif paragraph text.

A Sans-Serif headline
Sans-Serif paragraph text.

A Monospace headline
Monospace paragraph text.

A Cursive headline
Cursive paragraph text.

A Fantasy headline
Fantasy paragraph text.

FIGURE 3.4 Generic font families as displayed by Internet Explorer for Windows.

Safari 1.2.3

A Serif headline
Serif paragraph text.

A Sans-Serif headline
Sans-Serif paragraph text.

A Monospace headline
Monospace paragraph text.

A Cursive headline
Cursive paragraph text.

A Fantasy headline
Fantasy paragraph text.

FIGURE 3.5 Generic font families as displayed by Safari. Note Safari uses regular fonts for Fantasy and Cursive in headings.

Exploring Font Families

In the world of print, you can use just about any font family you want; you purchase and install the font on your computer if it's not already there, and you use it in the design of your document. When your design is complete, you then send the font to the printer along with the document, or you PDF your document so the fonts are converted to vectors (outlines), and you're done. In print, you can work with any of the thousands of available fonts because you have control over them all the way to the printing press.

On the Web, you simply don't have this freedom of choice as far as fonts are concerned. This is one of the most disappointing aspects of the Web for transitioning print designers; *you must trust that the viewers have the fonts in which you want your document to be displayed installed on their computers.* Fonts aren't part of the browser; they are served up for the all applications on a computer from the system software where they reside. Furthermore, it is impossible to know what flavor of any given font (Times, Times Regular, or Times Roman, for example) a user might have on their machine.

As much as you might want your Web pages' headlines to be displayed in Univers 87 Oblique, the odds of a user having that particular font are, to quote Elvis (Costello), less than zero. In fact, there is only a very short list of fonts that you can be sure users of both Windows and Macintosh have installed on their systems: Times, Arial, Verdana, and Courier.

Fonts Common to Both Mac and Windows

Here's a list of fonts with exactly the same names that came included on both my Windows XP and Mac OS X systems. You can probably use these pretty confidently as your "first-choice" fonts, but of course, always provide second, third, and even fourth choices and make sure to end your font-family declaration with a "last resort" font collection (either serif or sans-serif):

Arial	Franklin Gothic	Tahoma
Arial Black	Georgia	Times New Roman
Arial Narrow	Impact	Trebuchet MS
Century Gothic	Monotype	Verdana
Comic Sans MS	Palatino	Webdings
Courier New	Symbol	

CSS3 is the next version of CSS. It has been specified by the W3C but it is not currently implemented in any browsers, except partially in Opera.

Even Helvetica, perhaps the most popular sans-serif font of all time, is not included with Windows, but Windows has its own almost identical font, Arial.

"What about automatically downloading fonts as needed from my server to the user?" you ask (you did ask, right?). Good question. Although CSS 3 specifies a way you can request a font from your server in which to display the document, browsers do not currently support this capability. But it is nice to think about, and one day it may be a reality. (Even then, the browser will never install the font on the user's computer but merely use it to display the page).

Until the happy day when fonts are available on demand, to use specific fonts with CSS, you need to list the fonts, in order of preference, in which you would like the document to be displayed. This list must only be by family name—by that I mean you must use Helvetica or Times, not Helvetica Condensed or Times Expanded.

It is accepted practice to write a CSS declaration specifying a number of either serif or sans-serif fonts starting with the one you prefer first and ending with a generic font name such as serif or sans-serif like this (in this case, I'm working with sans-serif fonts)

```
font-family {"trebuchet ms", helvetica, arial, sans-serif}
```

Because Trebuchet MS is more than one word, it has to be in quotes. If you do this in an inline style that's already inside double quotes, use single quotes on the name, like this

```
<p style="font-family:'trebuchet ms', helvetica, arial,
sans-serif;">
```

or like this in the case of serif fonts

```
font-family: {charcoal, times, serif}
```

In the first example using the `font-family` property above I am saying to the browser, "Display this document in Trebuchet MS, and if you don't have it, use Helvetica. If you don't have either of those, use Arial, and if all else fails, use whatever generic sans-serif font you do have. *It is very important to make the last item of a font-family declaration a generic declaration of either serif or sans-serif as a final fallback.* This ensures that, at a minimum, your document at least displays in the right *type* (no pun intended) of font.

In the second example using the `font-family` property, I first declare Charcoal, a font only available on Macintosh, because I want Macintosh users to have the pleasure of viewing my document in that lovely font. However, because Windows users don't usually have Charcoal, they see the document displayed in the second choice, Times.

Setting Up to Style a Document

The best way to learn about all the different aspects of fonts is to style a document. So set up your XHTML editor (such as Macromedia Dreamweaver) and your browser to style the sample document (sample_xhtml_markup. htm) in the Chapter 3 folder on the Stylin' Web site (www.bbd.com/stylin). Here's how to proceed:

1. Download the sample documents folder from the Stylin' Web site and save it on your hard drive.

2. Navigate to the Chapter 3 folder and open the sample_xhtmml_ markup_htm file from the File menu of your HTML editor.

3. Also open the same file in a Web browser.

   It's fine to open the file in two applications at once, because you are only writing to the file from the editor and are simply reading it in the browser.

4. Each time you make a change to the HTML document and Save, flip to your Web browser (Alt-Tab on the PC or Command-Tab on the Mac) and refresh the page in the browser using the F5 function key (or Command-R in Safari).

Now you see the updated document displayed.

Using Embedded Styles (for Now)

To keep things simple, I'm going to show you how to write your CSS styles in a style element in the head of the document. I'll also show you how to remove the link to the external style sheet for now. Doing this means that you won't have to manage a separate style sheet, but the styles that you write will only be available to this one document. That's ideal for developing the layout of a specific page; later you'll create a separate style sheet that can supply styles to multiple pages. Review the start of Chapter 2 if this doesn't make complete sense.

Let's use the HTML document you created in Chapter 1 and modify it to include the style element in the document head, as illustrated by the highlighted code

```
<head>

<title>A Sample XHTML Document</title>

<meta http-equiv="Content-type" content="text/html;
charset=iso-8859-1" />
```

```
<meta http-equiv="Content-Language" content="en-us" />
```

```
<style type="text/css">
```

> Add CSS for specifying a font family in this blank line

```
</style>
```

```
</head>
```

The blank line between the opening and closing tag of the `style` element is where you add your CSS. When the browser encounters the opening tag of the `style` element, it stops interpreting the code as XHTML and starts interpreting it as CSS. When it encounters the closing tag of the `style` element, the browser reverts to treating the code as XHTML again. So anything you write within the `style` element must be in CSS syntax, the same syntax you use if the CSS is in a separate style sheet. This means any code within the `style` element is formatted like this:

```
selector {property1:value; property2:value; etc.}
```

You need to be aware of whether you are writing CSS or XHTML at any given moment during the development of your projects and make sure you format your code accordingly. In the case of the sample XHTML documents I provide at my Web site, www.bbd.com/stylin, the XHTML is already written, so once you add the `style` element using XHTML, you are working entirely in CSS.

Setting the Font Family for the Entire Page

To set the font family for the entire page, you first need to set it for the body of the document

```
<style type="text/css">
```

```
body {font-family: verdana, arial, sans-serif;}
```

```
</style>
```

Save your changes, flip to the browser, and refresh the page. What you see should look like **Figure 3.6**.

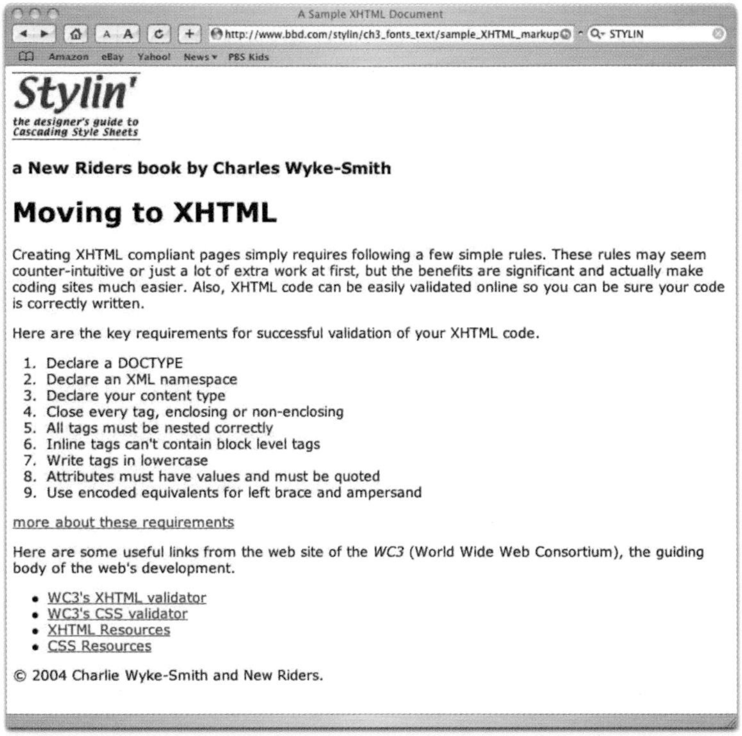

FIGURE 3.6 Setting the `font-family` property of the body element affects the whole document.

Because `font-family` is an inherited property, its value is passed to all its descendants, which, since `body` is the top-level element, are all the other elements in the markup. So with one line, you've made it so everything is in the desired font; bathe for a moment in that glow of CSS magic. OK, moving right along . . .

Sizing Fonts

You can use three types of values to size fonts. They are *absolute* (for example, pixels or inches), *relative* (for example, percentages or ems), and what I call the *sweatshirt keywords* (for example, x-small, small, large, and xx-large, among others). All three methods have advantages and disadvantages. Jeffrey Zeldman and other CCS mavens advocate keywords as the least problematic of the three (see A List Apart at www.alistapart.com/articles/sizematters/); but because the keyword method requires some sophisticated CSS to make fonts display at consistent sizes in all browsers and only offers a limited number of font sizes, here, I'm going to have you set font sizes in ems.

The Pros and Cons of Using Proportional Sizing

When you start to develop a style sheet, one key decision is the kind of units you will use to size type; absolute (points, inches, etc.) or relative (percentages, ems, etc.). The old way was to use points, but Internet Explorer, and other less-compliant browsers cannot scale type set in absolute units when the user selects a different size from a choice such as Type Size (exact wording varies between browsers) in the View menu. So now the trend is towards using relative sizes. Here are the pros and cons of doing that:

Pros:

- All type scales proportionally if the user uses the Text Size menu choice (it may be named differently in some browsers) to set the text larger or smaller. This is very user friendly and is an important step in making your site accessible to the visually impaired or to someone who has a super high-resolution monitor with pixels the size of grains of sand.

- As you fine-tune your design, you can proportionally change the size of all text by simply adjusting the body font-size; this changes the baseline size and all the other elements increase their size proportionally to that baseline.

Cons:

- If you are not careful, nested elements can display very small text, (using keyword sizing prevents this) because font sizing is inherited

- It is possible for users to "break" a CSS page layout that hasn't been designed for text sizing. For example, if the user sets type to large sizes from the View menu, a "floating-columns" layout can display weirdness like the right column being forced down below the content area because it is too large to remain in place. In Chapter 6, where we create advanced CCS-based page layouts, we'll review this problem, and ways to prevent it, in detail.

There is an excellent blog item and discussion on the thorny subject of sizing fonts by Richard Rutter at www.clagnut.com/blog/348/, so I'll not waste more space here except to say that if you care about people being able to size the type on your site, you need to read this. For an in-depth resource on font-sizing, check out the CSS-Discuss site at http://css-discuss.incutio.com/ ?page=FontSize.

Ems can be a strange, confusing unit at first, but they are simply a proportional value—think of them as decimal percentages where .9 em is the same as 90 percent of the baseline size.

Most browsers have a default size for 1 em (approximately 16 pixels high), and if you set an element to 1 em, it takes on that baseline size. If you want a piece of type to be three-quarters of that size, set it to .75 ems, if you want it to be half, set it to .5ems.

When working with ems, you should start by setting the body font-size value to 100 percent (which it is by default, but you should explicitly state it so that you can tweak overall sizes later; you also do this for the benefit of Internet Explorer, as I'll explain momentarily), and then you can set all other sizes in proportion to it. Here's how this works.

First, modify the body selector to look like this

```
<style type="text/css">
body {font-family: verdana, arial, sans-serif; font-size:100%;}
</style>
```

Although this doesn't produce a visible effect, you now have a tweakable baseline size. The reason you are using a percentage to set the baseline size is because if Internet Explorer sees a baseline size in ems, it *overscales*—that is, it scales ems in descendant selectors more than it should, both larger and smaller, when the user changes the text size. If the baseline size is set as a percentage, the correct proportions are maintained.

You might notice that the default sizes for common markup elements such as `<h1>` through `<h6>`, `<p>`, `<ul>`, and `<li>` are rather (read "very") large, and if you need to get any amount of content on the page, using these default sizes means the user must do lots of scrolling. Long hours behind market research mirrors have taught me that scrolling is one of the least loved aspects of Web browsing. Also, I simply find that these large default sizes give the page a horsey, poorly designed look.

But, when working in proportional ems, you can choose to make the overall font size a little smaller, because those users who want large text sizes can get them easily by selecting View > Text Size from the browser menu and choosing Larger (or similar, depending on the browser).

Let's say you decide that the new baseline size is going to be 12 points (from a visual standpoint, that is; you will use percents and ems to actually specify the sizes). You set the body font size to 76 percent. Now text in a paragraph is 76 percent of the browser's 16-point default size for paragraphs: 12 points.

Now, when you style the elements 1em equals 12 points, .75 equals 9pts and so on.

Some developers style the `html` tag (yes, you can do that) to 125 percent (20 points) and style its immediate child `body` to 50%. This results in all the descendants tags seeing 1em=10 points, so .9em equals 9 points, 1.2ems equals 12 points and so on which gives a very nice correlation of ems in the style sheet to points on the screen.

Remember, regardless of what units you use to style type, the browser has to convert them into pixels, because that's what the

Shouldn't that be 75% you ask? The answer is that a more consistent sizing result across browsers is obtained by rounding to an even number than an odd one, so 76% actually produces more consistent results than 75%!

screen uses. Every browser has a slightly different algorithm to perform that calculation, so the rounder the numbers the browser uses in the calculations, the more consistent the result from browser to browser. The importance of pixel-accurate type between browsers is a personal matter, but these are a couple of ways you can approach the issue of setting a baseline size for your type.

The bottom line is that if you are using a proportional value method (for example, ems) to size the fonts for the individual selectors, you are then able provide the majority of viewers with font sizes that are more aesthetically pleasing, that result in less scrolling, and that still give visually impaired users the option to override your font size decisions and increase the size of all type proportionally.

In the following examples, you work with the default of 100%, and later, when you start building sites, you can adjust this baseline value to suit the needs of each design.

From the 100% `font-size` baseline, let's set font sizes on each of the elements using ems, starting with the line under the logo that reads "a New Riders book . . ." (**Figure 3.7**). We do it this way because setting the baseline at 100% provides more consistent results across browsers than using 1em. However, we use ems for the elements because ems are a familiar and conventional unit for setting type.

FIGURE 3.7 Here's the original version of the header from the Chapter 1 example with default font styling.

This line is an `h3` element, so you're going to set it to .8em (I chose this number because I've done this before and I know that's a nice size for it). Here's what you write

```
<style type="text/css">

body {font-family: verdana, arial, sans-serif; font-
size:100%;}

h3 {font-size:.8em}

</style>
```

Figure 3.8 shows how this looks.

You can see that the headline is now much smaller. (You may be interested to know that by experimentation, I discovered its default size was equal to 1.2ems, or 16 × 1.2 = 19.2 points).

Let's now go on and set the font sizes for other elements in your markup, as follows

```
<style type="text/css">

body {font-family: verdana, arial, sans-serif; font-size:100%;}

h1 {font-size:.1em}

h3 {font-size:.8em}

p {font-size:.8em}

ol {font-size:.75em}

ul {font-size:.75em}

a {font-size:.7em}

</style>
```

This results in **Figure 3.9**.

A couple of points (no pun intended) about these styles: first, you didn't set a style for the list item (li) elements of the two lists, but you did for the ordered list (ol) and unordered list (ul) elements that respectively contain them. If you styled the li element, both lists would display in the same size, but because you styled the ol and ul elements instead, the li elements inherit their values, and you can later make the lists' items different sizes if you wish.

FIGURE 3.9 Here the font size for the various elements is set in ems, but the combination of ems and nested tags is making the text in the second list very small.

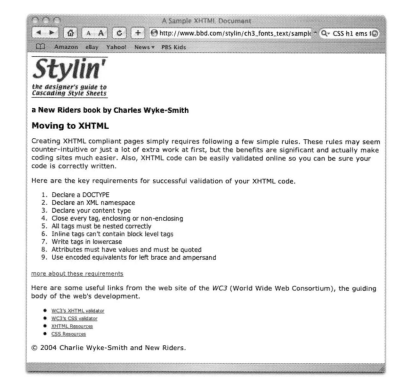

Inherited Styles in Nested Tags

Secondly, although you are already making a nice improvement to the unstyled layout with which you started, the font size for the bulleted unordered list (ul) is very small, even though it's set to the same size as the ordered list (ol).

This problem is caused by the fact that the ol element is set to .75 ems and the a elements nested down inside are set to .7ems. The net result is type in those a elements end up sized to .525ems (.7 x .75). Inheritance of font sizes can work for you, and, as here, against you. Fortunately, the fix here is easy; you simply set a contextual selector for this specific situation, like this

```
<style type="text/css">

body {font-family: verdana, arial, sans-serif; font-
size:1em;}

h1 {font-size:.1em}

h3 {font-size:.8em}
```

```
p {font-size:.8em}

ol {font-size:.75em}

ul {font-size:.75em}

ul a {font-size:inherit}

a {font-size:.7em}

</style>
```

You simply used the inherit value to tell the a element to get its font size from its containing element. Not only does this ensure that the a element displays in the desired size, but also, if you later want to change the size of the list items, you can just update the ol selector and the nested a element dutifully inherits the new size, and the problem is fixed (**Figure 3.10**).

FIGURE 3.10 Now that the inherited sizing issue is fixed, the list is much more readable.

Here are some useful links from the web site of the WC body of the web's development.

- WC3's XHTML validator
- WC3's CSS validator
- XHTML Resources
- CSS Resources

© 2004 Charlie Wyke-Smith and New Riders.

You can now test the scalability of your ems-based layout:

1. Select View > Text Size > Largest in the browser menu (this is the path in Internet Explorer—it will vary slightly in other browsers).

    Note that everything scales up nicely for viewers who are visually impaired.

2. Vary the value of font-size property of the body selector—try 80 percent and 120 percent, for example. Save and reload the page.

    Again, all the elements size proportionally. Those of you who have spent hours changing the size attribute of hundreds of font tags in dozens of pages after it's decided that the type sizes are all too big or too small will appreciate the power and convenience of this capability. Next time the client makes some comment like "The problem with you designers is you always make the type so bloody small", you can quadruple the font size of the entire site in about five seconds, and then politely say "Is *that* big enough for you?"

Let's move on to some other font-related CSS.

Font Properties

The relationship of font sizes is key to indicating the hierarchy of the text in your document. This is achieved through an understanding of the various font properties and an understanding of how font properties can be inherited through the hierarchy of your document. Let's take at the font properties now.

Font-Style Property

Example: `h2 {font-style:italic}`

Other values: `normal`, `oblique`

Font style determines whether a font is italicized or not. It's that simple. If you want a piece of text to be italicized, you write this

`p {font-style:italic;}`

You can also write `oblique` instead of `italic`, but generally, the result is the same. The difference between the two is that, supposedly, italic is simply a distortion applied to the regular font to make it lean to the right, whereas an oblique font is actually designed as a font in its own right and therefore, the theory goes, is more pure. These niceties are pretty much lost on the Web, where a font variation such as Helvetica Oblique can't be specified even though if exists as a font on the user's machine,, and oblique doesn't even alter the regular type in older browsers such as Netscape 4.7.

So, there are only two useful settings for the `font-style` property: `italic` to make regular text italicized, and `normal` to make a section within italicized type regular "upright" text. In this example,

`p {font-style:italic;}`

`span{font-style:normal}`

```
<p>This is italicized type with <span>a piece of non-italic
text</span> in the middle.</p>
```

the code produces the result in **Figure 3.11**.

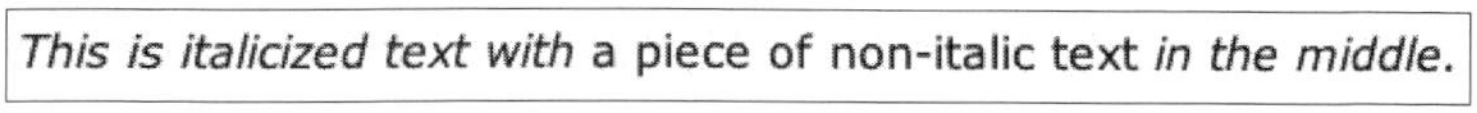

FIGURE 3.11 The normal value for the font-style property causes a specified section of type to appear normal within a bit of italicized text.

This is italicized text with a piece of non-italic text *in the middle.*

Note on the Value Normal

normal causes any of the possible effects of a property not to be applied. Why might you want to do this, you ask? As I showed you in the font-style example in the main text, setting font-style:normal leaves the text in its regular state, rather than italicized. The reason this option is available is so that you can selectively override a default or a global property you have set. Headlines h1 through h6 are bold by default, so if you want to unbold the h3 element, for example, you need to write h3 {font-weight: normal;}. If your style sheet states a {font-variant:small-caps;} so that all links are in small caps and you want one special set of links to be in regular upper- and lowercase type, you might write a declaration such as a.speciallink {font-variant:normal:}.

Font-Weight Property

Example: a {font-weight:bold}

Possible values: 100, 200, and so on to 900, or bold, bolder, lighter, normal

The W3C recommendations for implementing this property simply state that each successive higher value (whether numerical or "weight" values) must produce boldness equal to or heavier than the previous lower value.

bold and bolder give two weights of boldness. lighter allows you to go one step in the other direction if you want a section within bold type to be, well, lighter.

Figure 3.12 shows a little test I ran on some different browsers.

Can you see more than two weights for any given browser among these results? Nor can I. I even tried different fonts, but to no avail. There really are only two results for all the font-weight values—bold or normal. Boldness variations would be a nice way to show a hierarchy in all kinds of data, especially when you could easily generate the different numerical values mathematically from middleware (for example, ASP or PHP) code to automatically highlight results that cross certain thresholds. In the following section, I show you a relatively simple and useful representational method that the browser makers could give us designers. Certainly there's room for improvement here, as the results show.

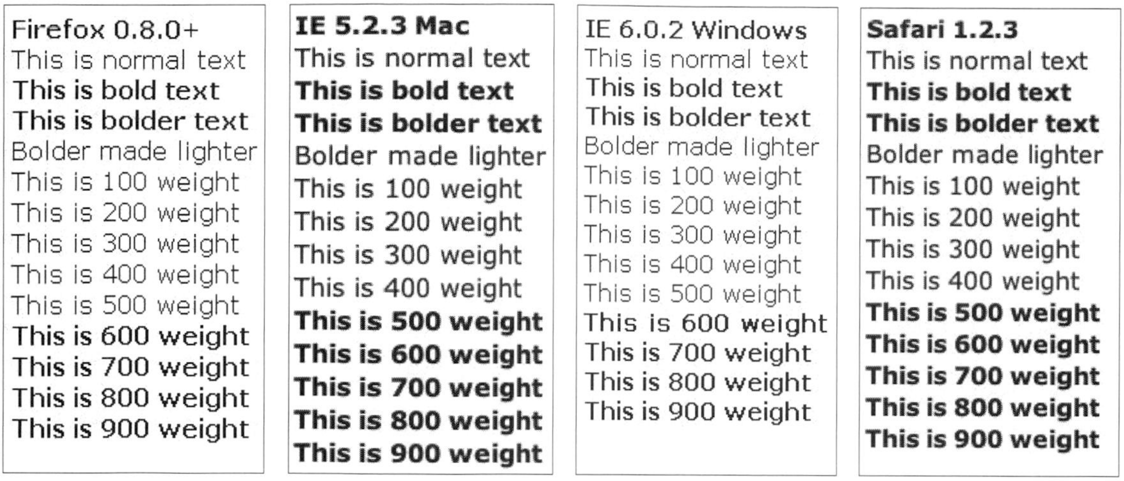

Firefox 0.8.0+	IE 5.2.3 Mac	IE 6.0.2 Windows	Safari 1.2.3
This is normal text	This is normal text	This is normal text	This is normal text
This is bold text	**This is bold text**	This is bold text	**This is bold text**
This is bolder text	**This is bolder text**	This is bolder text	**This is bolder text**
Bolder made lighter	Bolder made lighter	Bolder made lighter	Bolder made lighter
This is 100 weight	This is 100 weight	This is 100 weight	This is 100 weight
This is 200 weight	This is 200 weight	This is 200 weight	This is 200 weight
This is 300 weight	This is 300 weight	This is 300 weight	This is 300 weight
This is 400 weight	This is 400 weight	This is 400 weight	This is 400 weight
This is 500 weight	**This is 500 weight**	This is 500 weight	**This is 500 weight**
This is 600 weight	**This is 600 weight**	This is 600 weight	**This is 600 weight**
This is 700 weight	**This is 700 weight**	This is 700 weight	**This is 700 weight**
This is 800 weight	**This is 800 weight**	This is 800 weight	**This is 800 weight**
This is 900 weight	**This is 900 weight**	This is 900 weight	**This is 900 weight**

FIGURE 3.12 Here's how different browsers interpret different font-weight settings.

Font-Variant Property

Example: `blockquote {font-variant:small-caps;}`

Values: `small-caps, normal`

This property accepts just one value (besides `normal`) and that is `small-caps`. This causes all lowercase letters to be set in small caps, like this

`h3 {font-variant:small-caps;}`

I often use `small-caps` with the first-line pseudo-class, which allows you to specify a style for the first line of an element. Typically you would use it on a paragraph (see Chapter 2). Again, use this styling sparingly because text in all uppercase is harder to read because it lacks the visual cues provided by the ascenders and descenders of lowercase type.

The Font Property Shorthand

Example: `p {font: bold italic small-caps 12pt verdana, arial, sans-serif;}`

`<p>Here's a piece of text loaded up with every possible font property.</p>`

The code above produces the result in **Figure 3.13**.

FIGURE 3.13 It only takes one line of
CSS to create this font styling.

*Jumping ahead somewhat, you can
write the* font-size *property to
also include the* line-height *property (which is a text property rather
than a font property) by writing the
size as 12pt/150% or similar, which
in print parlance results in 12 on 18
point type. Line height is to CSS what
leading is to typesetting in the world
of print; you'll learn more about the*
line-height *property in the "Text
Properties" section next.*

> **HERE'S A PIECE OF TEXT LOADED UP WITH EVERY POSSIBLE FONT PROPERTY.**

The font property is a nifty shortcut that lets you apply all of the
font properties in a single declaration; this helps reduce the amount
of CSS you have to write to achieve your desired font styling. You
have to sequence the values in the correct order, however, so that
the browser can interpret them correctly.

Two simple rules apply:

Rule 1: Values for font-size and font-family must always be
declared.

Rule 2: The sequence for the values is as follows:

1. font-weight, font-style, font-variant, in any order, then

2. font-size, then

3. font-family

Text Properties

So now that you've looked at how to get the font you want, it's time
to look at how to style text. If you want to indent a paragraph, create
a superscript such as the 6 in 10^6, create more space between each
letter of a headline, and many other type formatting tasks, you need
to use the CSS text properties.

There are eight text-related CSS properties:

- text-indent
- letter-spacing
- word-spacing
- text-decoration
- text-align
- line-height
- text-transform
- vertical-align

Meet the Text Snake

You must understand a very important concept about how CSS manages text—CSS puts a box around the text inside an element. For example, if you put a block of text in a paragraph p element, CSS sees the actual text as a long skinny line of text in a box, even if it gets broken across multiple lines in order to fit in the container. To make this clear, in **Figure 3.14**, the border of the containing element (the paragraph) is in red, and the border of the text box is in green.

Both these boxes are normally invisible—you have to set their borders to see them, but they are always there.

Here is a long paragraph of text that just keeps going and going. Think of it as a long, thin snake contained within the paragraph's box. The paragraph is a containing box, but CSS also applies a box around the text text itself, and it is this inner box to which the text properties are applied. In this example, the containing element's box is in red and the inner box around the text is in green. As you can see from the way the inner box is drawn, CSS sees the text as one long strip, even though the width of the container causes it to be broken across several lines.

Figure 3.14 Text is contained within a long, skinny box that is often broken across multiple lines.

In this example, I marked up the text like this

```
<p><span>This is a long paragraph…(etc.)</span></p>
```

and applied the following styles

```
p {border:2px solid red:}
```

```
span {border:2px solid green;}
```

Note that the text box is broken across the lines and is only closed at the beginning of the first line and the end of the last line.

Knowing this can help you get things looking the way you want faster. For example, if you want to indent the first line of a paragraph, you can use the text property text-indent, as I did in Figure 3.14, and you then are moving the start position of the text box. Subsequent lines are not indented because to CSS, it's just one long piece of text.

If you want the whole paragraph indented, then you need to set the margin-left property of the paragraph; in other words, you have to push the whole container to the right. All you need to remember from all this is that text properties are applied to the long, thin, snake-like inner text box, not the box of the containing element.

In these examples, the paragraph border is displayed for clarity—normally it would not be shown.

Text-Indent Property

Example: `p {text-indent:3em;}`

Values: any length value (positive or negative)

Because I have already touched on it, let's start with the `text-indent` property. This property sets the start position of the text box in relation to the containing element. Normally, the left edge of the text box (the start of the first line, in the case of a multiple line block) and the left edge of the container are the same.

If you set a positive value to the `text-indent`, then the text moves to the right, creating an indented paragraph (**Figure 3.15**).

FIGURE 3.15 Set a positive value for the `text-indent` property to create an indented paragraph.

If you set a negative value, the first line hangs out to the left of the containing element. Be careful when you use negative margins to create a negative indent—in such a case, the first line of text actually hangs outside of its container, so make sure that there is a place for the hanging text to go. If the containing element abuts another element to its left, then the hanging text overlaps the latter element, or if it's close to the edge of the browser window, it is clipped (**Figure 3.16**).

FIGURE 3.16 This paragraph has a negative indent for the right margin but no corresponding left margin value, which causes the hanging text to be clipped.

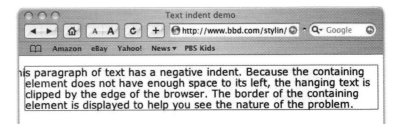

The way to avoid this problem is always to specify a positive left margin value greater than the specified negative indent. In Figure 3.16, the negative indent is –1.5 ems, but in **Figure 3.17**, there is also a left margin value of 2 ems.

FIGURE 3.17 This paragraph has a
negative indent for the right margin
and a corresponding left margin
value that creates enough space for
the hanging text on the right.

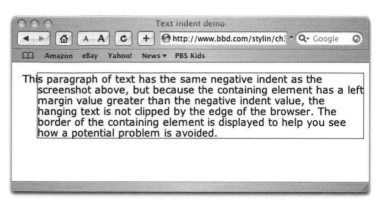

The code for the paragraph in Figure 3.17 is as follows

```
p {text-indent:1.5em; margin-left:2em; border: 1px solid red;}
```

Hanging paragraphs help give text that professionally styled look
and give the reader clear entry points into the text blocks.

It's good practice to set indents and related margins in ems so that
the indent remains proportional to the line length if the user (or
you) change the text size. In the case of a hanging indent, proportional sizing ensures that enough space for the hanging text is
created, regardless of how large the user might scale the font.

If space is tight and you don't want spaces between paragraphs, you
can set the margin top and margin bottom values of the paragraphs
to 0 and use indents or negative indents instead of vertical space to
provide a clear indication of where each paragraph starts.

Inherited Values with the Text-Indent Property

One more important note here: text-indent is inherited by child elements. For example, if you set a text-indent on
a div, all the paragraphs inside the div will have that text-indent value. However, it's not the defined value that's
passed down but the computed value. Here's an example that explains the implications of this fact.

Let's say you have a div containing text that's 400 pixels wide with a 5 percent text indent. If this is the case, the indent
for that text is 20 pixels (5 percent of 400). Within the div is a paragraph that's 200 pixels wide. As a child element, the
paragraph inherits any text-indent value, so it is indented too, but the value it inherits is the result of the calculation
made on the parent, that is, 20 pixels, not the defined 5 percent. As a result, it too has a 20-pixel indent even though it's
half the width of the parent element. This ensures that all the paragraphs have nice matching indents regardless of their
widths. Of course, you can override this behavior by explicitly setting a different text-indent for child elements.

Tracking *is the print term for the letter spacing applied to a block of text.* Kerning *is the term for adjusting the space between two specific characters.*

FIGURE 3.18 In this example, you can see how changing the letter-spacing value changes the look of your text.

Letter-Spacing Property

Example: p {letter-spacing: .2em;}

Values: any length values (positive or negative)

This property produces what print designers call *tracking*, the overall spacing between letters. Positive values increase letter-spacing, while negative values decrease it. I highly recommend you use relative values, such as ems or percentages, rather than absolute values, such as inches or pixels, so that the spacing remains proportional even if the user changes the font size. **Figure 3.18** gets you started.

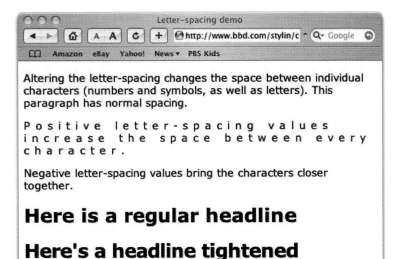

As you can see, you can give headlines that professional touch by tightening them up a bit; the default letter spacing appears more and more loose as the text gets larger.

Generally, body copy doesn't need changes to the letter spacing, although it's a personal preference, and you can give your pages a unique look if the type is a little tighter or looser than is typical. Just go easy, as too much either way makes the type hard to read. Note the text and headline I tightened in Figure 3.18 only have .05em (a twentieth of an em) of letter spacing removed from between each character; much more and the letters would start to mush into each other. Generally, very small values, such a 0.1em, give the desired result; although it's only a small amount of space, it is inserted (or removed) between every character).

Word-Spacing Property

Example: p {word-spacing: .2em;}

Values: any length values (positive or negative)

Word spacing is very similar to letter spacing except, as you might imagine, the space changes between each word rather than between each letter. The first observation you should make here is that CSS treats any character or group of characters with white space around them as a word. Second, even more than letter spacing, word spacing can easily be overdone and result in some very hard to read type (**Figure 3.19**). Easy does it.

FIGURE 3.19 Word spacing is one of those styles that is easy to overdo.

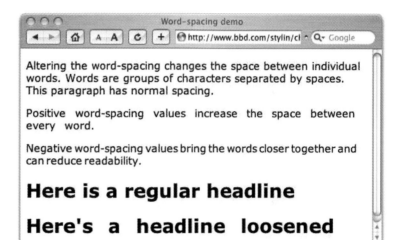

Text-Decoration Property

Example: .retailprice {text-decoration: strikethrough;}

Values: underline, overline, strikethrough, blink

No, you can't hang holly and little bells on it, but you can underline, overline, strike-through, and blink (but don't do it, please, because it is s-o-o-o-o annoying) text using this property.

The primary application of text decoration is controlling the underlining of links. Think long and hard before you add underlining to text that is not a link; in fact, unless it's a link, don't underline it. Perhaps if you have a column of numbers, you might underline the last one before the total, or something like that, but Web users are so used to underlining as the visual cue for a link that you are setting them up for frustration, disappointment, and a lot of useless clicking if you underline text that is not a link.

Text-Align Property

Example: `p {text-align: right;}`

Values: `left`, `right`, `center`, `justify`

There are only four values for this property: `left`, `center`, `right`, and `justify`. The text aligns horizontally with respect to the containing element and you must set the property on the containing element; in other words, if you want a `h1` headline centered with in a `div`, set the `text-align` of the `div`, not the `h1`. **Figure 3.20** shows the four possible `text-align` values in action.

FIGURE 3.20 Text alignment has four different values, each of which is demonstrated here.

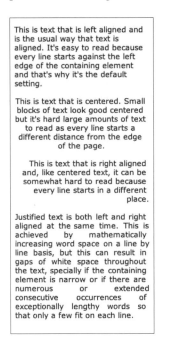

This is text that is left aligned and is the usual way that text is aligned. It's easy to read because every line starts against the left edge of the containing element and that's why it's the default setting.

This is text that is centered. Small blocks of text look good centered but it's hard large amounts of text to read as every line starts a different distance from the edge of the page.

This is text that is right aligned and, like centered text, it can be somewhat hard to read because every line starts in a different place.

Justified text is both left and right aligned at the same time. This is achieved by mathematically increasing word space on a line by line basis, but this can result in gaps of white space throughout the text, specially if the containing element is narrow or if there are numerous or extended consecutive occurrences of exceptionally lengthy words so that only a few fit on each line.

Line-Height Property

Example: `p {line-height: 1.5;}`

Values: any numerical value (no value type is needed)

`line-height` is the CSS equivalent of *leading* (pronounced like the metal) in the world of print. Leading creates space between the lines of a block of text. Leading is defined not as the height of the space between the lines, but as the distance between the baseline of one line and the next. For the sake of readability, leading is greater than the height of the type so that there is space between the lines. By default, browsers set leading proportionately to the

In case you're wondering where "leading" came from, in the early days of printing, a strip of lead was used to space the lines of type.

font size—typically at 118 percent of the font size according to my tests—so there is always consistent space between the lines no matter what the font size.

The simplest way to set the leading is to use the font: shorthand property and write a compound value for both font size and line height in one. For example:

```
div#intro {font: 1.2em/1.4;}
```

In this case, the leading is 1.4 times the font size of 1.2 ems. Note that you don't need any units, such as ems or pixels, specified for the line-height part of the value, just a number. In this case, CSS simply takes the calculated size of whatever number of onscreen pixels 1.2 ems works out to be and multiplies it by 1.4 to arrive at the line height. If you later increase the font size to 1.5 ems, the line height (leading) is still 1.4 times the calculated amount of 1.5 ems. If the line height had been specified in a fixed unit such as pixels and you increased the font size, then the lines of text would overlap one another.

It's worth noting that any line height greater than the text height is shared both above and below the text. Let's take a simple example in pixels to illustrate this point, although for the reasons I gave earlier, using pixels is not the ideal way to set line height. However, it's easier to understand the math if you use pixels here. If you have a font size of 12 pixels and you set the line height to 20 pixels, the browser adds 4 pixels of space above the line of type and four below; 12 + 4 + 4 = 20. In the normal course of events, you don't notice this because the overall look in a multiline paragraph of text is that there are 8 pixels of space between each line. However, this might have a bearing for you on the top and bottom line of type, which, in fact, only have 4 pixels of space above and below them respectively.

Vertical Centering of Single Lines of Text

It is natural to try using the vertical-align property to center elements vertically within a containing element, but it doesn't work. However, if you just want to center a single line of type with a containing element, that's doable. Tables have the valign attribute, which moves the contents of a table cell to the vertical center of the cell. In CSS, you can achieve vertical centering, for a single line of text at least, by setting its line height equal to the height of the containing element. Because the line height is split between the top and bottom of the text, the text ends up centered vertically.

Vertically entering a block of text, such as a p element, within a containing element is almost impossible, although with some extra divs, it is doable. Rather than get into a lengthy explanation here, I refer you to "Vertical Centering in CSS" (www.jakpsatweb.cz/css/css-vertical-center-solution.html).

You can do this, but it ain't pretty. Sometimes you just have to wonder why such a basic necessity wasn't addressed in the CSS spec.

Text-Transform Property

Example: `p {text-transform: capitalize;}`

Values: `uppercase, lowercase, capitalize, none`

`text-transform` changes the capitalization of text within an element. You can force a line of text to have initial letters capitalized, all text uppercase, or all text lowercase. **Figure 3.21** shows the various options.

FIGURE 3.21 The `text-transform` property can turn text into uppercase or lowercase as well as perform other party tricks.

This is text that is not transformed. It's displayed in the usual way that text is presented.

This Is Regular Text That Is Capitalized Using The Text-Transform Capitalize Value.

THIS TEXT IS STYLED USING THE TEXT-TRANSFORM UPPERCASE VALUE; IT IS IN ALL LOWERCASE LETTERS IN THE MARKUP, INCLUDING THE FIRST LETTER OF THE FIRST WORD.

this is text that is actually written in all caps in the markup but displays in lowercase because of the text-transform lowercase value.

`capitalize` capitalizes the first letter of every word. This emulates the style of many headlines in ads, newspapers, and magazines, except that a human applying such styling tends to leave the capitalization off minor words such as "of", "as", and "and", as in "Tom and Jerry Go to Vegas." CSS capitalization simply produces "Tom And Jerry Go To Vegas." However, it's a nice effect for headlines, and if your content is coming from a database or another source such as XML, you can get this effect without touching the markup.

Use `font-variant` if you want large and small caps. Think also about tightening up the visual appearance with a small negative `letter-spacing` value (see "Letter-Spacing Property" earlier in this chapter).

Vertical-Align Property

Example: `vertical-align:60%`

Values: any length `value`, `sub`, `sup`, `top`, `middle`, `bottom`

Vertical-align moves type up or down with respect to the baseline. As this example demonstrates, one of the most common uses is for superscript and subscripted numbers in formulas and mathematical expressions, such as x^4-y^{-5} or N_3O. It's also the correct way to style asterisks and other markers within text to indicate footnotes.

The XHTML tags `sup` and `sub` create superscript or subscript text automatically, but as **Figure 3.22** shows, it's worth using `vertical-align` and `text-size` in combination to produce a more pleasing result.

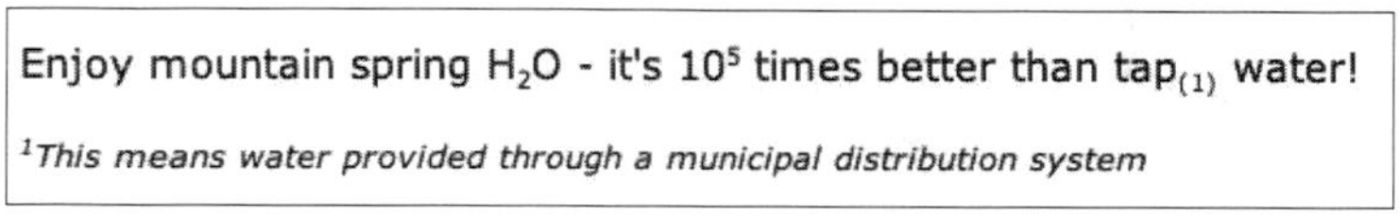

FIGURE 3.22 Vertical-align improves the appearance of the default XHTML tags for creating subscript and superscript

Enjoy mountain spring H_2O - it's 10^5 times better than tap[1] water!

[1]*This means water provided through a municipal distribution system*

Here's the code for this example

```
<style type="text/css">

body {font-family:verdana, arial, sans-serif; font-
size:100%;}


h4 {margin: 1.4em 20px .5em; color:#069;}

p {margin: 0 20px;}

p.largertext {font-size:2em; margin-top: 1em;}

span.raised {font-size:.4em; vertical-align:50%;}


p.custom sub {vertical-align:sub; font-size:65%;}

p.custom sup {vertical-align:65%; font-size:65%;}

p.customsmall {font-size:.8em;}


</style>

</head>
```

code continues on next page

```
<body>

<p class="largertext">Vertical-align <span class="raised">can
be used in all kinds of</span> interesting ways.</p>


<h4>This example uses default settings of the xhtml tags
"sub" and "sup"</h4>

<p>Enjoy mountain spring H<sub>2</sub>0 - it's 10<sup>5</sup>
times better than tap<sup>&dagger;</sup> water!</p>

<p><sup>&dagger;</sup><em>This means water provided through a
municipal distribution system</em></p>


<h4>This example uses classes for custom vertical alignment
and type sizes</h4>

<p class="custom">Enjoy mountain spring H<sub>2</sub>0 -
it's 10<sup>5</sup> times better than tap<sup>&dagger;</sup>
water!</p>

<p class="customsmall"><sup>&dagger;</sup><em>This means
water provided through a municipal distribution system</em></
p>

</body>
```

Using Font and Text Styles

Using the markup we developed in Chapter 1, let's look at how we can transform a very ordinary looking page into a more professional looking piece. **Figure 3.23** shows the unstyled markup:

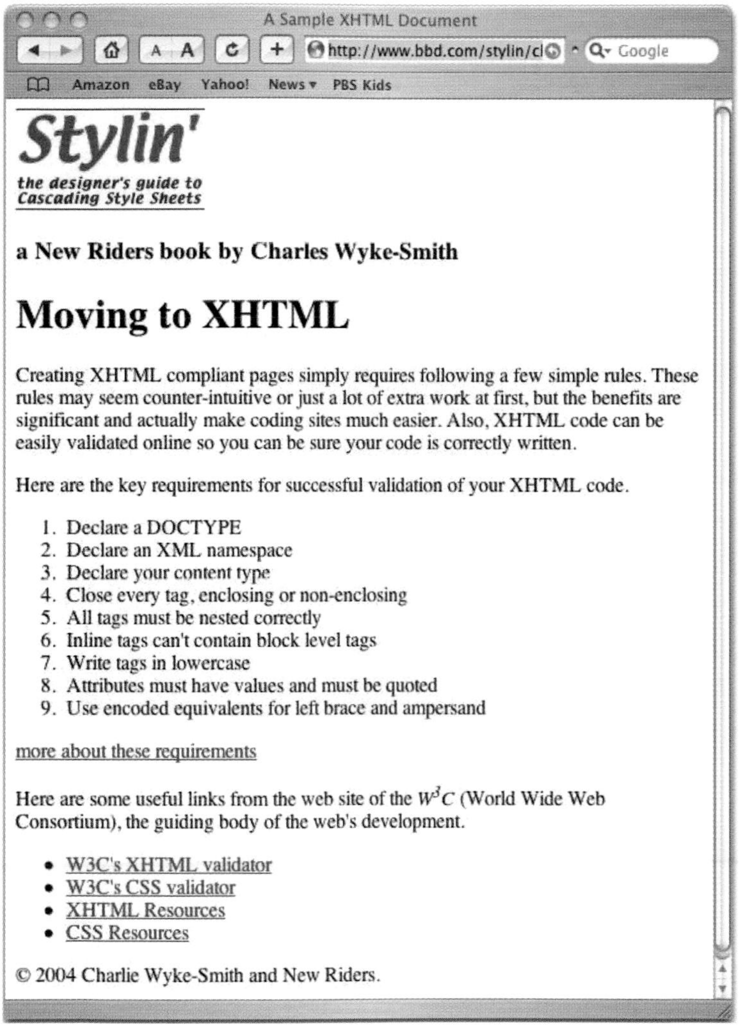

FIGURE 3.23 Here's our unstyled markup from the Chapter 1 example.

By applying only styles we learned in this chapter plus the margin property, the page suddenly looks like someone actually designed it (**Figure 3.24**).

FIGURE 3.24 Here's the Chapter 1 sample markup styled with font and text styles

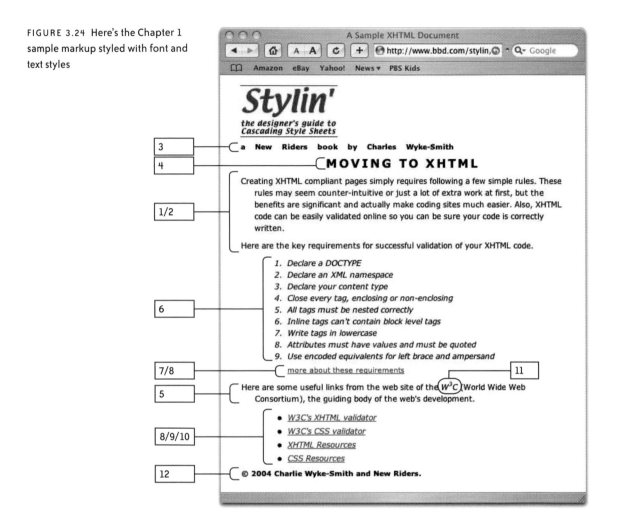

Here are the styles:

1. `body {font-family:verdana, arial, sans-serif; font-size:100%; margin:1em 2em;}`

These are baseline styles for the font and page margins. The `font-family` is inherited by all elements and the margins move all the elements in from the edges of the page.

2. `* {margin:0; padding:0;}`

Here we "neutralize" all the default margins on the elements that eat up so much vertical space in the unstyled version. We also do the same for the padding to enable us to apply consistent styles to the lists for all browsers. By removing all the default margins and padding, only elements that we decide should have them, have them.

3. `h3 {font-size:.7em; word-spacing:1em; letter-spacing:-.05em; margin:.5em 0;}`

   Here we've set tight letter spacing and wide word spacing.

4. `h1 {font-size:1.1em; text-transform:uppercase; text-align:center; letter-spacing:.2em; margin: .5em 0;}`

   The header is now centered with increased letter spacing and all capitals.

5. `p {font-size:.75em; line-height:1.5em; text-indent:-1.75em; margin: 0.5em 0 .75em 1.75em;}`

   Here we've reduced the type size, increased the line height, and set a negative indent for the first line.

6. `ol {margin-left:6em; font-size:.75em; line-height:1.5; font-style:italic;}`

   The large left margin indents the list. We've also italicized the list and increased line spacing for any lines that may wrap.

7. `a {margin-left:6.5em; font-size:.7em;}`

   We set the left margin to make the link sit under the list text.

8. `a:hover {text-decoration:overline underline;}`

   When the link is hovered, we get an interesting above and below underline. (Hovered behavior not shown in Figure 3.24.)

9. `ul {margin-left:6em; font-size:.75em; line-height:1.75; font-style:italic;}`

   This list is also indented and italicized.

10. `ul a {font-size:1em; margin:0;}`

    The list items are links so we style these differently from non-list links using a contextual selector

11. `sup {vertical-align:35%; font-size:65%;}`

    A custom treatment of the sup tag.

12. `div#homepagefooter p {font-size:.7em; font-weight:bold;}`

    We've created small bold type for the footer.

Remember that once styles like these are in a style sheet, they are applied to all the pages that link to it, so you can get a whole Web site's-worth of mileage out of the work you put into styling a page like this.

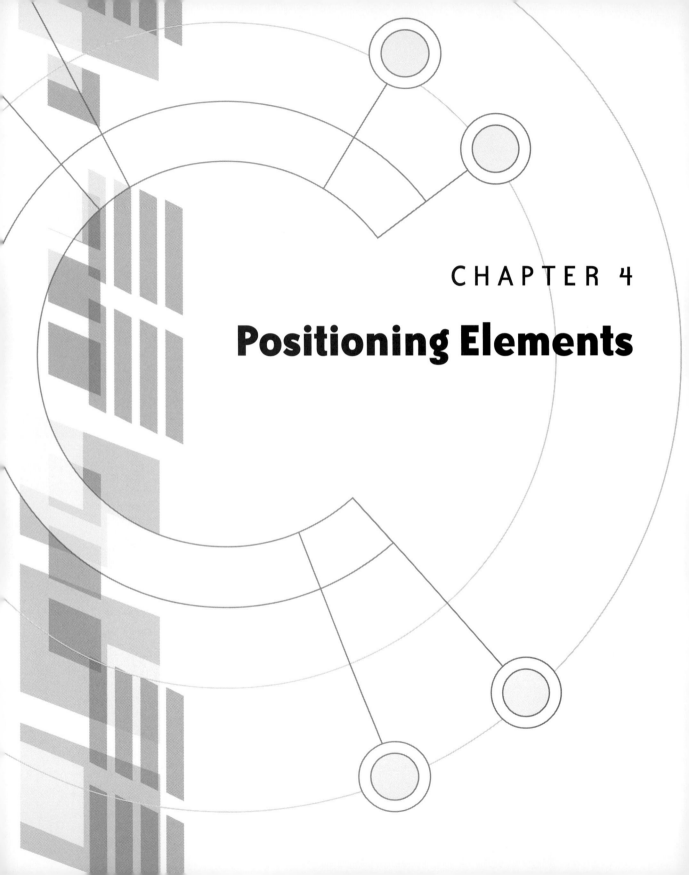

CHAPTER 4

Positioning Elements

Learn about how the box model works and why it's important to understand

Find out how CSS margins enable you to create space around elements

Learn how to use padding to position content within elements

Discover how to style borders

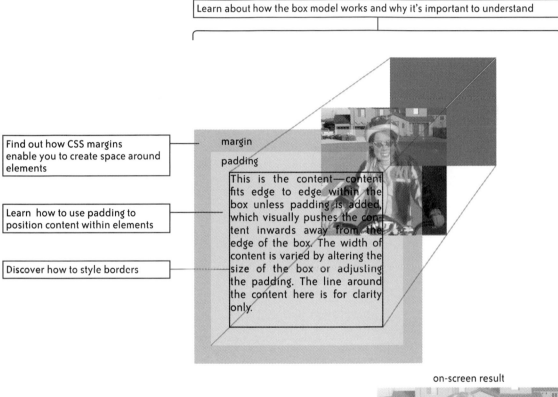

margin

padding

This is the content—content fits edge to edge within the box unless padding is added, which visually pushes the content inwards away from the edge of the box. The width of content is varied by altering the size of the box or adjusting the padding. The line around the content here is for clarity only.

on-screen result

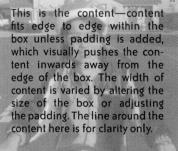

This is the content—content fits edge to edge within the box unless padding is added, which visually pushes the content inwards away from the edge of the box. The width of content is varied by altering the size of the box or adjusting the padding. The line around the content here is for clarity only.

Since the earliest days of the Web, designers have used tables to create an underlying layout grid for Web pages. This meant adding nasty presentational hacks—such as spacer GIFs, line breaks, and non-breaking spaces—into the markup to achieve the desired layout. With CSS, you can position XHTML elements with great accuracy without adding presentational elements into your markup that pollute the content and make the code difficult to decipher.

With the application of CSS properties, such as margins, padding, and borders, and CSS techniques, such as floating and clearing, you can achieve the same—or even better—results than in the past. You can do this while keeping your markup lean and clean, and while sharing the styles you write between like elements of your layout, to achieve lightweight and easy-to-read code.

How well you succeed with these techniques depends on how well you understand the *box model*, the `position` *property*, and the `display` *property*. The box model describes the positioning controls that exist for every element in your markup. The `position` property defines the positional relationship between these elements on the page. The `display` property determines whether elements stack or sit side-by-side, or even display on the page at all. Let's look at each in turn.

Understanding the Box Model

To learn more about the box model see www.w3.org/TR/REC-CSS2/box.html.

Since every element you create in your markup produces a box on the page, an (X)HTML page is actually an arrangement of boxes.

By default, the border of each element box isn't visible and the background of the box is transparent, so I understand if you're wondering where all the boxes are. With CSS, it's easy to turn on the borders and color the backgrounds of the boxes. Then you can start to see your page structure in a whole new light.

In **Figure 4.1**, you can see two paragraphs of text, each of which is styled with borders on and a light gray background, like this

```
p {border: 1px solid #333; background-color:#EEE}
```

To do more than simply use the XHTML layout presented by the browser, you must understand how to control the appearance and placement of element boxes. Step one is to understand the box model (**Figure 4.2**) This box model diagram shows the properties that make up each box.

FIGURE 4.1 Spacing between the two paragraphs on this page is created by their margin settings.

Here's a paragraph of text. Note the border is turned on and the background is colored, so it's now clear that the content is contained in a box.

Here's another paragraph so that you can see that there are default margins (spacing around the outside of the box) that creates vertical space between the paragraphs that creates the effect of an empty line between each paragraph.

FIGURE 4.2 The box model diagram shows how padding pushes in from the border and margins push out from it.

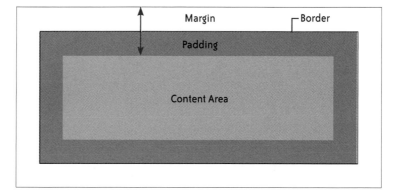

Note that the exact widths of thin, medium, *and* thick *are not actually defined in the CSS specifications, and so these widths may vary between browsers. The line styles, with the exception of* solid, *which is a simple unbroken line, also are not explicitly defined in the CSS specifications; a dashed line may have different dash and space lengths from browser to browser.*

You can adjust three aspects of the box with CSS:

Border. You can set the thickness, style, and color of the border.

Margin. You can set the distance between this box and adjacent elements.

Padding. You can set the distance of the content from the border of the box.

A simple way to think about these properties is that margins push outward from the border and padding pushes inward from the border.

Because a box has four sides, properties associated with margin, border, and padding each have four settings for the top, right, bottom, and left of the box.

The Box Border

Border has three associated properties:

Width. This includes thin, medium, thick, or *any unit* (ems, px, %, and so on).

Style. This includes none, hidden, dotted, dashed, solid, double, groove, ridge, inset, and outset.

Color. This includes any color value (for example, RGB, hex, or keyword).

You can style the border properties for all four sides of a box at once like this

```
p {border-style: solid}
```

or for just one side, like this

```
p {border-left-style: solid}
```

or you can use shorthand (see "Shorthand Styling" on the next page) to specify four different styles for the four sides at once

Borders are applied in this order: top, right, bottom, left

```
p {border-style: solid dashed double inset}
```

However, it's fairly unlikely that you will want to specify a different style for each side because four different types of border on the same box looks, well, bad. On the other hand, it is common to specify the same color and style for all four sides but have some sides have different weights (thicknesses). In such a case, you can use two rules to achieve the desired result. In the following example, the first rule contains the styling common to all four sides (along with a couple of pixels of padding all around to keep the text from touching the edges of the box) and the second rule specifies the differences between them

```
h2.headbox {border:solid #AAA; padding:2px;}
```

Widths are applied in this order: top, right, bottom, left

```
h2.headbox {border-width:3px 1px 1px 3px;}
```

which results in **Figure 4.3**.

FIGURE 4.3 Here, two border styles are applied to a box.

Graphic heading

A common way to style a box is to make all four sides the same color, style, and thickness, in which case you can just write something like this

Puts a thick red line around the paragraph

```
p.warning {border: 4px solid #3FF}
```

It is very helpful to temporarily display the border of a box during development so that you can clearly see the effect of styles such as margins and padding. By default, the styles for element boxes are that the border width is set to medium, the border style is set to none, and the border color is set to black. However, because the border style is set to none, the box doesn't display. So all you need to do to quickly display a paragraph's box, for example, is write this

```
p {border: solid}
```

This sets the border style to solid and the box appears. Note, however, that adding borders can alter the layout because borders add dimension to the element. An alternate way to display a box is to add a background color so that the box does not change size.

Shorthand Styling

It gets tedious to write a separate style for each of the four sides of an element, whether you are specifying margins, padding, or borders. CSS offers some shorthand ways to specify these one after another within a single declaration. In such a declaration, the order of the sides of the box is always top, right, bottom, left. You can remember this as TRouBLe, which you will be in if you forget, or you can visualize the order as the hands on a clock going around from 12. So, if you want to specify the margins on an element, instead of writing

```
{margin-top:5px; margin-right:10px; margin-bottom:12px;
margin-left:8px;}
```

you can simply write

```
{margin: 5px 10px 12px 8px}
```

Note that there is just a space between each of the four values; you don't need a delimiter such as a colon or comma.

You don't have to specify all four elements; if you miss any, the opposite side's value is used as the missing value

```
{margin: 12px 10px 6px}
```

In this example, because the last value, left, is missing, the right value is used and the left margin is set to 10px.

In this next example

```
{margin: 12px 10px}
```

only the first two values, top and right, are set, so the missing values for bottom and left are set to 12px and 10px, respectively.

Finally, if only one value is supplied

```
{margin: 12px}
```

then all four sides are set to this value.

If you want some of the values to be zero, you can write 0 without supplying a value type like this

```
{border: 2px 0 0 4px;}
```

The Box Padding

Padding adds space between the box's content and the border of the box. As part of the inside of the box, it takes on the color of the box's background. **Figure 4.4** shows two paragraphs, one with and one without padding.

> Without padding, any border that you add to an element such as this paragraph is very close to the content; not always the desired result.

> Even a small amount of padding gives the content some visual breathing space. Note that the padding area around the content also takes on the background color; it makes perfect sense that the background color extends to the border and does not just color the area behind the content itself.

When you build page layouts from elements that have content in them, padding is an important tool you can use to create white space around the content. Where designers once used to clog markup with presentation code by adding table cell padding and spacer GIFs to create white space, you can now achieve the same effect economically by adding CSS padding styles.

The Box Margins

Margins are slightly more complex than borders and padding. First, most block level elements (paragraphs, headings, lists, and so on) have default margins. In **Figures 4.5–4.7**, you can see the effect of margins very clearly.

FIGURE 4.5 Here you can see how the default margins appear in a browser.

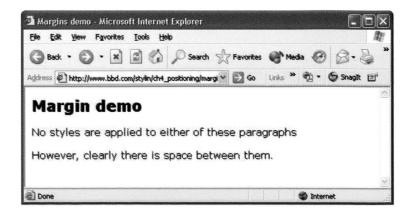

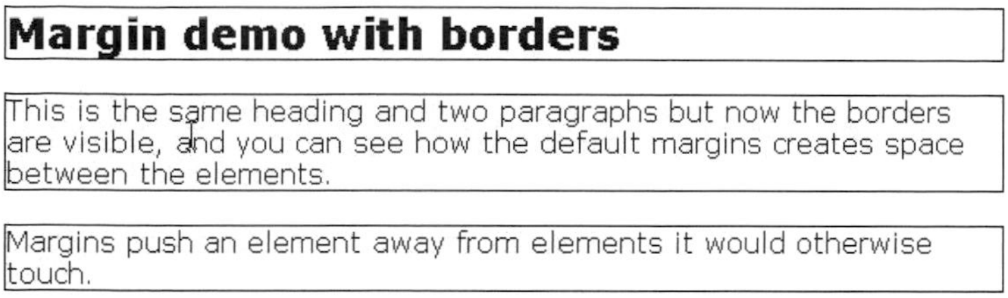

FIGURE 4.6 If you display the header and paragraphs with borders turned on, you can clearly see how the margins create space between them.

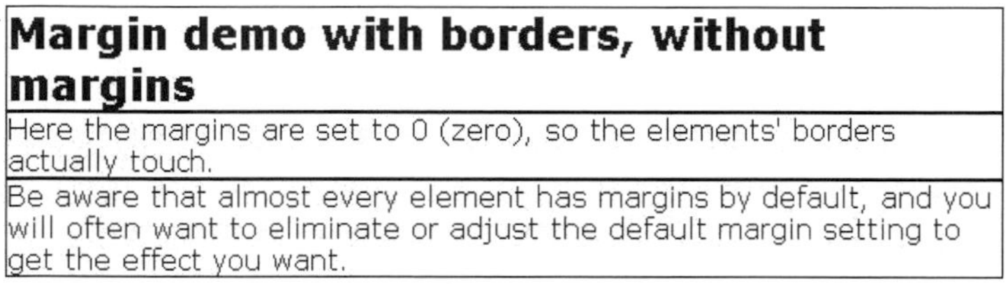

Margin demo with borders

This is the same heading and two paragraphs but now the borders are visible, and you can see how the default margins creates space between the elements.

Margins push an element away from elements it would otherwise touch.

FIGURE 4.7 Removing the margins causes the borders of all three elements to touch.

Margin demo with borders, without margins

Here the margins are set to 0 (zero), so the elements' borders actually touch.

Be aware that almost every element has margins by default, and you will often want to eliminate or adjust the default margin setting to get the effect you want.

It's good practice to place the following declaration at the top of a style sheet (usually in the second line after the body declaration)

The asterisk selector means "any element"

```
* {margin:0; padding:0}
```

This sets the default margins and padding of *all* elements to zero so that you don't get confused by which margins and padding the browser sets and which you set. Once you put this in your style sheet, all the default margins and padding disappear.

Often, you will want to mix units when you set margins for text elements such as paragraphs. In such a case, the left and right margins of a paragraph might be set in pixels so that the text remains a fixed distance from a navigation sidebar, but you might set the top and bottom margins in ems so that the vertical spacing between paragraphs is relative to the size of the paragraphs' text, like this

When only two margin values are stated, the first defaults to top and bottom, the second to left and right

```
p {font-size: 1em; margin: .75em 30px;}
```

In this example, the space between the paragraphs is always three quarters of the height of the text; if you increase the overall type size in the body tag, not only does the paragraphs' text get bigger, but the space between the paragraphs also increases proportionately. The left and right margins, set in points, remain unchanged. We'll look at this concept further when we start constructing page layouts in Chapter 5.

COLLAPSING MARGINS

Say the following out loud: "Vertical margins collapse." You need to remember this important fact. Let me explain what this means and why it's important. Imagine that you have three paragraphs, one after the other, and each is styled with this rule

```
p {width:400px; height:50px; border:1px solid #000;
margin-top:50px; margin-bottom:30px; background-color:#CCC;}
```

Because the bottom margin of the first paragraph is adjacent to the top margin of second, you might reasonably assume that there are 80 pixels (50 + 30) between the two paragraphs, but you'd be wrong. The distance between them is actually 50 pixels. *When top and bottom margins meet, they overlap until one of the margins touches the border of the other element.* In this case, the larger top margin of the lower paragraph touches first, so it determines how far apart the elements are set—50 pixels (**Figure 4.8**). This effect is known as *collapsing*.

FIGURE 4.8 Vertical margins collapse; they overlap until one element touches the border of the other.

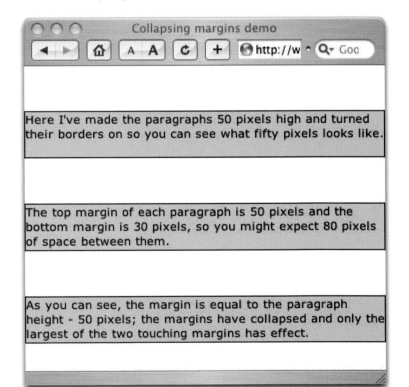

Although vertical margins collapse, horizontal margins do not. Instead, horizontal margins act as you would expect—margin settings are added together to create space between horizontally adjacent elements. In Figure 4.8, if you set horizontal margins instead of vertical margins with the same values, the distance between the elements would be 80 pixels.

This collapsing margin effect ensures that when an element is first or last in a group of headings, paragraphs or lists, for example, the element can be kept away from the top or bottom of the page or the containing element. When the same elements appear between other elements, both margins are not needed, so they simply collapse into each other and the largest one sets the distance.

How Big Is a Box?

This is a question that has apparently baffled browser developers and even the World Wide Web Consortium (W3C). This issue is at the heart of some of the most frustrating aspects of CSS for beginner and expert alike.

Let's go step by step and review the box model in a little more depth. We discuss setting the width of a box here, but you can apply the same (il)logic to the height also.

You can set the width of an element box (hereafter simply called a box) using the width property

```
p {width:400px}
```

Then you can turn the background color on so that you can see the box without affecting its width in any way

```
p {width:400px; background-color:#EEE}
```

Figure 4.9 shows a 400-pixel-wide element with background color on.

FIGURE 4.9 By setting the width property, the element does not default to the width of the containing element. In this case, the containing element is the body element, which is always the width of the browser window.

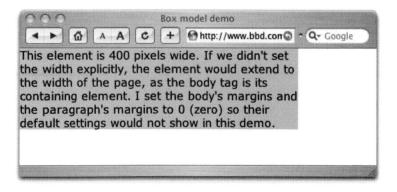

Without any padding, the content is this width also and it touches the sides of the box. That makes perfect sense, but this logic goes out of the window when you start adding padding and borders. Let's add a padding of 20 pixels to each side of the content, like this

```
p {width:400px; background-color:#EEE; padding:0 20px;}
```

You might expect that if you pad a 400-pixel-wide box by 40 pixels, the content gets squeezed down to 360 pixels, but you would be wrong. Instead, in the wonderful, wacky world of CSS, the box gets bigger by 40 pixels (**Figure 4.10**).

FIGURE 4.10 Adding padding causes the box to get wider.

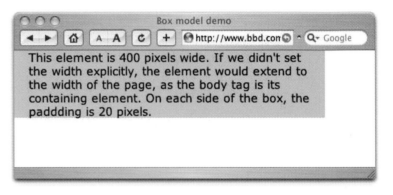

If you then add a 6-pixel border to the right and left sides of the box

```
p {width:400px; margin: 0; padding:0 20px;  border:#000
solid;  border-width: 0 6px  0 6px;  background-color:#CCC;}
```

the box grows wider by 12 pixels (**Figure 4.11**). Now the original 400-pixel-wide box is a total of 452 pixels wide (6 + 20 + 400 + 20 + 6 = 452).

FIGURE 4.11 Adding borders causes the box to grow even wider.

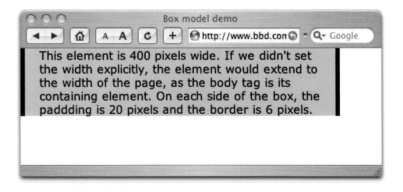

Let's now add right and left margins to create space around the sides of the element (**Figure 4.12**)

```
p {width:400px; margin: 0 30px; padding:0 20px;  border:#000
solid;  border-width: 0 6px  0 6px;  background-color:#CCC;}
```

FIGURE 4.12 Margins create space around an element.

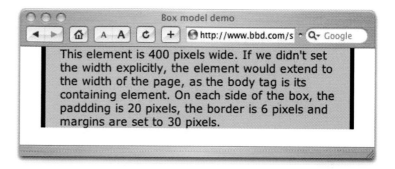

FIGURE 4.12 Margins create space around an element.

Adding margins, 30 pixels to each side in this case increases the overall space occupied by the element since the margins are outside of the box. However, although you might reasonably expect the border of the box and the padding within *not* to increase the box's width, they do.

These sizing issues can have important implications as you fine-tune your work. When you have a tight layout where every pixel is accounted for and you decide to add to the padding or border thickness of element, you then have to subtract the corresponding amount from the box width value to keep the overall dimensions the same. You have to keep your wits about you as you make these kinds of adjustments, but that's the way the CSS box model works.

To make matters more confusing, Internet Explorer 5 and 5.5 for Windows handles the box model completely differently, by behaving the way you might expect and by maintaining the box width when padding is added by squeezing down the content. Internet Explorer 6 behaves like Internet Explorer 5 in Quirks mode (or with no DOCTYPE). However, Internet Explorer 6 works according to the "correct" version described above if the DOCTYPE is set to Transitional or Strict.

The takeaway from this box model discussion is that, with all modern, standards–compliant browsers, when you set the width of an element, you are really setting the width of the content within it, and any padding, borders, and margins you set increase the overall space the element occupies over and above the specified width value.

Now let's look at the other key component you need to understand when it comes to creating CCS-based layouts—the position property.

The Position Property

At the heart of CSS-based layouts is the `position` property. The `position` property determines the reference point for the positioning of each element box.

Let's look at what this means.

There are four values for the `position` property: `static`, `absolute`, `fixed`, and `relative`. `static` is the default. These terms didn't seem to map to what they actually do when I first encountered them; to help you avoid puzzling over what each does, let's take a quick look at each using a simple example with four paragraphs. In each case, I will leave paragraphs 1, 2, and 4 in the default `static` positioning and alter the `property` value of paragraph 3. I have deleted the class `specialpara` for the third paragraph in the markup (not shown), so I can change its `position` property without affecting the other paragraphs.

Static Positioning

First, let's see our four paragraphs all with the default position of `static` (**Figure 4.13**).

With `static` positioning, each element is simply laid out one after the other, so the paragraphs appear one under the next, with their default margin settings creating the space between them.

To break away from this sequential layout of elements provided by the default `static` positioning, you must change a box's positioning property to one of the three other values.

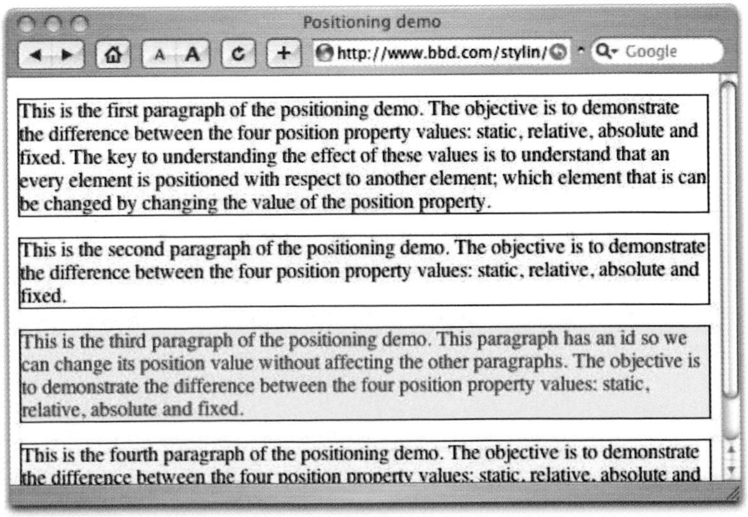

FIGURE 4.13 Static positioning is the default. Block level elements stack up on top of one another, separated by their default margins.

Relative Positioning

Let's set the third paragraph to the `relative` position. You can move the third paragraph with respect to its default position using the properties `top`, `left`, `bottom`, and `right`. Normally, providing values for just `top` and `left` produces the result you want. In this example

```
p#specialpara {position:relative; top:30px; left:20px;}
```

produces the results in **Figure 4.14**.

FIGURE 4.14 When you are using relative positioning, you can move an element from its default position but the space it originally occupied is retained.

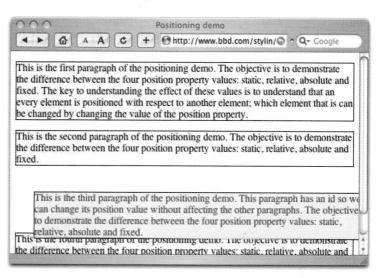

Now the top of your paragraph is moved down by 30 pixels and left by 20 pixels. However, as you have noticed, although the element moves relative to its original position, nothing else changes; the space occupied by the original static element is retained as is the positioning of the other elements.

The lesson here is that if you move an element in this way, you must allow space for it. In the example shown in Figure 4.14 above, you might take the next step of adding a `margin-top` value of 30 pixels or greater to the fourth paragraph to move it down; this prevents it from being overlapped by the repositioned third paragraph.

You can also use negative values for top and left to move an element up and to the left.

Absolute Positioning

Absolute positioning is whole different animal from `static` and `relative`, since this type of positioning takes an element entirely out of the flow of the document. Let's modify the code you used for relative positioning by changing `relative` to `absolute`

```
p#specialpara {position:absolute; top:30px; left:20px;}
```

Figure 4.15 shows the results.

FIGURE 4.15 Absolute positioning removes an element from the document flow entirely.

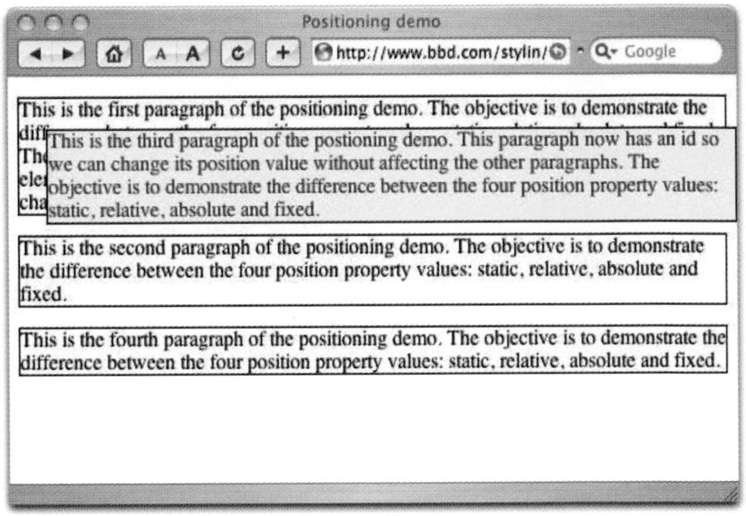

In Figure 4.15, you can see that the space previously occupied by the element is gone. The absolutely positioned element has become entirely independent of the surrounding elements in the markup, and it is now positioned with respect to the top-level element, body. And this brings us neatly to the important concept of *positioning context*, which is a recurring subject in the rest of this chapter.

Let's start thinking about this concept by saying that *the default positioning context of an absolutely positioned element is the body element.* As Figure 4.15 shows, the offset provided by the top and left values moves the element with respect to the body element—the top ancestor container in our markup hierarchy— not with respect to the element's default position, as is the case with relative.

Because the absolutely positioned element's positioning context is body, the element moves when the page is scrolled to retain its relationship to the body element, which also moves when the page scrolls.

Before we see how we can use a different element than body as the positioning context for an absolutely positioned element, let's cover the last of the four positioning properties—fixed positioning.

Fixed Positioning

Fixed positioning is similar to absolute positioning except that the element's positioning context is the viewport (the browser window, or the screen of a handheld device, for example), so the element does not move when the page is scrolled. **Figures 4.16** and **4.17** show the effect of fixed positioning.

FIGURE 4.16 At first glance, fixed positioning seems to work just like absolute positioning.

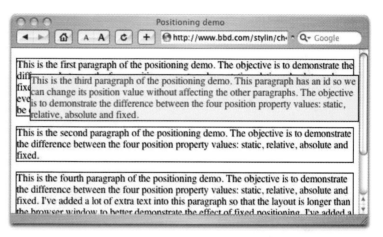

FIGURE 4.17 But when you scroll the page, the fixed element remains exactly where it is.

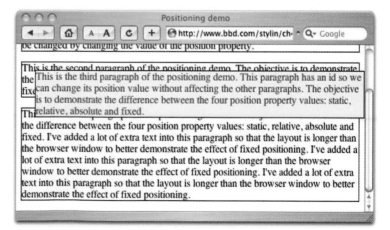

This "nailed-to-the-browser" effect enables you to simulate the effect of now-deprecated frames. For example, you can create a navigation element that stays put when the page scrolls without all the headaches of managing multiple documents in a frameset. However, `position:fixed` does not work in Internet Explorer for Windows. You can find a neat workaround to make fixed positioning work in Internet Explorer for Windows at TagSoup.com (http://devnull.tagsoup.com/fixed).

Positioning Context

Because positioning context is such an important concept to grasp if you want to escape from table-based layouts, some more explanation is useful. Put simply, *contextual positioning* means that when you move an element using the properties `top`, `left`, `right`, or `bottom`, you are moving that element with respect to another element; that other element is known as its *positioning context*. As you saw in "Absolute Positioning" earlier, the positioning context of an absolutely positioned element is `body`; that is, unless you change it.

`body` is the containing element of all other elements in your markup, but you can use any ancestor element as the positioning context of another element by changing the ancestor's `position` value to `relative`.

With this markup

```
<body>

<div id="outer">The outer div

<div id="inner">The inner div</div>

</div>

</body>
```

If you use margins and padding carefully, in most cases, all you need to achieve your layout is static positioning. Many beginning CSS designers mistakenly set the position property of almost every element only to find it hard to control all these freed-up elements. Don't change the position *property of an element from* static *unless you really need to.*

if you set the inner div's `position` property to `absolute`, it is positioned relative to `body`, because `body` is the default positioning context. Setting the `top` and `left` properties of the inner div moves it with respect to `body`, as you saw in Figure 4.15.

If you then set the `position` property of the outer div to relative, the positioning context of the inner div is the outer div. Setting the `top` and `left` properties of the inner div moves it with respect to the outer div. If you then set the `left` and `top` position properties of the outer div to anything other than zero, the inner div also moves to maintain its positioning relationship.

This ability to set the positioning context of any element, in combination with floating and clearing (coming up next), gives you the control you need to organize your markup into a multicolumn page layout.

Floating and Clearing

Another powerful technique you can use to organize your layout on the page involves combining *floating* and *clearing*, using the float and clear properties. Floating an element is another way of moving it out of the normal flow of the document. Elements that follow a floated element will sit next to the floated element if there is room. Think of floating as dynamic relative positioning; the behavior is predetermined, and you just have to invoke it.

The clear property enables you to stop elements moving up next to a floated element. If, for example, you have two paragraphs and only want the first to sit next to the floated element, even though both would fit, you can "clear" the second one so it positions under the floated element. Let's look at both these properties in more detail.

The Float Property

The float property is primarily used to flow text around images, but it is also the basis for one of the ways to create multicolumn layouts. Let's start with the basics.

The most common use for float is to make text flow around an image; in this respect, float works like the HTML property align. Here's an example

```
img {float:left; margin:0 4px 4px 0;}
```

This markup sets the image's float to the left so that the text wraps around it (**Figure 4.18**).

FIGURE 4.18 Here I used the float property to make text wrap around an image, with a small margin on the right and bottom of the image so the text does not touch it.

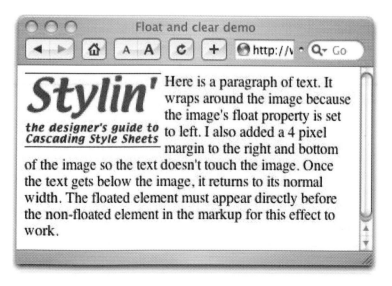

There are many more rules that govern floats, *and you can read about them in Eric Meyer's book* Cascading Style Sheets 2.0 Programmer's Reference *(2001, McGraw-Hill Osborne Media). It's a very useful reference for any serious CSS programmer.*

For the float to work, the markup should look like this with the image first

```
<img ......./>

<p>...the paragraph text...</p>
```

In short, when you float an image or any element, you are asking it to be pushed up as far as possible to the left (or right, in the case of float:right) of the parent element. The elements that follow the floated element in the markup wrap around the element until they clear the bottom of it, and then normal layout resumes.

From here, it's a simple step to use float to form columns. By writing this,

```
p {float:left; width:200px; margin:0;}

img {float:left; margin:0 4px 4px 0;}
```

you create float for both the image and the text, which results in **Figure 4.19**.

FIGURE 4.19 When both elements are floated, the text becomes a column instead of wrapping around the image.

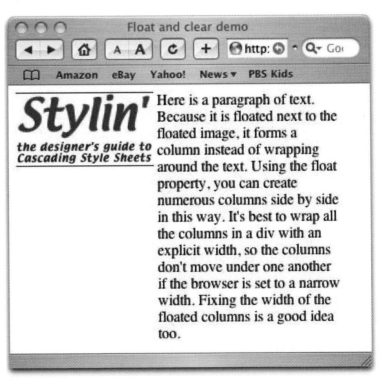

When you float both the paragraph *and* the text, the text-wrapping effect stops and the text forms a column next to the image. This is the principle of creating multicolumn layouts using floats. As long as each element is floated, they line up like columns. If you do this with three floated, fixed-width divs, you get three containers into which you can put other non-floated elements (although they too can be floated if you wish). You'll see all of this in action in Chapter 5.

The Clear Property

The other property that is frequently used with float is clear. You have seen that text can wrap itself around a float. In the case of images, if a number of images are next to a float, the first one that can entirely clear (that is, start below the bottom of) the floated element resumes normal positioning. But sometimes you want an element to clear a float when it wouldn't normally do so.

To demonstrate this point, **Figure 4.20** shows an example of a listing where each item comprises an image with text next to it, achieved by floating the images. It's like the example shown in Figure 4.18, but repeated three times. Each image should float next to its associated text down the page. However, when there is not enough text to clear the bottom of a floated image, as in paragraph 2 in Figure 4.20, the next image/paragraph pair moves up next to the float also.

FIGURE 4.20 In this example, float alone isn't producing the result we want.

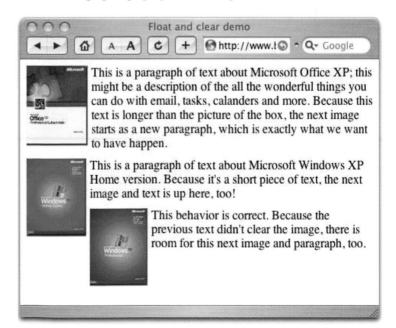

In this example, the float property is behaving just like it should; the third item has room to sit next to the previous floated element, so it does. Of course, this is not what we want. The fix here is to add a non-floated element into the markup that has a clear property applied to it to force the third item to start below the second. Here's the markup with an extra div element and an associated style added

```
<style type="text/css">
```

Creates space between each item

```
p {margin:0 0 10px 0;}

img {float:left; margin:0 4px 4px 0;}

.clearthefloats {clear:both;}

</style>

</head>

<body>

<img src="images/office_xp.gif" />

<p>

This is a paragraph of text about Microsoft Office XP…

</p>

<img src="images/win_home.gif" />

<p>

This is a paragraph of text about Microsoft Windows XP…

</p>

<div class="clearthefloats"><!-- this div is not floated and
its clear property is set to both--></div>

<img src="images/win_pro.gif" />

<p>

Now the next image and paragraph…

</p>

</body>
```

The value of both on the clear property means the div clears (sits below) elements floated both left and right. You could have used the value left in this case, but by using both, if you switch the float on the images to right later, the clear still works.

With the additional markup, the page now looks correct (**Figure 4.21**).

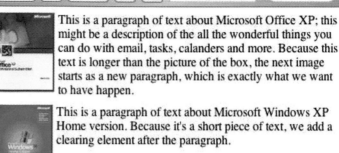

After all my earlier comments about avoiding presentational markup, you might be wondering why I'm adding markup just to achieve a presentational effect. Well, it's because this is the simplest way to force-clear elements when you are just starting out with CSS. Just recently, the CSS gods worked out a way to clear elements without adding any presentational markup. You'll learn about this in Chapter 5 but if you can't wait, check out Position is Everything (www.positioniseverything.net/ easyclearing.htm).

This new "cleared" element added between the second and third paragraphs is now positioned (invisibly, because it has no content associated with it) beneath the second image. Because the third image and paragraph follow this cleared element in the markup, they are positioned below it, and the desired layout is achieved.

Clearing floats is an important technique to master when you are creating CSS layouts. We will study this further, but this is enough information to get you started using floats as the basis of all-CSS page layouts. Before we get started using floats, there's just one more important property to understand—`display`.

The Display Property

Just as every element has a `position` property, every element also has a `display` property. Although there are quite a number of `display` property values, the most commonly used elements have a default `display` property value of either `block` or `inline`. (Most of the other `display` values relate to tables.) The difference between `block` and `inline` is simple:

- `Block` elements, such as paragraphs, headings, and lists, sit one above another when displayed in the browser.

- `Inline` elements such as a, span, and img, sit side by side when they are displayed in the browser and only appear on a new line if there is insufficient room on the previous one.

The ability to change `block` elements to `inline` elements, and vice versa, is a powerful capability that allows you, for example, to transform a row of links that normally sit next to each other into a vertical stack that you can use as sidebar navigation (with no br elements required); more on this particular trick when we look at styling lists later in the book.

One other value for `display` worth mentioning here is `none`. When an element's `display` property is set to `none`, that element, and any elements nested inside it, is switched off and is not visible on the page. Any space that was occupied by the element is removed; it's as if the related markup did not exist. (This contrasts with the `visibility` property, which simply has the values `visible` or `hidden`. If an element's `visibility` is set to `hidden`, the element is hidden but the space it occupies remains.) Later, you'll learn how to toggle the `display` property of elements between `none` and another value to enable functionality such as drop-down menus. JavaScript can also toggle this property to cause elements to appear or disappear when defined user actions occur.

Now let's put the information you have learned in this chapter to work and start creating entirely CSS-based layouts.

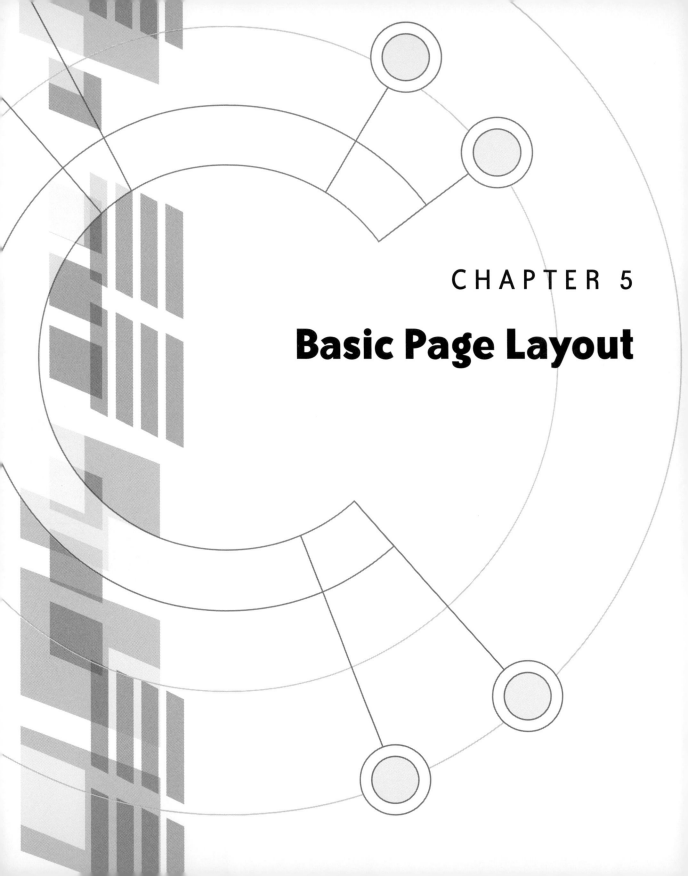

CHAPTER 5

Basic Page Layout

Set the top margin correctly

Create a centered header

Position columns absolutely

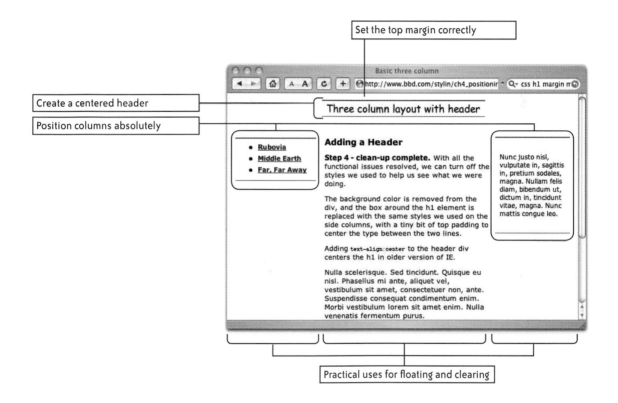

Basic three column

http://www.bbd.com/stylin/ch4_positionir   css h1 margin m

Three column layout with header

- Rubovia
- Middle Earth
- Far, Far Away

Adding a Header

Step 4 - clean-up complete. With all the functional issues resolved, we can turn off the styles we used to help us see what we were doing.

The background color is removed from the div, and the box around the h1 element is replaced with the same styles we used on the side columns, with a tiny bit of top padding to center the type between the two lines.

Adding text-align:center to the header div centers the h1 in older version of IE.

Nulla scelerisque. Sed tincidunt. Quisque eu nisl. Phasellus mi ante, aliquet vel, vestibulum sit amet, consectetuer non, ante. Suspendisse consequat condimentum enim. Morbi vestibulum lorem sit amet enim. Nulla venenatis fermentum purus.

Nunc justo nisl, vulputate in, sagittis in, pretium sodales, magna. Nullam felis diam, bibendum ut, dictum in, tincidunt vitae, magna. Nunc mattis congue leo.

Practical uses for floating and clearing

OK, we're ready to start creating some actual page layouts where CSS controls the positioning of elements. These examples are simple, easily reproduced layouts that show you the basics. They also demonstrate that you can create clean and attractive layouts without extraneous graphics and lots of little boxes everywhere.

It's easy to forget that the purpose of a Web page is to connect the user with the content; I try to ensure that anything I add to a page is content or an element that helps the user either access that content or understand the relationships between the various types of content. The proximity in which elements are placed to one another and a few rules (meaning, in this case, thin lines) are often all a Web page needs. The other elements are usually eye candy, meant to give the page appeal and individuality. But too much of that clutters the page and distracts the viewer.

Simple designs not only render most consistently across a wide variety of user agents, but they make it easier for the viewer to interact with the content. As soon as the viewer starts to wonder where to go or what to do next because of poor organization or excessive screen junk, the interface becomes the focus, not the content. A well-designed interface is, in this respect, invisible to the user.

Enough philosophy; let's start with a simple two-column layout.

A Simple Two-Column Layout

In the first example, I introduce a very common layout; it contains a narrow left column for navigation and a right column that houses the rest of the page's content. In this example, the navigation column is a fixed width, but the content area is fluid—that is, it changes width depending on the width of the browser window.

First, let's start with the XHTML Strict template, which you can download from www.bbd.com/stylin.

The body of the document should be styled to look like this

```
<body>
<div id="nav">     ⎤— Start of navigation div
    <ul>
        <li><a href="#">Link 1</a></li>
        <li><a href="#">Link 2</a></li>
```

```
            <li><a href="#">Link 3</a></li>
        </ul>
    </div>
```

Start of content div

```
    <div id="content">
        <h1>A Simple Two Column Layout</h1>
        <p><strong>Step x - bold text here…</strong> More text
        here…</p>
        <p>More text here…</p>
        <p>More text here…</p>
        <p>More text here…</p>
    </div>
    </body>
```

The markup has two divs: the first is the navigation div, which is a set of links organized within a list, and the second is the content div, which is a heading and some paragraphs. It looks like this in the browser (**Figure 5.1**):

FIGURE 5.1 Here's how the unstyled markup for our two-column layout looks.

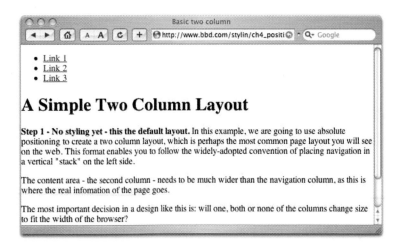

The first step in creating your two-column layout is to break the navigation out of the flow of the document by positioning it absolutely, like this

```
body {margin:0px; padding:0px;}

div#nav {position:absolute; width:150px; border-right:2px
solid red;}
```

Note that you also need to set the margins and padding of the body to zero to remove any default settings. In addition, you should set the width of your navigation to 150px to create the width of the column and temporarily turn on the right border so that you can see exactly where the div is now positioned. Here's what you get (**Figure 5.2**):

FIGURE 5.2 The navigation is taken out of the flow of the document, but the content is too far to the left.

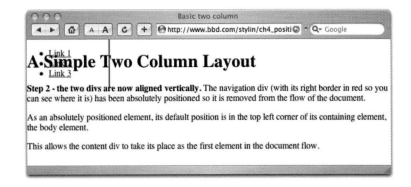

The navigation is now absolutely positioned, and by setting the left and top to zero, you ensure that its top left corner is aligned with the top left corner of its containing element, body.

Now is the winter of our "div content". The content area now takes the navigation div's place as the first element in the regular flow of the document, so it also moves to the top left corner of the parent body element. The page looks a bit of a mess at this point. However, the tops of both elements are now aligned, and all you have to do next is push the content div over to the right (**Figure 5.3**). We do this by setting its left margin

```
body {margin:0px; padding:0px;}i
```

Temporary 2px border will be removed soon, so not accounted for in margin-width of div#content

```
div#nav {position:absolute; width:150px; left:0px; top:0px;
border-right:2px solid red;}
```

```
div#content {margin-left:150px;}
```

FIGURE 5.3 There it is—a two-column layout with just three lines of CSS. Now it's cleanup time.

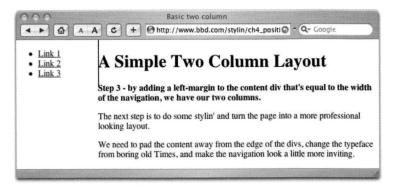

Now that you have your two-column layout, you need to think about making it look more presentable.

You can have some fun playing with this yourself, but here are a few ideas to get to you started (**Figure 5.4**)

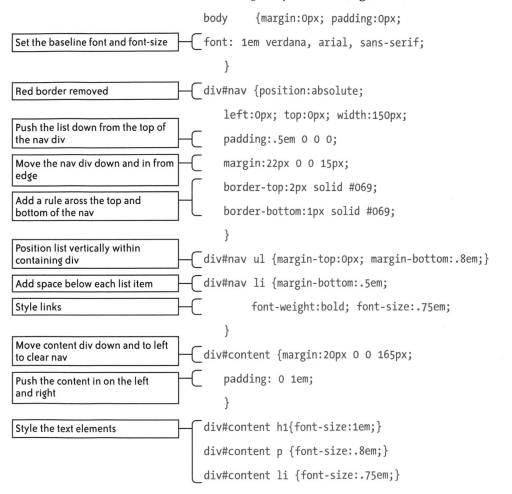

Set the baseline font and font-size

Red border removed

Push the list down from the top of the nav div

Move the nav div down and in from edge

Add a rule aross the top and bottom of the nav

Position list vertically within containing div

Add space below each list item

Style links

Move content div down and to left to clear nav

Push the content in on the left and right

Style the text elements

```
body      {margin:0px; padding:0px;
           font: 1em verdana, arial, sans-serif;
          }

div#nav {position:absolute;
          left:0px; top:0px; width:150px;
          padding:.5em 0 0 0;
          margin:22px 0 0 15px;
          border-top:2px solid #069;
          border-bottom:1px solid #069;
         }

div#nav ul {margin-top:0px; margin-bottom:.8em;}

div#nav li {margin-bottom:.5em;
            font-weight:bold; font-size:.75em;
           }

div#content {margin:20px 0 0 165px;
             padding: 0 1em;
            }

div#content h1{font-size:1em;}

div#content p {font-size:.8em;}

div#content li {font-size:.75em;}
```

FIGURE 5.4 Here is the finished layout, which has been enhanced with some text and border styles.

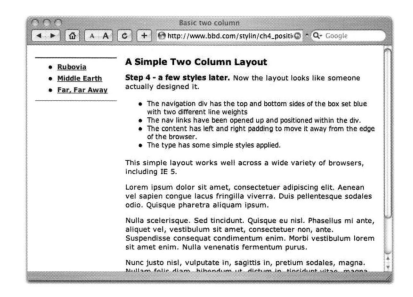

FIGURE 5.4 Here is the finished layout, which has been enhanced with some text and border styles.

Here's more detail on what I did to make the layout look better:

1. I wanted to align the top of the navigation div with the top of the content div and bring them both down from the top of the page a little, so I put 20 pixels of top margin on the content div first. I then found that I needed a couple more pixels on the navigation div to compensate for the thickness of its top rule.

2. I padded the navigation div with 5 pixels on each side to move it away from the browser on the left and the content on the right.

3. I compensated for the extra 10 pixels this added to the width of the navigation div by adding 15 pixels to the left margin of the content div. Note that I changed the margin style to the shorthand version so that I could specify the other three sides at the same time.

Three-Column Layout

If creating a two-column layout makes sense to you, then you won't have any trouble understanding how to transform it into a three-column layout.

In this case, you use the same markup structure as you did for the two-column layout, but you add one more div for the right column at the end

```
<body>

<div id="nav">

    <ul>

        <li><a href="#">Link 1</a></li>

        <li><a href="#">Link 2</a></li>

        <li><a href="#">Link 3</a></li>

    </ul>

</div>

<div id="content">

    <h1>A Simple Three Column Layout</h1>

    <p><strong>Step x - bold text here…</strong> In this
example, we are going to use absolute positioning to create
a three column layout, which is also a very common page
layout you will see on the web. This format enables you to
follow the widely-adopted convention of placing navigation
in a vertical "stack" on the left side, and use the right
side for things like testimonials, promotions, ads or other
links.</p>

    <p>In this design, we'll fix the width of the side
columns and let the content column fill the rest of the
browser's width.</p>

</div>

<div id="rightcolumn">

    <p>This is temporary filler for the right column. We'll
put something more interesting in here later.</p>

</div>

</body>
```

The unstyled code looks like **Figure 5.5**.

FIGURE 5.5 Here's our unstyled
markup for a three-column layout.

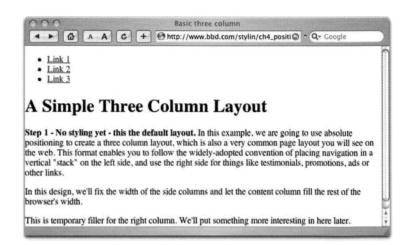

FIGURE 5.5 Here's our unstyled
markup for a three-column layout.

*In a fluid design like this, you have
to position the right column with
a right value of 0 to make it always
position against the right edge of the
browser. In a fixed-width layout, you
can simply set a high left value to
position this column.*

Because the content for the right column is styled as a paragraph,
when it is displayed in the browser, it simply appears as another line
of text in the unstyled layout.

The next step is to position the two side columns absolutely: the
only difference between the two columns in the way you do this is
that the left column is positioned with the `left:0px;` style and the
right column is positioned with the `right:0px;` style.

Here's the markup

```
body {margin:0px; padding:0px;}
```

```
div#nav {position:absolute; width:150px; top:0px; left:0px;
border-right:2px solid red;}
```

```
div#rightcolumn {position:absolute; width:125px; top:0px;
right:0px; border-left:2px solid red;}
```

and here's how this looks. (**Figure 5.6**):

FIGURE 5.6 The side columns are
now in position.

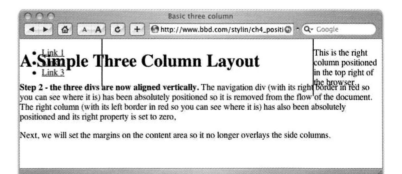

I made the inner borders of the columns red so you can clearly see where the columns ended up. I also changed the text in the right column.

The next step is to set the left and right margins on the content area so it doesn't overlay the side columns

```
body {margin:0px; padding:0px;}

div#nav {position:absolute; width:150px; left:0px; top:0px;
border-right:2px solid red;}

div#content {margin-left:150px; margin-right:125px;}

div#rightcolumn {position:absolute; width:125px; top:0px;
right:0px; border-left:2px solid red;}
```

Now the positioning work is done (**Figure 5.7**).

FIGURE 5.7 With the left and right margins set on the content area, the three-column layout is ready for some cosmetic styling.

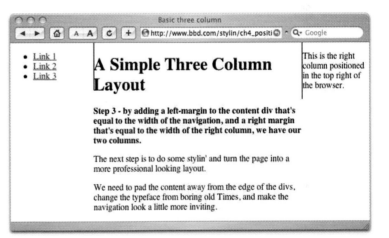

For this layout, I use exactly the same set of CSS rules as I did on the two-column layout, except for the changes highlighted below. Here is the CSS of the three-column layout styled to a more finished level

```
body {margin:0px; padding:0px; font: 1em verdana, arial,
sans-serif;}

div#nav {position:absolute; left:0px; top:0px; width:150px;
    padding:.5em 0 0 0; margin:22px 0 0 15px;
    border-top:2px solid #069; border-bottom:1px solid #069;}

div#nav ul {margin-top:0; margin-bottom:.8em;}
```

code continues on next page

```
div#nav li {margin-bottom:.5em; font-weight:bold; font-
size:.75em;}
```

Margin to make room for the right column
```
div#content {margin:20px 150px 0 165px; padding: 0 1em;}
```

```
div#content h1{font-size:1em;}
```

```
div#content p {font-size:.8em;}
```

```
div#content li {font-size:.75em;}
```

The new right column
```
div#rightcolumn {position:absolute; width:125px; top:0px;
right:0px;

    margin:20px 15px 0 0; padding:1em   .5em;

    border-top:2px solid #069; border-bottom:1px solid #069;}
```

Styling for the text in the new right column
```
div#rightcolumn p {font-size:.75em;}
```

The result is shown in **Figure 5.8**.

FIGURE 5.8 Simple! Here's the complete three-column layout.

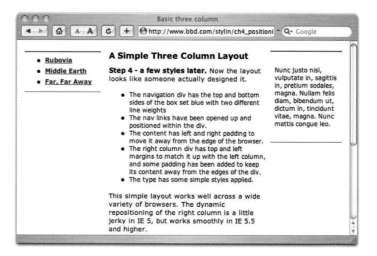

Three-Column Layout with Header

Many three-column layouts also have a header across the top of the page, so let's add one. If you start by working from the three-column markup and styles, you can add another div for the header and modify the positioning of your left and right columns to make room for the header at the top of the page. Because both the header and the content are in the flow of the document, once you have the header in place, the content is pushed down and appears correctly below it.

Use the markup from the completed three-column layout and add this line after the opening body tag

```
<div id="header"><h1>Three column layout with header</h1></div>
```

Then add these styles to the CSS—the logical place is right after the body styles

```
div#header {height:60px; background-color:#CCC;}
```

```
div#header h1 {margin-top:0px;}
```

Now your layout looks like **Figure 5.9**.

FIGURE 5.9 The new header pushes the content div down, but not the absolutely positioned sidebars.

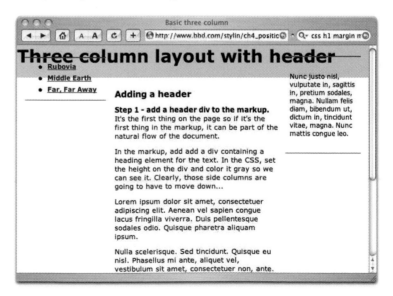

This example is the simplest way to create this three column layout. For flexibility, you might want to add a container div around the content and the left and right column divs and then set its position to relative. Then the content and the left and right columns will always be positioned relative to the depth of the header rather than requiring the hardcoded 60px for the top *property. This way, adding more content to the header won't require adjusting the* top *property.*

If you are wondering why I set the top margin of the h1 element to zero, it's because in some browsers, such as Safari and Firefox, the h1's top margin pushes the header away from the top of the browser, leaving a gap. This doesn't happen in Internet Explorer for Windows.

The content area is pushed down when you add the header, but you have to move those absolutely positioned sidebars by modifying their CSS; they are no longer in the flow of the layout once they are absolutely positioned. So, you need to add the height of the header onto their current top values

```
div#nav {position:absolute; left:0px; top:60px; width:150px;

    padding:.5em 0 0 0; margin:22px 0 0 15px;

    border-top:2px solid #069; border-bottom:1px solid #069;}
div#rightcolumn {position:absolute; width:125px; top:60px;
right:0px;

    margin:20px 15px 0 0; padding:1em  .5em;

    border-top:2px solid #069; border-bottom:1px solid
#069;}
```

Now things are starting to shape up (**Figure 5.10**).

FIGURE 5.10 The sidebars are now correctly positioned.

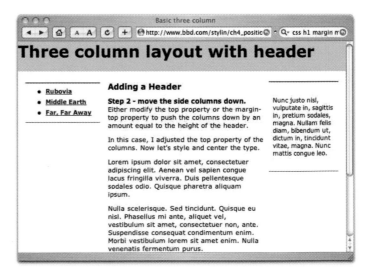

Next, we can get to work styling the text in the header. I want to make it a lot smaller (surprised?) and center it so that it remains centered as the browser width changes. To achieve this, I set a width on the h1 so that it is large enough to contain the text. With the width specified, it no longer defaults to the full width of the header div.

Then I apply left and right margin values of `auto` to center it in the header div. `auto` is a useful size to specify; it effectively means "as large as you can be." So with that applied on both sides, the element sits in the middle of its container, whatever size that container is.

Using margins set to `auto` is the best method of horizontal centering with CSS, as long as the element has a specified width. Here's the code

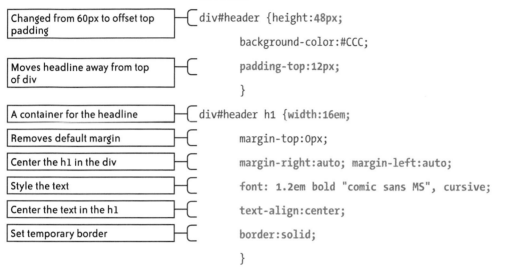

Changed from 60px to offset top padding	`div#header {height:48px;`
	`background-color:#CCC;`
Moves headline away from top of div	`padding-top:12px;`
	`}`
A container for the headline	`div#header h1 {width:16em;`
Removes default margin	`margin-top:0px;`
Center the h1 in the div	`margin-right:auto; margin-left:auto;`
Style the text	`font: 1.2em bold "comic sans MS", cursive;`
Center the text in the h1	`text-align:center;`
Set temporary border	`border:solid;`
	`}`

Even this small change makes your layout more pleasing (**Figure 5.11**).

FIGURE 5.11 The headline is sized and centered in the header.

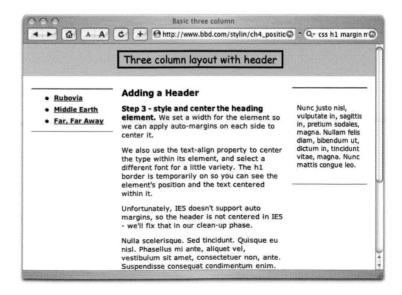

Now the headline centers correctly no matter what the browser's width is. All that you have left to do is restyle the headline box in the same way as you restyled the sidebar divs.

Here's the completed CSS

```
body {margin:0px; padding:0px; font: 1.0em verdana, arial,
sans-serif; }
```

Added to ensure older browsers center the heading

```
div#header {height:48px; text-align:center; margin-top:0px;
padding-top:12px;}
```

```
div#header h1 {width:16em; margin-top:0px; margin-right:auto;
margin-left:auto;

     font: 1.2em bold "comic sans MS", arial, sans-serif;
text-align:center;

     padding:0 0 .1em; border-top:2px solid #069; border-
bottom:1px solid #069;}
```

```
div#nav {position:absolute; left:0px; top:60px; width:150px;

          padding:.5em 0 0 0; margin:22px 0 0 15px;

          border-top:2px solid #069; border-bottom:1px
solid #069;}
```

```
div#nav ul {margin-top:0; margin-bottom:.8em;}
```

```
div#nav li {margin-bottom:.5em; font-weight:bold; font-
size:.75em;}
```

```
div#content {margin:20px 150px 0 165px; padding: 0 1em;}
```

```
div#content h1{font-size:1em;}
```

```
div#content p {font-size:.8em;}
```

```
div#content li {font-size:.75em;}
```

```
div#rightcolumn {position:absolute; width:125px; top:60px;
right:0px;

     margin:20px 15px 0 0; padding:1em  .5em; border-
top:2px solid #069; border-bottom:1px solid #069;}
```

```
div#rightcolumn p {font-size:.75em;}
```

And here's how the completed layout looks (**Figure 5.12**):

FIGURE 5.12 Voila! The finished result.

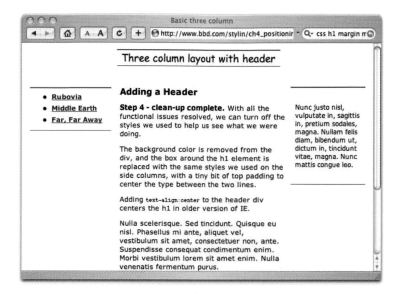

Well, that was easy wasn't it? These are nice, simple, solid layouts that work well in a variety of browsers, old and new. Unfortunately, some other structural elements that are popular on many sites and that are easily achieved with table-based layouts, such as full-length columns and footers that automatically position themselves below the other content, are harder to achieve with CSS. That, however, won't stop us from doing these things.

Three-Column Layouts with Float and Clear

The next demo uses five visual elements: a header, three columns, and a footer. This demo is about as simple as it can be, but the structure it demonstrates can be the foundation of complex and beautifully designed pages. The page you create is going to be only 450 pixels wide, with three columns—each 150 pixels across.

The objective is to float the three columns side by side under the header and then have the footer run across the bottom. The footer will be the width of the page, and will sit directly under whichever of the three columns is longest.

The first step, as always, is to write the markup

```
<body>

<div id="header">This is the header</div>

<div id="contentarea">

<div id="column1">These divs will float side by side to
create columns. This is div 1 with a little text to give it
some height…</div>

<div id="column2">This is div 2 with a little less text so
it's a different height than the other two…</div>

<div id="column3">The objective is that no matter which
the three divs is longest, the footer sits below it…</div>

</div><!--end contentarea-->

<div id="footer">This is the footer</div>

</body>
```

Then you start with some simple styles to color the backgrounds of the elements so you can see their positions (**Figure 5.13**). Here are the styles

```
div#header {width:450px; background-color:#CAF;}

div#contentarea {width:450px; background-color:#CCC;}

div#column1 {width:150px; background-color:#FCC;}

div#column2 {width:150px; background-color:#CFC;}

div#column3 {width:150px; background-color:#AAF;}

div#footer {width:450px; background-color:#FAC;}
```

About Footers

A footer is like a header, but it runs across the bottom of the page rather than the top, and it often contains a second set of major navigation links as well as some minor links such as a link to a privacy policy or a link to the site's terms of use and copyright information. Also, if the viewer has scrolled to the bottom of a long page, the footer links can provide main-choice options so the viewer doesn't have to scroll back to the top again.

You can add a footer to the designs you've seen earlier in this chapter in the same way you added the header. However, if the absolutely positioned columns happen to be longer than the content area (which, being in the document flow, pushes the footer downward), the columns will extend over the footer. What you need, and will create, is a page structure where the bottom of the longest column, whichever one it happens to be, sets the position for the top of the footer.

FIGURE 5.13 This shows the basic markup with each div a different color.

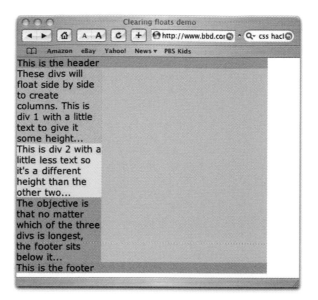

I added one extra structural element to the markup—a div that contains the three column divs, called contentarea. The purpose of this element is to enclose the three columns so that as any of the columns get longer, the bottom of this container gets pushed down, and the footer that follows gets pushed down too. Without it, the footer moves up as close as possible to the header.

Now, while you can see that this "wrapper" div surrounds the three columns in the markup, this is not what is happening in the browser. The CSS recommendations do not require a div to enclose floated elements, but by using clear, you can make it do just that and thereby get your footer to position correctly below the longest column.

Let's start by floating the three columns, which pushes each one up and to the left as far as possible. Here, I've set it up so that there is room for the columns to still be side by side (**Figure 5.14**). Here's the CSS

```
div#header {width:450px; background-color:#CAF;}

div#contentarea {width:450px; background-color:#CCC; border:
solid;}

div#column1 {width:150px; background-color:#FCC; float:left;}

div#column2 {width:150px; background-color:#CFC; float:left;}

div#column3 {width:150px; background-color:#AAF; float:left;}

div#footer {width:450px; background-color:#FAC;}
```

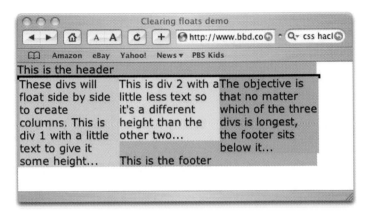

Contrary to the CSS specification, in Internet Explorer for Windows, the `div` does surround the float, so it already shows the result displayed in Figure 5.15, but this does not happen in other more standards-compliant browsers. Be sure to clear the wrapper as described, or your layout will only work in Internet Explorer. This is just another reason why it is important to develop in a standards-compliant browser and then adjust for Internet Explorer afterward.

Divs don't like to be empty. If you don't have any content for a div, simply put a comment inside it. Some people put a period or a similar small element in these "clearing" elements and then add a couple of extra rules to set the `line-height` and `height` of the div to zero so that content is not visible. The important thing is not to have this extra element take up space in your page. Sometimes you have to experiment to achieve that.

You can see that the footer, in its effort to move up against the container div, is jammed up under the second, shortest column.

I also turned on the border of the `div#contentarea` so you can see it. The top and bottom edge of the div touch, forming a solid black rectangle. You can see three sides of this rectangle because those sides add to the width of the div. The bottom edge of the box is obscured by the three columns. The div has no vertical height because it contains only floated elements and, therefore, behaves as if it is empty. But that's not what you want; you have to devise some way to make that div's box open up and surround the columns.

The way to do this (until I show you the really good, but more complex, way to do it in "The Alsett Clearing Method" later in the chapter) is to add a non-floated element into the markup after the column divs and then force the containing div to clear it. This opens the div up to the height of the tallest column. To do this, you add an extra div into the markup as shown here

```
<div id="contentarea">

<div id="column1">These divs will float side by side to
create columns. This is div 1 with a little text to give it
some height…</div>

<div id="column2">This is div 2 with a little more text so
it's a different height than the other two…</div>

<div id="column3">The objective is that no matter which of
the three divs is longest, the footer sits below it…</div>

<div class="clearfloats"><!-- --></div>

</div><!--end contentarea-->

<div id="footer">This is the footer</div>
```

Notice that this new element is positioned *after* the floated columns but *before* the container div closes and that it has the class "clear-floats". Now you need to add a style for this class

```
div#header {width:450px; background-color:#CAF;}

div#contentarea {width:450px; background-color:#CCC;
border:solid;}

div#column1 {width:150px; background-color:#FCC;
float:left;}

div#column2 {width:150px; background-color:#CFC;
float:left;}

div#column3 {width:150px; background-color:#AAF;
float:left;}

div#footer {width:450px; background-color:#FAC;}

div.clearfloats {clear:both;}
```

Now the `contentarea` div is forced to enclose the columns so it can clear the non-floated element, and the footer, which follows the container in the flow, is positioned correctly beneath the columns (**Figure 5.15**).

FIGURE 5.15 The containing element is forced to enclose the non-floating div, thus forming a boundary below the columns that the footer cannot move above.

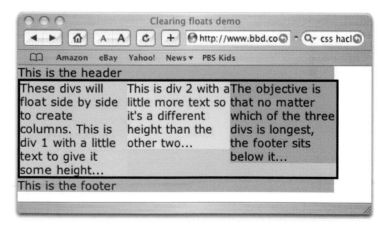

Just to show you that the footer is always below the longest column, I'll add some text to the center column to make it the longest one. I'll also turn off the border of the container div now that you know it's doing its job (**Figure 5.16** on the next page).

Because I added this extra markup purely to achieve a presentational effect, it's not ideal in terms of keeping this markup structural, but it's a simple way to get the result I want and its relatively simple to understand. Now that you get the idea of how this works, let's look at a more complex, all-CSS method for enclosing floats that requires no additional elements in the markup.

FIGURE 5.16 The footer always appears below the longest column.

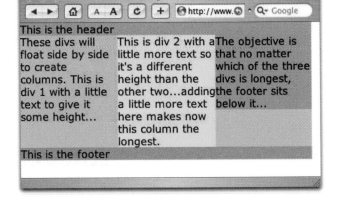

The Alsett Clearing Method

This is a superior method of clearing floats to the "clearing div" method in the previous example since it requires no additional markup.

Named after its creator, Tony Alsett (www.csscreator.com), the Alsett Clearing Method uses the CSS :after pseudo-class to insert a hidden bit of non-floated content (instead of a div) at the appropriate place in the markup. The clear is then applied to this non-floated content.

:after enables you to define a string of characters to be inserted after the content of an element. You set up the required CSS as a class and then add the class to the containing element. Here's the complete page markup for this demo; in this markup, I'm using the Alsett method to force the div to enclose the floated elements. You can see the results in **Figure 5.17**.

Here's how it works

```
<!DOCTYPE html PUBLIC "-//W3C//DTD XHTML 1.0 Strict//EN"

    "http://www.w3.org/TR/xhtml1/DTD/xhtml1-strict.dtd">

<html xmlns="http://www.w3.org/1999/xhtml" lang="en" xml:
lang="en">

<head>

<title>Clearing floats demo</title>

<meta http-equiv="Content-type" content="text/html;
charset=iso-8859-1" />

<meta http-equiv="Content-Language" content="en-us" />
```

FIGURE 5.17 There's not much visual difference between this page and Figure 5.16, but here the clearing is achieved with the Alsett method.

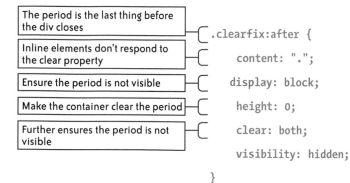

Clearing floats demo

http://www.bbd.c

This is the header

These divs will float side by side to create columns. This is div 1 with a little text to give it some height...

This is div 2 with a little more text so it's a different height than the other two...the third column now is the longest so it sets the footer position.

This version uses the Alsett clearing method which uses the CSS :after psuedo-class to add content and force the container to enclose the floats, and only requires a class to be added to the markup, instead of a "clearing" element.

This is the footer

```css
<style type="text/css">

body {margin:0px; padding:0px; font: 1.0em verdana, arial,
sans-serif;}

div#header {width:450px; background-color:#CAF;}

div#contentarea {width:450px; background-color:#CCC;}

div#column1 {width:150px; background-color:#FCC; float:left;}

div#column2 {width:150px; background-color:#CFC; float:left;}

div#column3 {width:150px; background-color:#AAF; float:left;}

div#footer {width:450px; background-color:#FAC;}
```

The period is the last thing before the div closes

Inline elements don't respond to the clear property

Ensure the period is not visible

Make the container clear the period

Further ensures the period is not visible

```css
.clearfix:after {

    content: ".";

    display: block;

    height: 0;

    clear: both;

    visibility: hidden;

}
```

code continues on next page

A fix for IE Mac

```
.clearfix {display: inline-block;}
```

The Holly hack for a bug in IE6 for Windows

```
* html .clearfix {height: 1%;}

.clearfix {display: block;}

</style>


</head>

<body>

<div id="header">This is the header</div>

<div id="contentarea" class="clearfix">

<div id="column1">These divs will float side by side to
create columns. This is div 1 with a little text to give it
some height…</div>

<div id="column2">This is div 2 with a little more text so
it's a different height than the other two…adding a little
more text here makes now this column the longest.</div>

<div id="column3">This version uses the Alsett clearing
method which uses the CSS :after psuedo-class to add content
and force the container to enclose the floats, and only
requires a class to be added to the markup, instead of a
"clearing" element.</div>

</div><!--end contentarea-->

<div id="footer">This is the footer</div>

</body>

</html>
```

Using comments in this code, I provided a superficial explanation of this method; if you want to learn all about the whys and wherefores of how this method actually works, go to Big John and Holly "Hack" Bergevin's site, Position Is Everything (www.positioniseverything.net). Here you'll also find lots of great information on floats in general.

What's good about this method is that you don't need to know how it works to use it. You can just paste the styles into your style sheet and add the class to any element that you want to enclose floats; using it is simple.

A couple of observations, though. First, in Internet Explorer for Windows, divs *will* enclose floats without any clearing even though this is not correct behavior. As a result, when working with floated elements you shouldn't assume that what you see in Internet Explorer works everywhere. If you want a container to enclose floats, use one of these two methods demonstrated above to ensure cross-browser clearing. Second, Internet Explorer has some buggy behaviors having to do with floats such as the guillotine bug, which can cut off the bottom of elements that contain both links and floats (this Internet Explorer bug and others are well documented at Position Is Everything). The version of the Alsett method used here addresses these Internet Explorer float bugs—another reason it's superior to the "clearing div" method I showed you first. You can strip the Alsett clearing code down to the highlighted lines in the markup above, but note that two of the lines of comments (highlighted) are also part of an Internet Explorer hack to fix the guillotine bug, so you must keep them in your CSS.

CHAPTER 6

Advanced Page Layout

Learn how background images can be tiled or arranged in vertical or horizontal rows

Learn what makes a good background image—and what makes a poor one

Find out how to use background images to create the illusion of full-length columns

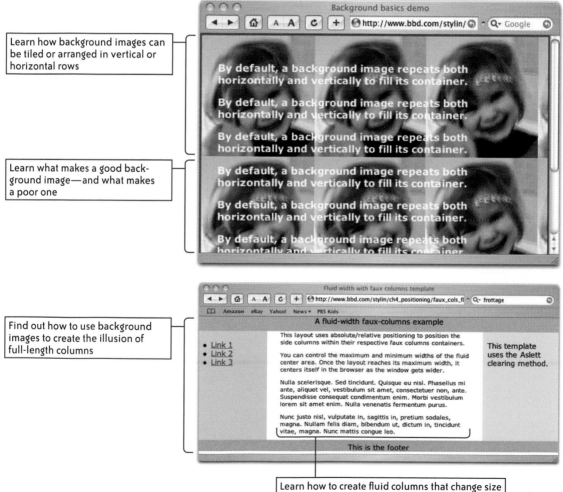

Learn how to create fluid columns that change size as the user changes the browser window's size

Now that you know how to create a basic layout, we're going to go a bit further. First, you'll learn how to create and control background images, which can really liven up your layouts. You'll also learn how to create faux columns and fluid columns—these techniques allow your design to resize elegantly as the user changes the size of his or her browser window.

By the time you're finished with this chapter, you'll be armed with the knowledge you need to create pretty complex, and very practical, CSS-based Web sites. And, you'll be ready to move on to the next chapter where we create an actual real-world site.

A Digression on Backgrounds

Before you learn to create the effect of full-height columns in your CSS-based layouts, you'll need to understand backgrounds. There's actually quite a lot to know about them, but at this point, I'm going to stick with the key information you need to use CSS (rather than XHTML) to add a background graphic into a div and to make that graphic repeat to fill the entire div. This is the method you'll use to create the illusion of columns for the viewer.

The Two Ways to Add Graphics

From a design point of view, it's interesting to consider whether it's best to add graphics into the background of a div using CSS or directly into the div as content using XHTML markup.

For example, if you are adding a bio of the CEO to a corporate Web site, then the CEO's picture is definitely part of the content and should be added into the markup with an img tag. On the other hand, if the graphic is a texture you want to add behind the page for visual interest, then that is presentational and you shouldn't add it to the markup; instead, add it as a background element using CSS.

As an extension of this thinking, it's good practice to store content graphics and presentational graphics in separate folders. If you decide to redesign the site using the same content, you have the XHTML and content images entirely separate from the CSS and presentational images, so it's easy to ditch the old presentation and keep the content. This organization is also helpful if you ever syndicate content from your site—syndicators just want your content, which they use in the context of their own presentation, and if your site is organized in this way, then it is easy for you to separate its content from its presentational elements.

The bottom line? Add presentational graphics as backgrounds using CSS.

The URL path to background images must be relative to the CSS file, not the XHTML file.

Background Basics

Although several properties are associated with backgrounds, you only need to look at two of them right now: `background-image` and `background-repeat`.

The `background-image` property has only one value—the URL of the image. The syntax works like this

```
background-image:url(my_image_path/my_image.jpg)
```

Let's use this property to add an image into the background of a div

```
body {margin:0px; padding:0px; font: 1.0em verdana, arial,
sans-serif;}

div#maindiv {border: 3px solid #F33; padding:25px;

background-image:url(images_pres/lucy_blur_v_small.jpg);}

div#maindiv p {color:#FFF; font-weight:bold;}
```

You'll get the result shown in **Figure 6.1**.

FIGURE 6.1 By default, the `background-repeat` property repeats an image both horizontally and vertically.

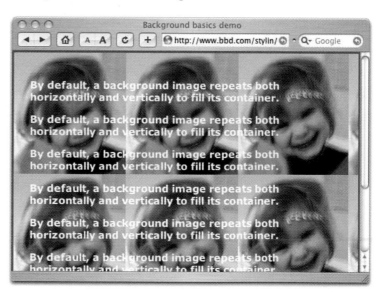

If the background image is smaller than its container, by default, it fills the container by repeating, or *tiling,* both horizontally and vertically. You can control the repeating effect using the `background-repeat` property.

To have the image only appear once, deactivate tiling by setting the background-repeat property to no-repeat, like this

```
div#maindiv {border: 3px solid #F33; padding:25px;
background-color:#666; background-image:url(images_pres/lucy_
blur_v_small.jpg); background-repeat:no-repeat;}
```

Now your page should look like **Figure 6.2**.

FIGURE 6.2 If you set the value of the background-repeat property to no-repeat, then the image only appears once.

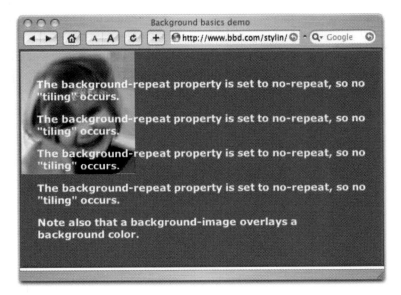

Now the image appears only once—this is known as the origin image. If tiling is active, all subsequent images emanate from this one. (The default origin image position is top-left, but you can change that with the background-position property; see Appendix A).

If you set background-repeat to repeat-x, then the image only repeats horizontally, along the x-axis (**Figure 6.3**).

If you set background-repeat to repeat-y then the image only repeats vertically, along the y-axis (**Figure 6.4**).

What is wonderful about background images is that they add a great sense of depth to your designs and open up a whole world of creative possibilities. That said, it's important to be aware that you need to carefully choose background images so that they don't interfere with the readability of the type that overlays them. Sometimes lowering the contrast of a background image and then lightening it can help reduce readability problems.

FIGURE 6.3 If you set the value of the background-repeat property to repeat-x, then the image only repeats horizontally.

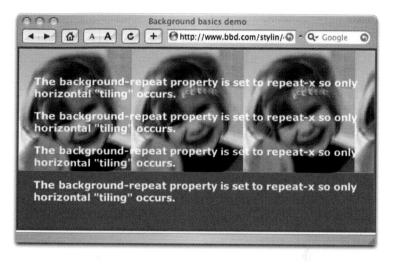

FIGURE 6.4 If you set the value of the background-repeat property to repeat-y, then the image repeats vertically.

Building Full-Length Columns

Now that you understand the basics of backgrounds, you can start building pages that use full-length columns. Although you can't force divs to be longer than their content, you can use background images to create the illusion that they extend all the way down the page. The fact that you must have graphics to achieve this effect and that you have to rework the background graphic if the columns need to change color or width can make this technique a little tedious and rather against the concept of doing it all with CSS, but it does the job very effectively. So, armed with your newfound knowledge of background images, you are ready to tackle the wonderful faux-column technique.

Faux-Column Technique

I think the French name that someone out in CSS land gave to this technique (which was devised by CSS luminary Doug Bowman) certainly sounds more exotic than fake columns, which is what they really are. Let's continue with the three-columns-floated example from the previous chapter and turn it from a simple demo into a page template with full-length columns that you can use it as the basis for creating real Web sites.

The first step is to adjust the page width to 774 pixels, a width that works well on virtually everyone's monitor since it has slightly fewer pixels than today's worst-case scenario—an 800-pixel-wide monitor. Later we'll also make the page position in the center of the browser window. That's because, by default, the page displays in the top-left corner of the browser window on larger monitors.

To set the page width, first specify a width of 774 pixels for the header and for the footer, then recalculate the widths of the three columns so that they add up to 774 pixels.

Also, because we are getting this template ready for prime time, I'm going to use, and recommend that you always do too, the asterisk (*) wild-card selector, which when used on its own as shown in the following code example, zeros out the margins and padding on *every* element; from this point on, any margins and padding are set as you need them. This eliminates the difference in the default margins and padding between different browsers. For example, Safari uses padding to indent lists while Internet Explorer uses margins. If you kill both the padding and margins and then start from scratch using *either* padding *or* margins, then you can get consistent results across all browsers. Here's how the code looks

```
body { font: 1.0em verdana, arial, sans-serif;}

* {margin:0; padding:0;}

div#header {width:774px; height:32px; background-color:#CAF;
text-align:center; padding-top:6px;}

div#column2 p {font-size:.8em;}

div#contentarea {width:774px; background-color:#FFF;}
```

```
div#column1 {width:150px; background-color:#CCC; float:left;}

div#column2 {width:454px; background-color:#FFF; float:left;}

div#column3 {width:170px; background-color:#DDD; float:left;}

div#footer {width:774px; background-color:#FAC;}

/* and the Alsett Clearing Method code must go here
```

See Chapter 5 for this code or go to www.bbd.com/stylin.

Figure 6.5 shows how our template looks so far.

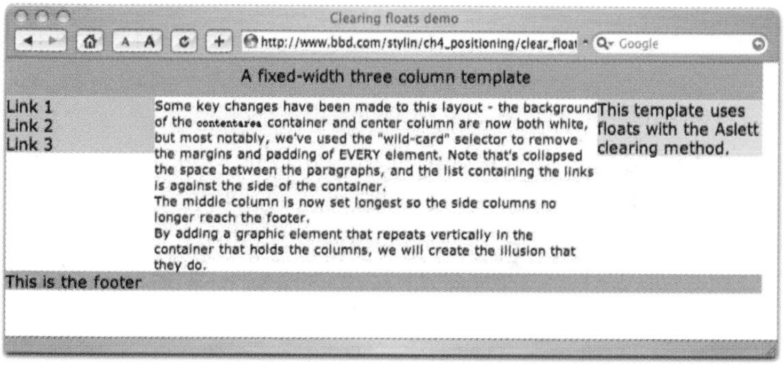

FIGURE 6.5 This is the start of a three-column-floated template.

The first step in creating the floated columns is to create a graphic in Adobe Photoshop or your favorite graphics application that can be repeated as a background down the page. The graphic should look like a horizontal slice of the background of the content area; you have to match the color and width of each column. Next, export your graphic as a GIF (the preferred format for graphic rather than pictorial images) and save it in a folder you can reference with a URL from your page. In my case, I put this graphic in a graphics folder called images_pres at the same level as my XHTML document. **Figure 6.6** shows what my faux-column artwork looks like, I've surrounded it by black so you can see it properly.

FIGURE 6.6 The column artwork matches the colors and widths of the three columns. Here it is surrounded by black for clarity.

Because the browser repeats a background graphic as many times as necessary, you can make it as little as one pixel high, but I always make a repeating graphic like this somewhat taller, in this case 12 pixels high, so that it is still small enough to load quickly, but large enough that the browser can calculate the number of repeats quickly, too.

Now you need to modify your CSS to add this element to the contentarea div that encloses the three columns and set it to tile vertically; this will make it repeat down the page as many times as needed to fill the container.

```
div#contentarea {width:774px;

         background-color:#FFF;

         background-image:url(images_pres/faux_columns.gif);

         background-repeat: repeat-y;}
```

Figure 6.7 shows how your template should look now.

FIGURE 6.7 The vertically repeating background blends perfectly with the divs of the side columns that overlay it, thus creating the illusion of full-length columns.

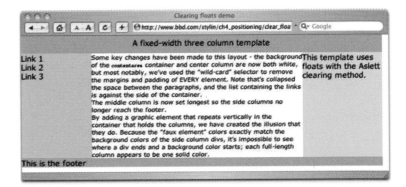

By comparing Figure 6.6 and Figure 6.7, you can see just how far the sidebar divs actually extend. But by forcing the graphic element to vertically repeat in the background, you've created the illusion of full-length columns. Because you've set the clearing method for the container that holds the columns, it gets bigger as any of the three content divs are filled with enough content to push down on it. The background then automatically repeats more to fill the space, and the columns magically extend downward.

Now it's time to center the layout in the browser window. As mentioned earlier, this 774-pixel, fixed-width layout fits nicely on 800×600 resolution monitors. In order to center the layout, you have to add a wrapper around all the other divs, like this

```
<body>

<div id="mainwrap">

<div id="header"><p>A fixed-width three column template</p></
div>
```

31 percent of Web surfers still use 800×600 resolution monitors, according to the The Counter.com's (www.thecounter.com/stats/) November 2004 global stats.

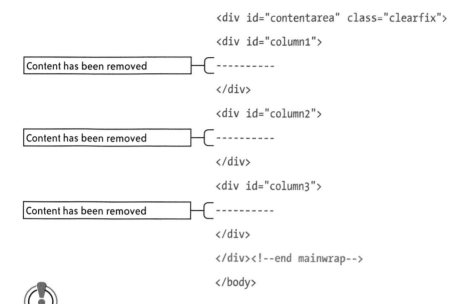

```
<div id="contentarea" class="clearfix">

<div id="column1">
```

Content has been removed ┤ ─ ─ ─ ─ ─ ─ ─ ─ ─ ─

```
</div>

<div id="column2">
```

Content has been removed ┤ ─ ─ ─ ─ ─ ─ ─ ─ ─ ─

```
</div>

<div id="column3">
```

Content has been removed ┤ ─ ─ ─ ─ ─ ─ ─ ─ ─ ─

```
</div>

</div><!--end mainwrap-->

</body>
```

It is important to set the wrapper div to the width of the layout so that there is space on each side of it for the margin auto-sizing to do its thing. Again, auto *means as large as possible, so both margins go as large as they can, pushing the div and the layout within it into the center of the browser window.*

Note that Internet Explorer 5 for Windows doesn't support auto margins. You can force Internet Explorer 5 for Windows to center the layout by adding text-align:center *to the* body *selector, but then you also have to add* text-align:left *on the* mainwrap *div to prevent the entire layout from inheriting this centered text property.*

Next we apply auto margins to the left and right sides of the "meta-wrapper" div we just created. That way both margins become as large as possible, centering the div and your layout within it. I also use the text-align property on the body tag to make the centering work in older browsers that don't understand auto margins

```
body {margin:0px; padding:0px; font: 1.0em verdana, arial,
sans-serif; text-align:center;}
```

```
div#mainwrap {width:774px; margin-left:auto; margin-right:
auto; text-align:left;}
```

At this point, you can also add some new styles to the margins on the content areas

```
div#column1 ul {margin: 20px 0 0 26px;}
```

```
div#column2 p {font-size:.8em; margin:1em 30px;}
```

```
div#column3 p {margin: 20px 10px 0 10px;}
```

Figure 6.8 shows what the template looks like now.

FIGURE 6.8 Adding a div wrapper with auto margins to enclose the header, the three columns, and the footer allows you to center the layout. Adding some margins to the elements in the columns moves them away from the edge of their containing divs and opens up the paragraphs.

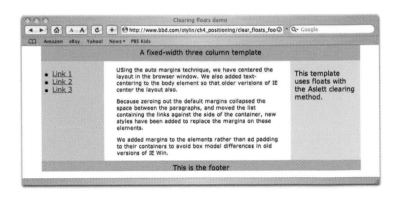

Although there is a simple hack to get around this width difference issue, it's often easiest to get the result you want by using margins on the contained elements, rather than padding on the container, which avoids Box Model issues entirely.

Download the floated-faux-columns template containing this code from www.bbd.com/stylin.

Note that you can simply add padding to the divs themselves, which would be an alternative way of moving the elements away from the edge of the divs. However, when you add padding or borders to elements, you invoke the tedious box model differences between the browsers (see Chapter 4). In standards-compliant browsers, padding and borders are added to the width or height of an element, but Internet Explorer 5.x (and 6.0 in Quirks Mode) for Windows would reduce the area available to the content within the element by the amount of padding and border applied, leaving the divs the same width. The outcome would be that—with a floated layout inside a fixed-size wrapper like you have here—as the layout gets wider, the right-floated column may be forced to wrap and may end up under the left column. Not a pretty sight.

Here's the complete CSS page and markup to this point

```
<!DOCTYPE html PUBLIC "-//W3C//DTD XHTML 1.0 Strict//EN"
    "http://www.w3.org/TR/xhtml1/DTD/xhtml1-strict.dtd">
<html xmlns="http://www.w3.org/1999/xhtml" lang="en" xml:
lang="en">
<head>
<title>Clearing floats demo</title>
<meta http-equiv="Content-type" content="text/html;
charset=iso-8859-1" />
<meta http-equiv="Content-Language" content="en-us" />
<style type="text/css">
body {margin:0px; padding:0px; font: 1.0em verdana, arial,
sans-serif; text-align:center;}
```

```
* {margin:0; padding:0;}

div#mainwrap {width:774px; margin-left:auto; margin-right:
auto;   text-align:left;}

div#header {width:774px; height:32px; background-color:#CAF;
text-align:center; padding-top:6px;}

div#column2 p {font-size:.8em; margin:1em 30px;}

div#contentarea {width:774px; background-color:#FFF;
background-image:url(images_pres/faux_columns.gif);
background-repeat: repeat-y;}

div#column1 {width:150px; background-color:#CCC; float:left;}

div#column1 ul {margin: 20px 0 0 26px;}

div#column2 {width:454px; background-color:#FFF; float:left;}

div#column3 {width:170px; background-color:#DDD; float:left;}

div#column3 p {margin: 20px 10px 0 10px;}

div#footer {width:774px; background-color:#FAC; text-align:
center; padding-top:6px;}
```

See Chapter 5 for this code or go to
www.bbd.com/stylin

```
/* and the Alsett Clearing Method code must go here */

</style>


</head>

<body>

<div id="mainwrap">

<div id="header"><p>A fixed-width three column template</p></
div>

<div id="contentarea" class="clearfix">

<div id="column1"><p>

<ul>

<li><a href="#">Link 1</a></li>

<li><a href="#">Link 2</a></li>

<li><a href="#">Link 3</a></li>

</ul>
```

code continues on next page

```
</p></div>

<div id="column2">

<p>Using the auto margins technique, we have centered the
layout in the browser window. We also added text-centering to
the body element so

that older verisions of IE center the layout also.</p>

<p>Because zeroing out the default margins collapsed the
space between the paragraphs,

and moved the list containing the links against the side of
the container, new styles have been added to replace the
margins on these elements.</p>


<p>We added margins to the elements, rather than add padding
to their containers, to avoid box model differences in old
versions of IE Win.</p>

</div>

<div id="column3">

<p>This template uses floats with the Alsett clearing
method.</p></div>

</div><!--end contentarea-->

<div id="footer">This is the footer</div>

</div><!--end mainwrap-->

</body>

</html>
```

Columns for Fluid Center Layouts

Let's now add faux-columns to a fluid layout. Your first thought, smart reader, may be, "Yes, but how can this fixed width background for the faux columns work if the center is fluid? How can the center area of the background change size?" Here's the answer: It can't. But with some simple modifications to the existing layout example, you can have faux columns for a fluid layout.

First make two separate graphics, one for the background of each column. Then put a second container div around the three columns, with an ID of container2 or whatever. Put the left column background in the background of one container with the background-position set to left, and put the right column background in the background of the other container with the background-position set to right. At this point, each side column works independently of, although identically to, the other, regardless of the width of the center column. Finally, modify the overall layout so the center column resizes as the browser window is resized. As usual, this kind of explanation is longer (and no doubt, more confusing) than a simple demo, like the following:

1. First, add a second container div around the columns. Note how the new container is nested inside the other, original one

```
<div id="mainwrap">

<div id="header"><p>A fixed-width three column template</p></div>

<div id="contentarea" class="clearfix">

<div id="contentarea2" class="clearfix">

<div id="column1">
```

Content has been removed. ----------

```
<div>

<div id="column2">
```

Content has been removed. ----------

```
</div>

<div id="column3">
```

Content has been removed. ----------

```
</div>

</div><!--end contentarea2-->

</div><!--end contentarea-->

<div id="footer">This is the footer</div>

</div><!--end mainwrap-->

</body>
```

2.   Now create two separate column artwork elements as shown in **Figure 6.9**.

FIGURE 6.9 These are the two pieces of artwork for the faux-column fluid layout. Each has the same width and color as its respective side column div.

3.   Next, add the CSS for the two containers

```
div#contentarea {width:774px; background-color:#FFF;
background:url(images_pres/faux_left.gif) repeat-y top
left;}

div#contentarea2 {width:774px; background-color:#FFF;
background:url(images_pres/faux_right.gif) repeat-y top
right;}
```

We have used shorthand for the background property to set the image, repeat, and position in one line of CSS.

You can use this concept to create independent columns on any layout.

A Robust Fluid Layout

Converting the fixed-width layout to a fluid center column layout involves a number of changes to the markup. Here are the three main changes.

1.   Most notably, you must remove all the `width:774px` declarations off the containers, since they now have to change size as the browser width changes. Without an explicit declaration, the containers default to `width:auto`, which is just what you want.

2.   You also need to change from the floating method of arranging the columns to the relative/absolute technique. Absolutely positioned elements (the side columns, in this case) use the positioning context of their closest absolutely positioned ancestor (the column container). By using the top and left settings for the left column and the top and right settings for the right column, you can move the columns up into the top corners of their respective containers.

One big advantage of this method of positioning the side columns is that you can now reorganize the markup so that the center column with the page content comes first; the side columns are absolutely positioned, so it doesn't matter where they appear in the markup. There are two benefits to doing this. First, users with disabilities, who might be using a screen reader or non-mouse navigation device to step through the markup, will encounter the content immediately. Second, search engines tend to rank content that is placed near the top of the markup highest, so this arrangement can help your content rank higher in search engines.

3. The new fluid layout has some constraints on just how fluid it can be. Fluid sizing is definitely user friendly, because the layout can be adjusted to match the available screen real estate. The problems with fluid layouts, however, are that, by narrowing the browser window, the user can either crush the content until the side columns overlap and the content disappears or stretch the browser so wide that text lines become very long. Both of these options make it hard for the user's eye to move from the end of one line to the start of the next. By constraining the maximum and minimum widths to which the layout can size, you give the user the benefits of a fluid layout, while avoiding these two problems.

CSS2 introduced the `max-size` and `min-size` properties, which enable you to set how wide or narrow an element can size. By using these properties on your `mainwrap` that encloses the whole layout, you can control the range of your fluid layout. As a final touch, in the following markup, I also used auto margins so that if the user sets the browser wider than the maximum width allowed for the layout, the layout centers itself in the browser window.

Let's look at the new markup

```
<body>

<div id="mainwrap">

<div id="header"><p>A fluid-width faux-columns example</p></
div>

<div id="contentarea" class="clearfix">

<div id="contentarea2" class="clearfix">


<div id="column2">

<p>This layout uses absolute/relative positioning to position
the side columns within their respective faux columns
containers.</p>

<p>You can control the maximum and minimum widths of the
fluid center area.
```

code continues on next page

Once the layout reaches its maximum width, it centers itself in the browser as the window gets wider.</p>

<p>Nulla scelerisque. Sed tincidunt. Quisque eu nisl. Phasellus

mi ante, aliquet vel, vestibulum sit amet, consectetuer non, ante. Suspendisse

consequat condimentum enim. Morbi vestibulum lorem sit amet enim. Nulla venenatis

fermentum purus.</p>

<p>Nunc justo nisl, vulputate in, sagittis in, pretium sodales,

magna. Nullam felis diam, bibendum ut, dictum in, tincidunt vitae, magna.

Nunc mattis congue leo.</p>

</div><!--end column2-->

<div id="column1">

<ul>

<li><a href="#">Link 1</a></li>

<li><a href="#">Link 2</a></li>

<li><a href="#">Link 3</a></li>

</ul>

</div><!--end column1-->

<div id="column3">

<p>This template uses the Alsett clearing method.</p>

</div><!--end column3-->

</div><!--end contentarea2-->

</div><!--end contentarea-->

<div id="footer">This is the footer</div>

</div><!--end mainwrap-->

</body>

Note that column2, the center content area, appears before the two side columns, column1 and column3, in this markup.

Here is the CSS:

```
<style type="text/css">

body {font: 1.0em verdana, arial, sans-serif;

    text-align:center;

    }

* {margin:0; padding:0;}

div#mainwrap {min-width:780px; max-width:960px;

    margin-left:auto; margin-right:auto;

    text-align:left;

    }

div#header {height:32px; background-color:#CAF; text-align:
center;}

div#contentarea { background-color:#FFF;

    background:url(images_pres/faux_left.gif) repeat-y top
left;

    position:relative;

    }

div#contentarea2 {background-color:#FFF;

    background:url(images_pres/faux_right.gif) repeat-y top
right;

    position:relative;

    }

div#column1 {width:150px;

    position: absolute;

    top:0px; left:0px;

    background-color:#CCC;

    overflow:hidden;

    }
```

Left labels (callouts):

- Centers the layout in IE 5 → `text-align:center;`
- Sets the max and min widths → `div#mainwrap {min-width:780px; max-width:960px;`
- Centers the layout in SCBs → `margin-left:auto; margin-right:auto;`
- Stops elements from inheriting the body's text-center → `text-align:left;`
- Temporary placeholder styles for header → `div#header {height:32px; background-color:#CAF; text-align: center;}`
- Ensures bg is white if faux graphic doesn't load → `div#contentarea { background-color:#FFF;`
- Faux-column graphic left column → `background:url(images_pres/faux_left.gif) repeat-y top left;`
- Set positioning context for left sidebar div → `position:relative;`
- Faux-column graphic right column → `background:url(images_pres/faux_right.gif) repeat-y top right;`
- Set positioning context for right sidebar div → `position:relative;`
- Contextual positioning in contentarea container → `position: absolute;`
- Positions col within contentarea container → `top:0px; left:0px;`
- Left column bg color → `background-color:#CCC;`
- Prevents overlarge elements breaking out of column → `overflow:hidden;`

code continues on next page

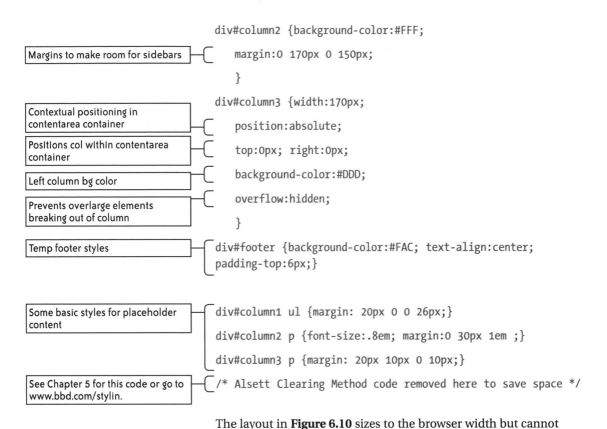

Margins to make room for sidebars

Contextual positioning in contentarea container

Positions col within contentarea container

Left column bg color

Prevents overlarge elements breaking out of column

Temp footer styles

Some basic styles for placeholder content

See Chapter 5 for this code or go to www.bbd.com/stylin.

```css
div#column2 {background-color:#FFF;
    margin:0 170px 0 150px;
}
div#column3 {width:170px;
    position:absolute;
    top:0px; right:0px;
    background-color:#DDD;
    overflow:hidden;
}
div#footer {background-color:#FAC; text-align:center;
padding-top:6px;}


div#column1 ul {margin: 20px 0 0 26px;}

div#column2 p {font-size:.8em; margin:0 30px 1em ;}

div#column3 p {margin: 20px 10px 0 10px;}

/* Alsett Clearing Method code removed here to save space */
```

The layout in **Figure 6.10** sizes to the browser width but cannot become too wide or narrow. It works in all modern, standards–compliant browsers, and it doesn't have the issues associated with floats wrapping the right column under the left if columns become too wide (from an overly large image, for example).

FIGURE 6.10 This layout is fluid but has maximum and minimum constraints to prevent the layout from getting too wide or too narrow.

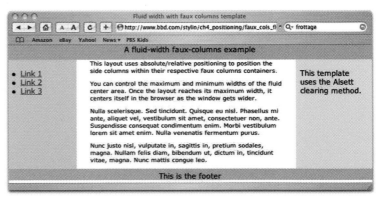

The side columns each have an overflow:hidden declaration to visually trim graphics or other elements that are wider than the column rather than have them spill out over other areas.

Note also that it is the use of positioning context (see Chapter 4) that makes this layout work. The side columns are absolutely positioned, which means that by default, their positioning context is body. In order to have the layout center in the screen after it reaches maximum width, the columns can't be positioned relative to body (which is always the width of the browser window), because if this was the case, the sidebars would stay at the edge of the browser, even as the rest of the layout moved away from the browser edges. By setting the column containers' position property to relative, they provide the positioning context for the sidebar divs; the side columns then move with the rest of the layout.

To see this for yourself, temporarily remove position:relative from each of the container divs. Then save and reload and open up the browser wider than the maximum width value so that the layout starts to move away from the browser's sides. If you do so, you will see that those side columns remain at the edge of the browser window because their positioning context has reverted to the default, body.

I will show you how to work extensively with this template in the next chapter.

A Template With Negative Margins

I want to finish with one more template, which I call the "Wyke-Switch." For some time, I have been thinking about a simple way to create a three-column layout where the second column with content appears first in the markup. There is good reason for wanting to do this, since search engines rank content at the beginning of the markup as more relevant than content further down. Leading your markup with a long list of links and other non-content material that appears in the left sidebar can work against your search engine visibility.

Also, there is an accessibility issue. If someone is reading your page with a screen reader, or using the keyboard to step through the markup, it's much more considerate to present the content first; otherwise the user has to make his or her way through the left column before getting to the page's content. While adding Skip Links options can help alleviate this problem (see Jim Hatcher's excellent article at www.jimthatcher.com/skipnav.htm for more on this), why not simply have the content appear first in the markup?

So how do we write CSS for markup sequenced like this:

1. Center Content column

2. Left navigation column

3. Right sidebar column

so it can appear in the browser like this?:

1. Left navigation column

2. Center Content column

3. Right sidebar column

Here's the answer I came up with: use negative margins to exchange the position of the left and center columns. We have seen how margins with positive values—values greater than zero—allow us to move one element away from another. Now we will explore how margins with negative values—values less than zero—can be used to move an element into the space occupied by another.

Let's look at a simple three-column example, using floats to get the columns to sit side by side.

Here is the markup (it goes within the Strict template found at www. bbd.com/stylin)

```
<div id="header">Content first in markup demo</div>
```

A wrapper for the three columns ——⎡ `<div id="contentarea">`

```
<div id="column2">Column 2. This is the first column in the
markup. The center column is the page's content.</div>
```

```
<div id="column1">Column 1. This is the second column in the
markup. This is the left navigation.</div>
```

```
<div id="column3">Column 3. This is the right column and
third in the markup. The wrapper round the three columns is
floated left like the three columns, to force it to enclose
the three columns. Because of this no matter which of the
three columns is longest, the footer sits below it…</div>
```

```
</div><!--end contentarea-->
```

```
<div classs="clearthis"><!--clearing element--></div>
```

```
<div id="footer">This is the footer</div>
```

What is most notable about this markup is the order of the three columns: 2, 1, 3.

Here is some CSS to layout this markup out as three columns

```
body {font: 0.8em verdana, arial, sans-serif;}
* {margin:0px; padding:0px;}
div#header {width:650px; background-color:#CAF;}
div#contentarea {width:650px; background-color:#CCC;}
div#column1 {float:left; width:150px; background-color:#FCC;}
div#column2 {float:left; width:350px; background-color:#CFC;}
div#column3 {float:left; width:150px; background-color:#AAF;}
div#footer {width:650px; background-color:#FAC;}
.clearthis {clear:both; height:0; linne-height:0;}
```

Clears the footer below longest column

which looks like this (**Figure 6.11**):

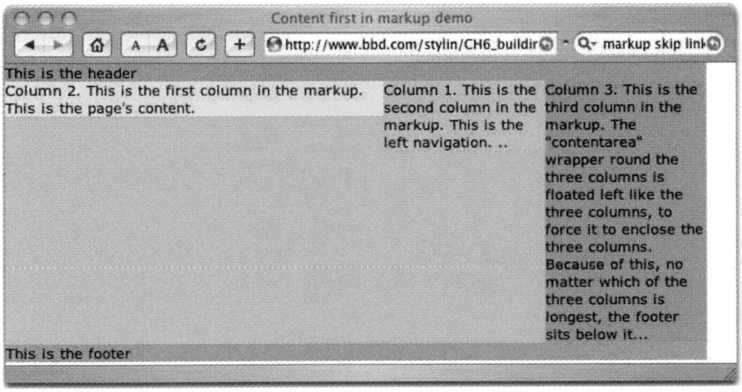

FIGURE 6.11 This layout reflects the sequence of the markup where column 2 appears before column 1.

What we need to do now is switch the position of the first and second columns. Let's start by moving column 2, currently left-most, into its correct position by applying a left-margin with a positive value of 150 pixels to push it over far enough to make room for column 1, the 150 pixel wide navigation column

```
div#column2 {float:left; width:350px; margin-left:150px;
background-color:#CFC;}
```

This moves the column over the correct amount in a standards-compliant browser, such as Safari (**Figure 6.12**).

FIGURE 6.12 A left margin of 150 pixels pushes the content column into the correct position.

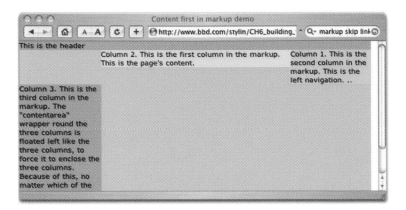

But, IDWIMIE—Internet Explorer for Windows seems to have a small problem (**Figure 6.13**).

FIGURE 6.13 Internet Explorer for Windows doubles the left-margin on a left-floated element. Don't ask why, just accept...

Learn more about this Internet Explorer bug on Big John and Holly the Hack's Position is Everything site (www.positioniseverything.net).

For some unknown reason, Internet Explorer for Windows doubles the left margin on a left floated element, and does the same for the right margin on right floated elements. This is a known bug.

A smart fellow called Steve Caslon, however, came up with the fix for this bug; change the element from a block-level element to an inline element, like this (**Figure 6.14**)

```
div#column2 {float:left; width:350px; margin-left:150px;
display:inline; background-color:#CFC;}
```

FIGURE 6.14 With the Caslon hack applied, Internet Explorer correctly displays the left-margin on the left-floated element.

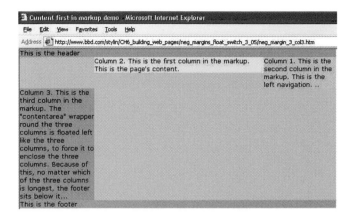

Because the layout in other browsers is not affected by this change, I didn't bother to hide it in a hack. The purists amongst you might want to write a nice little backslash comment hack for this, so only Internet Explorer can see it.

FIGURE 6.14 With the Caslon hack applied, Internet Explorer correctly displays the left-margin on the left-floated element.

Much better. Internet Explorer for Windows now correctly positions this element. Column 3 is "wrapped" down to the line below, since we still have to make room for it by moving column 1 into the correct position.

Now we are going to move column 1 over into the space we created for it in the last step. We need to move it to the left by the width of column 2 (350 pixels) plus its own width (150 pixels)—a total width of 500 pixels. We do this by setting a negative margin on the element, which moves it without disrupting the position of column 2 (**Figure 6.15**)

```
div#column1 {float:left; width:150px; margin-left:-500px;
background-color:#FCC;}
```

FIGURE 6.15 The left negative margin moves the navigation column into its correct position and makes room for the right column to take its place.

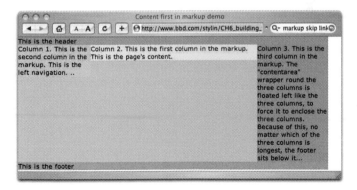

With column 1 in position, column 3 is able to move up to take the space vacated by column 1.

So there is a simple way you can create a layout that does not follow the sequence of the markup.

CHAPTER 7

Creating Interface Components

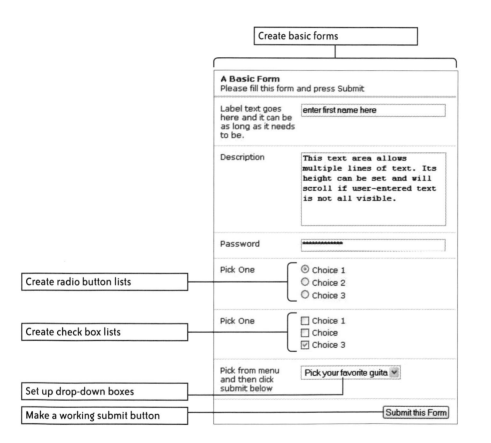

Create basic forms

A Basic Form
Please fill this form and press Submit

Label text goes here and it can be as long as it needs to be.

enter first name here

Description

This text area allows multiple lines of text. Its height can be set and will scroll if user-entered text is not all visible.

Password

Pick One
- Choice 1
- Choice 2
- Choice 3

Create radio button lists

Pick One
- Choice 1
- Choice
- Choice 3

Create check box lists

Pick from menu and then click submit below

Pick your favorite guita

Set up drop-down boxes

Make a working submit button

Submit this Form

Customers | Members | Dealers | Distributors
Our Services
FAQs
Sign Up
Support
What's New

Gold program
Silver program
Bronze program
By Region

Make a hover effect

Learn to create both simple and nested drop-down menus

The Web pages you create consist of the content that you are presenting as well as a number of interface components that are virtually the same on every site—navigation links, forms, lists, and tables are the most common examples. In this chapter, I'm going to show you how to write valid XHTML markup for these components and then style them with CSS. Along the way, we'll build a CSS library of components that you can use as a starting point for your pages. You'll be able to open the sample files, copy the markup into your XHTML, copy the styles into your style sheet, and then just fine-tune them for your particular needs. As you work with CSS, you will find yourself creating a library of your favorite component styles that you can copy into your project style sheets, thereby saving yourself hours of time rebuilding components you have already made.

Understanding Lists

There are three types of lists: unordered, ordered, and definitions. They have similar markup but should be used based on their content.

- **Unordered lists** are bulleted by default. You can change this bullet to a hollow circle or a square, or you can even replace the bullet with a graphic or an entity such as ~ (tilde).

- **Ordered lists** are numbered by default. You can change the numbers to letters of the alphabet or to roman numerals.

- **Definition lists (or nested lists)** contain subitems; you might use this type of list for a glossary of terms.

The markup for lists is very simple. Here's the code for an unordered list

```
<ul>

<li>Gibson</li>

<li>Fender</li>

<li>Rickenbacker</li>

<li>Washburn</li>

</ul>
```

This unordered list opens with an unordered list (ul) tag, contains a number of list (li) items, and then closes with another ul tag.

An ordered list is very similar except the list tag is `ol` instead of `ul`. In an ordered list, each item is sequentially labeled using numbers, letters, or roman numerals, depending on the value of the `list-style-type` property. You can place the label either outside of the list or within in it using the `list-style-position` property.

Figure 7.1 shows some examples of different types of unordered and ordered lists.

FIGURE 7.1 Here are examples of the various sorts of unordered and ordered lists you can create.

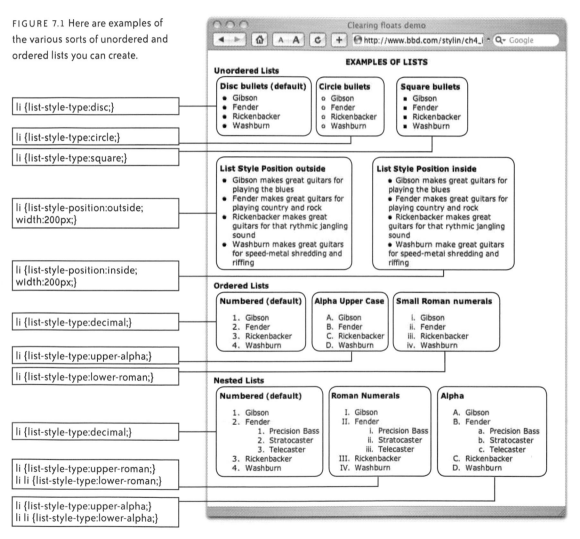

Styling Lists

Lists are the basis for navigation and menus; after all, navigation elements usually consist of a list of pages you can visita menu is a list of choices. So there is a movement within the CSS community toward styling navigation and menus as lists. One very important advantage of this thinking is that if the user is viewing the page in a user agent—perhaps a cell phone—that cannot apply the CSS styles, the XHTML list markup is enough to render the navigation or menus in meaningful ways. Even if that doesn't make sense now, it will by the time you have read through this section. Let's begin by styling a set of navigation links that you might find on the left sidebar of almost any site.

Here's the markup for an unordered list inside of a div, so you can see it in relation to a containing element (in the context of left navigation, the container would be the left column)

```
<div id="listcontainer">

<ul>

<li>Gibson</li>

<li>Fender</li>

<li>Rickenbacker</li>

<li>Washburn</li>

</ul>

</div>
```

First, let's display the div so we can see our unstyled list inside it (**Figure 7.2**).

```
body {font: 1.0em verdana, arial, sans-serif;}

div#listcontainer {border:1px solid #000; width:160px; font-size:.75em; margin:20px;}
```

Second, let's turn on the borders of the ul and the li elements so that we can see the position of the individual elements of the list (**Figure 7.3**).

```
ul {border:1px solid red;}

li {border:1px solid green;}
```

FIGURE 7.2 Here's an unordered list inside a div with its border on.

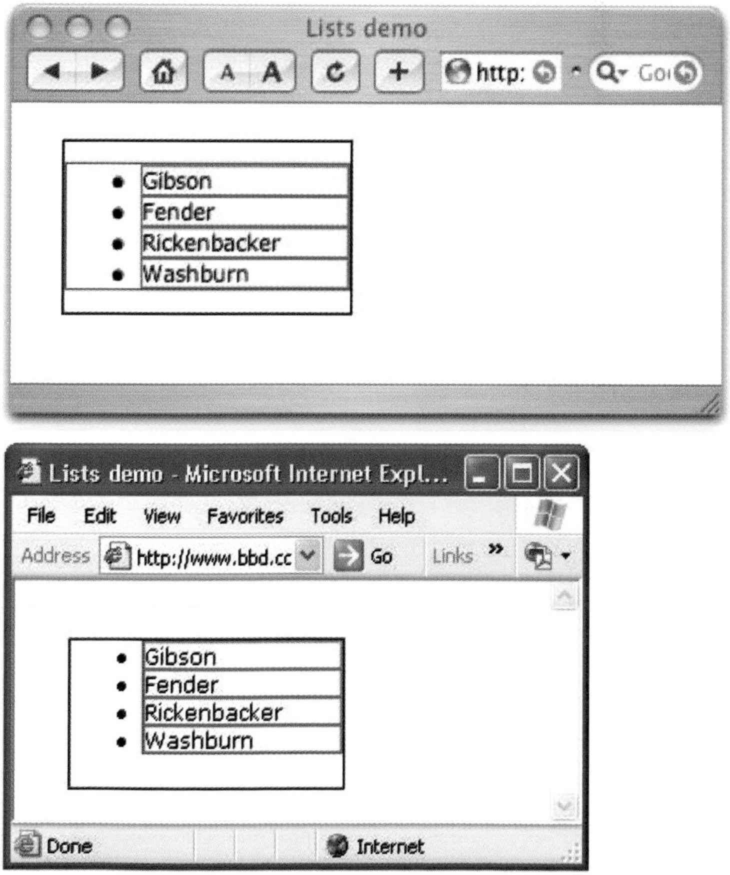

FIGURE 7.3 With the `ul` and `li` borders turned on, it's clear that Safari (top) and Internet Explorer (bottom) have different default styles for lists.

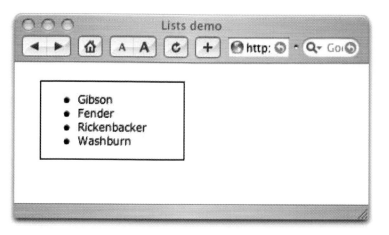

In Figure 7.3, the `ul` has a red border and each `li` has a green border. As you can see, Safari uses padding on the `ul` to indent the list (the green elements are pushed away from the `ul` red container) and also adds small top and bottom margins to separate the list from surrounding items. Internet Explorer uses a margin on the `ul` to indent the list (note the `ul` is wrapped tight around the `li` elements and both are moved away from the div), and Internet Explorer only adds a bottom margin, not a top one. These differences can make it hard to have lists look the same across browsers. The only way to overcome these discrepancies is first to reset the margin and padding values on lists to zero and then restyle them.

So let's set the `ul` and `li` margins and padding on both types of list elements to zero (**Figure 7.4**).

```
ul {border:1px solid red; margin:0; padding:0;}

li {border:1px solid green; margin:0; padding:0;}
```

FIGURE 7.4 Now Safari (top) and Internet Explorer (bottom) present the list identically. Note that once the bullets move outside of the `ul` in Internet Explorer, they are not displayed.

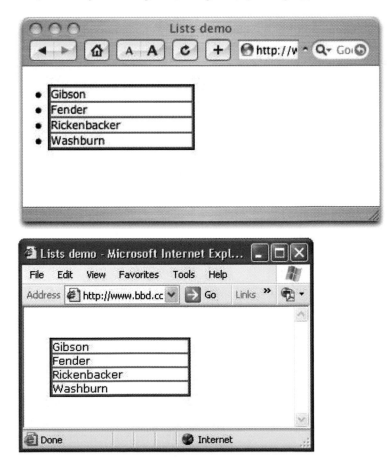

Now the list looks the same on both Safari and Internet Explorer. Note that the bullets, which belong to the li elements, are now hanging outside of the div. If the div was right against the edge of the browser window, the bullets wouldn't even be visible. So it's clear that we have to apply some minimal amount of left margin or padding to the ul to ensure that the bullets are within the div and are not over-lapping another element, or, as is the case in Internet Explorer, are not even displayed. So let's set the left margin (**Figure 7.5**).

```
div#listcontainer {border:1px solid #000; width:160px; font-
size:.75em; margin:20px;}

ul {border:1px solid red; margin:0 0 0 1.25em; padding:0;}

li {border:1px solid green; margin:0;}
```

FIGURE 7.5 By setting a left margin of 1.25 em on the ul, the bullets are brought back into the div.

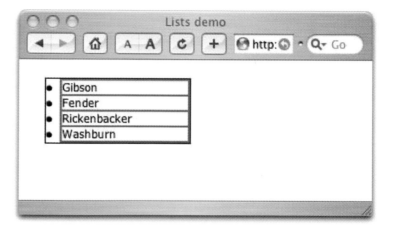

Note that I used the shorthand style to set *all* the margins, not just the left margin. If you don't keep the others explicitly set at zero, the default top and bottom margins, which are different for each browser, will reappear. Also, now we have placeholders ready for the other three values in case we want to change them later.

Let's change the space between the list items since they're a little too close together

```
div#listcontainer {border:1px solid #000; width:160px; font-
size:.75em; margin:20px;}

ul {border:1px solid red; margin:0 0 0 1.25em; padding:0;}

li {border:1px solid green; margin:0; padding:.3em 0;}
```

The obvious way to do this is to set the margin-top or margin-bottom on the li elements, but I prefer to use identical top and bottom padding. This keeps the li elements touching instead of creating space between them, which gives us some more options for styling. To show you why it's better to increase the padding than to change the margin, I'll replace the boxes around the elements with neat horizontal lines between each item (**Figure 7.6**).

FIGURE 7.6 Adding the horizontal lines is the first step in giving the list a more designed look.

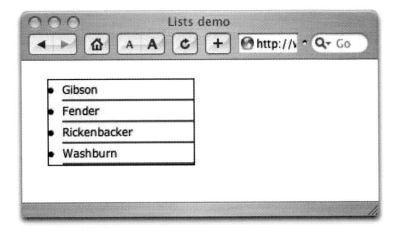

By adding the top and bottom padding to increase the height of the li elements instead of creating space between them, the top and bottom edges of the li elements are exactly halfway between each line of type. Now when you style either their top or bottom edges, you get a rule exactly halfway between them.

Now let's do some more cleanup on this list (**Figure 7.7**).

1. Remove the bullets.

2. Set the margins on the ul element so that the list is better positioned within the div.

3. Indent the list items so they are not flush with the edge of the rules.

Here are the changes to the markup

```
body {font:1em verdana, arial, sans-serif;}

div#listcontainer {border:1px solid #000; width:160px; font-size:.75em; margin:20px;}

ul {border:0; margin:10px 30px 10px 1.25em; padding:0; list-style-type:none;}

li {border-bottom:2px solid #069; margin:0; padding:.3em 0; text-indent:.5em}
```

FIGURE 7.7 The list looks better, but it could use a rule above the first item.

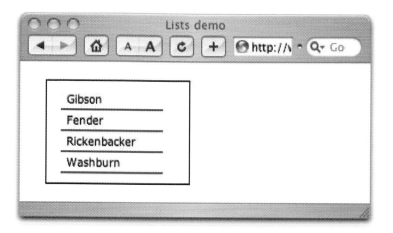

The most notable modification made at this step was using the list-style-type property, with a value of none, to remove the bullets. The text-indent property moves the text in slightly from the left edge of the rule, and the new margins on the ul position the list nicely within the container.

The list would certainly look better if we added a line across the top of the first item (**Figure 7.8** on the next page). The ideal solution is to add a border-top to just the first list item. There is a simple way to do that with the CSS pseudo-class :first-child. Sadly, IDWIMIE—Internet Explorer does not understand that pseudo-class.

This means that we either add the :first-child pseudo-class and accept, zen-like, that it will not appear in Internet Explorer, or we come up with a work-around. Let's use the pseudo-class first, and then think about a work-around for our less-compliant but popular friend Internet Explorer. Here's the code

```
body {font:1em verdana, arial, sans-serif;}

div#listcontainer {border:1px solid #000; width:150px; font-size:.75em; margin:20px;}

ul {border:0; margin:12px 20px 10px 1.25em; padding:0; list-style-type:none;}

li {border-bottom:2px solid #069; margin:0; padding:.3em 0; text-indent:.5em}

li:first-child {border-top:2px solid #069;}
```

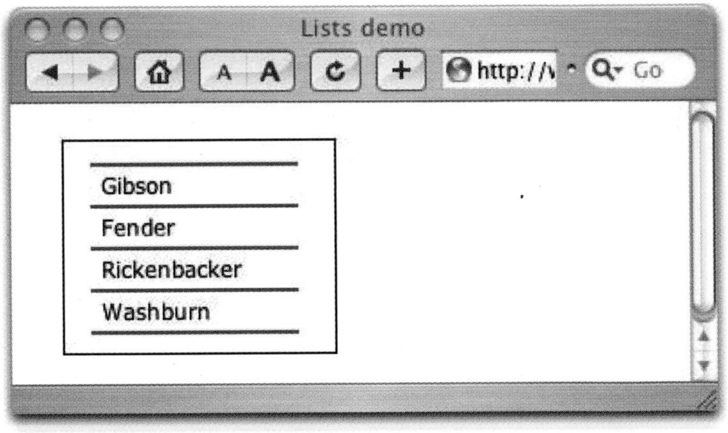

FIGURE 7.8 Here we've added a top line using the `:first-child` pseudo-class.

Now take a look at a simple fix for Internet Explorer. When the bullet was removed, the ul element shrank down to the same width as the list items. We can create our top rule by applying the style to the top of the ul, which contains all the list items. Instead of using the markup I just listed, you could use the following, which makes the top line appear in Internet Explorer too

```
body {font:1em verdana, arial, sans-serif;}
```

```
div#listcontainer {border:1px solid #000; width:150px; font-size:.75em; margin:20px;}
```

```
ul {border:0; margin:12px 20px 10px 1.25em; padding:0; list-style-type:none; border-top: 2px solid #069}
```

```
li {border-bottom:2px solid #069; margin:0; padding:.3em 0; text-indent:.5em}
```

Sometimes you can find easy work-arounds like this for Internet Explorer, and sometimes you have to accept that not everyone is going to get the same experience. As long as everyone gets an acceptable experience, that's OK.

We now have something that looks a lot like a set of navigation links. All we need to do is turn what are now lines of text into links and we'll have an attractive and functional navigation element (**Figure 7.9**). This is quite simple using this code

```
<div id="listcontainer">

<ul>

<li><a href="gibson.htm">Gibson</a></li>

<li><a href="fender.htm">Fender</a></li>

<li><a href="rickenbacker.htm">Rickenbacker</a></li>

<li><a href="washburn.htm">Washburn</a></li>

</ul>

</div>
```

Note how the link tags are closest to the content and nested inside the list items.

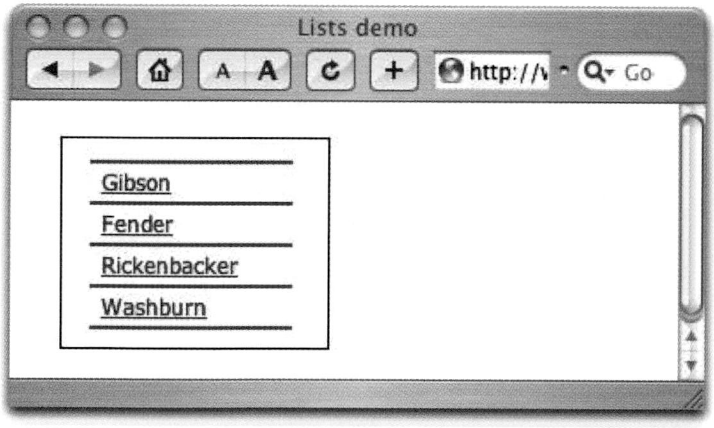

FIGURE 7.9 With links added into the markup, the text now appears underlined.

Basic Link Styling

Now let's give your links some styles. First, let's remove the underlining from them in their normal, "sitting-there-waiting-for-something-to-happen" state, and then, when the users rolls the cursor over the link, let's have it change color.

Also, since this is the last step to complete your navigation component, you should do some clean up: you need to adjust the ul bottom margin, add context to the selectors so that only the elements within your listcontainer div are affected by the styles, and add a hack (actually, two hacks) to make the line above the first list item appear in Internet Explorer for Windows.

Here's the final code for your list-based navigation component

```
body {font:1em verdana, arial, sans-serif;}

div#listcontainer {border:1px solid #000; width:150px; font-size:.75em; margin:20px;}

div#listcontainer ul {border:0; margin:12px 20px 12px 1.25em; padding:0; list-style-type:none;}

div#listcontainer li {border-bottom:2px solid #069; margin:0; padding:.3em 0; text-indent:.5em}

div#listcontainer li:first-child {border-top:2px solid #069;}

div#listcontainer a {text-decoration:none; color:#069;}

div#listcontainer a:hover {color: #FCC;}

html div#listcontainer ul {border-top:2px solid #069;}
```

A hack for Internet Explorer for Windows

FIGURE 7.10 Here's the finished menu, complete with a rollover highlight.

The Star Hack and the Backslash Hack

A *hack* is the term for using CSS in ways other than the way it was intended to be used. Hacks are used to enable CSS to be targeted to, or hidden from, specific browsers. A very common use of a hack is to provide alternate code for Internet Explorer.

The Star Hack

You have seen that the great-granddaddy of all ancestor elements is the html element; all elements are its descendants. However, Internet Explorer is unique in that it has an unnamed element that is a parent of the html element, so by referencing this element in a selector, you create a rule that is only read by Internet Explorer. Because this element has no name, you reference it with * (known as star), the wildcard CSS selector. The most common way to use the star selector is like this

```
div * ul {…some CSS…}
```

Here, the ul is not selected if it is a child of the div, but it is if it is a grandchild. You use the * to say that it doesn't matter what the in-between child element is.

So, to create a rule that is only read by Internet Explorer, you write

```
* html …more specific selectors… {…some CSS…}
```

For example

```
div#box {border:1px solid blue;}
```

```
* html div#box {border:1px solid red;}
```

In this example, all browsers set the border to blue, except Internet Explorer for Windows and Internet Explorer for Mac, which read the second rule also, and display the box border in red.

However, the more compliant Internet Explorer for Mac can interpret both the * selector and some CSS that Internet Explorer for Windows cannot interpret. So you need some way to ensure that only Internet Explorer for Windows reads the star hack rule. You do this by putting the star hack rule inside a pair of comments, which are written in a special way to take advantage of a strange, unique behavior of Internet Explorer for Mac.

The Backslash-Comment Hack

If you write a comment with a backslash right before the closing *, like this

```
/* this a comment \*/
```

Internet Explorer for Mac does not think the comment has ended and ignores all the CSS that follows until it encounters a comment that is closed in a normal way. (If you like to add comments after, or on the same line as, your selectors, don't do it here, since the positioning of the comments is what makes this hack work.)

For example,

```
/* a hack for IE Win only \*/
```

```
* html div#listcontainer ul {border-top:2px solid #069;}
```

```
/*end of hack */
```

Here, Internet Explorer for Mac ignores the line with the * html selector, even though it is perfectly capable of reading it; it thinks the first comment doesn't close until the end of the second one, so the * html selector is hidden from it. The combination of the star and backslash hacks gives you a rule that is only read by Internet Explorer for Windows.

Creating CSS-Based Menus

You can download the CSS from the Stylin' site (www.bbd.com/stylin).

When I approach the problem of creating drop-down menus from list markup, I want to be able to take a list, with nested lists for the drop-downs, and have it work without needing to add any additional markup—just vanilla XHTML list markup and my CSS. What follows is how to create CSS drop-down menus from "ID-and-class-free" lists. All that's required is context—a surrounding div with an ID, so the correct CSS styles are applied to the list within. Certainly, once you have the CSS, these drop-down menus are very simple to incorporate in a site.

Your first step toward drop-down menus is to create the horizontal menu from which they drop—a useful element in its own right.

Horizontal Navigation Components

Drop-down menus contain subcategories, which fall from each main category in a horizontal list. Drop-down menus are more flexible and space-efficient than vertical menus. Traditionally, drop-down menus have involved JavaScript, and often lots of it. Each drop-down menu required its own chunk of code, which was complex to modify or to develop as part of a dynamic site where such navigation would be expected to automatically reflect changes to site organization. With CSS, you can greatly simplify the creation of menus because the only markup that is required is lists, and one relatively small piece of CSS code can control the behavior of numerous menus without additional code being required as items are added to the menus.

So let's take a look at these advantages in action by first creating a horizontal navigation element, and then adding drop-down subcategories (**Figure 7.11**).

FIGURE 7.11 Here's a basic horizontal navigation element.

| Customers | Members | Dealers | Distributors |

This component is based on a simple list inside a div, like this

```
<div id="listmenu">
 <ul>
  <li><a href="#">Customers</a></li>
  <li><a href="#">Members</a></li>
```

```
<li><a href="#">Dealers</a></li>

<li><a href="#">Distributors</a></li>

</ul>
```

`</div>`

But to get to the horizontal menu shown in Figure 7.11, we have to start more simply (**Figure 7.12**).

FIGURE 7.12 Here's the humble beginning of our horizontal drop-down menu.

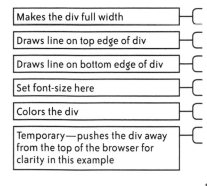

Start with some simple styles for the div; draw a line on its top and bottom edge, set its font size and the color of its background, and use a `top-margin` to push it away from the top of the browser.

Here's the markup

```
<style type="text/css">

body {font:1em verdana, arial, sans-serif;}

* {margin:0; padding:0;}

div#listmenu {

    width:100%;

    border-top:1px solid #069;

    border-bottom:1px solid #069;

    font-size:.8em;

    background-color:#CCF;

    margin-top:20px;

    }

</style>
```

Callout	Code line
Makes the div full width	`width:100%;`
Draws line on top edge of div	`border-top:1px solid #069;`
Draws line on bottom edge of div	`border-bottom:1px solid #069;`
Set font-size here	`font-size:.8em;`
Colors the div	`background-color:#CCF;`
Temporary—pushes the div away from the top of the browser for clarity in this example	`margin-top:20px;`

The unstyled list is stacked by default, so the next thing we need to do is get it to lay out horizontally by floating the list elements (**Figure 7.13**). Let's move the list over from the left edge of the div and color the background of the list items while we're at it.

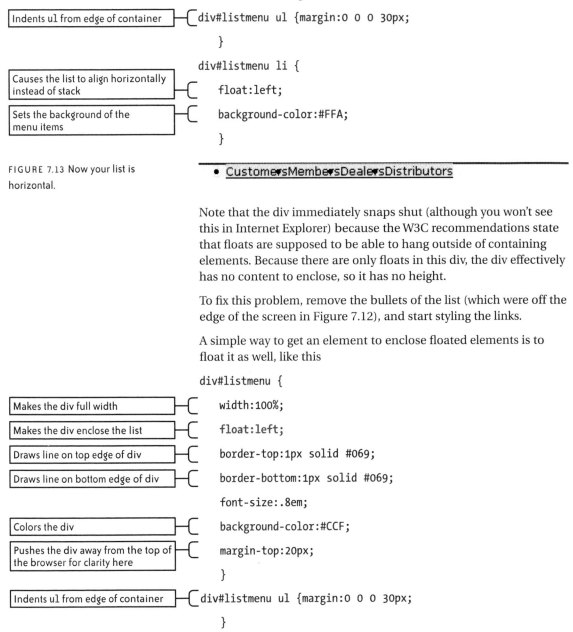

Indents ul from edge of container	`div#listmenu ul {margin:0 0 0 30px;`
	`}`
	`div#listmenu li {`
Causes the list to align horizontally instead of stack	`float:left;`
Sets the background of the menu items	`background-color:#FFA;`
	`}`

FIGURE 7.13 Now your list is horizontal.

• <u>Custome▾sMembe▾sDeale▾sDistributors</u>

Note that the div immediately snaps shut (although you won't see this in Internet Explorer) because the W3C recommendations state that floats are supposed to be able to hang outside of containing elements. Because there are only floats in this div, the div effectively has no content to enclose, so it has no height.

To fix this problem, remove the bullets of the list (which were off the edge of the screen in Figure 7.12), and start styling the links.

A simple way to get an element to enclose floated elements is to float it as well, like this

	`div#listmenu {`
Makes the div full width	`width:100%;`
Makes the div enclose the list	`float:left;`
Draws line on top edge of div	`border-top:1px solid #069;`
Draws line on bottom edge of div	`border-bottom:1px solid #069;`
	`font-size:.8em;`
Colors the div	`background-color:#CCF;`
Pushes the div away from the top of the browser for clarity here	`margin-top:20px;`
	`}`
Indents ul from edge of container	`div#listmenu ul {margin:0 0 0 30px;`
	`}`

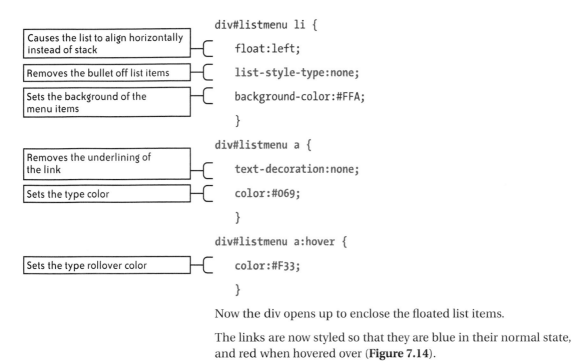

```
div#listmenu li {

    float:left;

    list-style-type:none;

    background-color:#FFA;

}

div#listmenu a {

    text-decoration:none;

    color:#069;

}

div#listmenu a:hover {

    color:#F33;

}
```

Causes the list to align horizontally instead of stack ─┤ `float:left;`

Removes the bullet off list items ─┤ `list-style-type:none;`

Sets the background of the menu items ─┤ `background-color:#FFA;`

Removes the underlining of the link ─┤ `text-decoration:none;`

Sets the type color ─┤ `color:#069;`

Sets the type rollover color ─┤ `color:#F33;`

Now the div opens up to enclose the floated list items.

The links are now styled so that they are blue in their normal state, and red when hovered over (**Figure 7.14**).

FIGURE 7.14 Links now turn red when the user rolls the pointer over them.

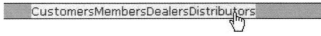

Although we now get a nice rollover effect on the link, there is no visual separation between the list items. A few new styles take care of that

```
div#listmenu li {

    float:left;

    list-style-type:none;

    background-color:#FFA;

    padding:0 6px;

    border-right:1px solid #069;

}

div#listmenu li:first-child {

    border-left:1px solid #069;

}
```

Causes the list to align horizontally ─┤ `float:left;`

Removes the bullet off list items ─┤ `list-style-type:none;`

Sets the background of menu items ─┤ `background-color:#FFA;`

Space on sides of menu item's text ─┤ `padding:0 6px;`

Creates dividing lines ─┤ `border-right:1px solid #069;`

The first vertical line on the menu ─┤ `border-left:1px solid #069;`

code continues on next page

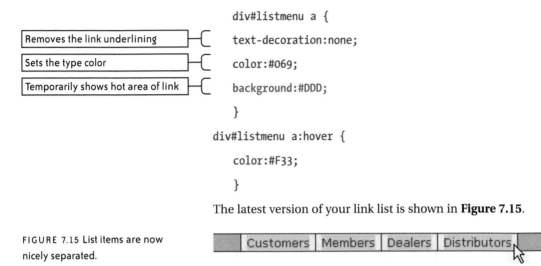

```
div#listmenu a {

text-decoration:none;

color:#069;

background:#DDD;

}

div#listmenu a:hover {

color:#F33;

}
```

Removes the link underlining

Sets the type color

Temporarily shows hot area of link

The latest version of your link list is shown in **Figure 7.15**.

FIGURE 7.15 List items are now nicely separated.

To create the dividing lines, in the preceding code, we first added a right border to each link, and that's four lines done. To create the very first dividing line, we used the :first-child pseudo-class to add a left border to the first list item. Because Internet Explorer for Windows does not recognize the :first-child pseudo-class, a bit later, you'll use a hack to fix this.

I've temporarily colored the backgrounds of the links gray so that you can see that they do not fill the entire list item space. This is a problem, because if you move the mouse into a yellow area, the link does not respond, as illustrated in Figure 7.15. You have to get onto the gray area of the link itself for the link to change color. What you want to do is make the link fill the list item space.

The problem is that links are inline elements that do not take width, height, or padding settings, so to provide settings to make a link fill its list item, you need to convert it to a block element. Then you can move the padding off the list item and onto the link; it then fills the list item and the whole area is "hot." Now modify your markup to look like this

```
div#listmenu li {

    float:left;

    list-style-type:none;

    background-color:#FFA;

    border-right:1px solid #069;

}
```

```
div#listmenu li:first-child {
    border-left:1px solid #069;
}
div#listmenu a {
    padding:0 6px;
    text-decoration:none;
    color:#069;
    background:#DDD;
}
div#listmenu a:hover {
    color:#F33;
}
```

Creates space each side of menu item's text

Now the link fills the list item and moving the mouse into any part of it causes the link to change color (**Figure 7.16**).

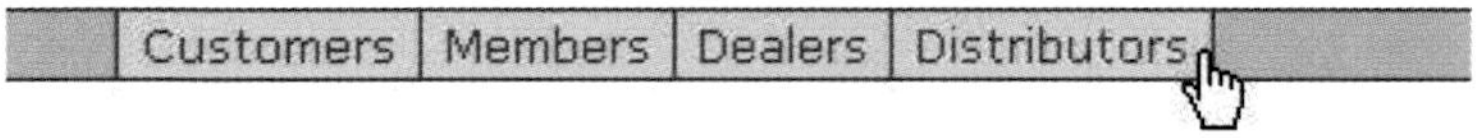

FIGURE 7.16 List items are now nicely separated.

All that you have to do now is take the temporary gray color off the link so the yellow background color of the list item is visible again, and have that background change color when it's rolled over by adding a :hover pseudo-class for the list items

```
div#listmenu li:hover {
    background-color:#FFF;
}
div#listmenu a {
    padding:0 6px;
    text-decoration:none;
    color:#069;
}
div#listmenu a:hover {
    color:#F33;
}
```

Sets the background of the menu items

which looks like **Figure 7.17**.

FIGURE 7.17 Now your background changes color when the user points to it.

Mousing onto any part of the list item causes the color of the list item to change color, except, yet again, in Internet Explorer for Windows.

Internet Explorer for Windows can only respond to the :hover pseudo-class when it is on a link, whereas more compliant browsers can provide a hover response on any element—in this case a list item. So although we have finished writing some solid CSS for this component, we must now do two more things to help poor old Internet Explorer for Windows—get Internet Explorer for Windows to display the first vertical line and get it to respond to the hover on the list item.

First add the vertical line to the left of the first list item. We can use the star hack to provide some CSS that is only read by Internet Explorer for Windows.

Up to now, we have only used the ul element to provide a left margin from which to indent the list from the left edge of the div. Because it only contains floated elements (the list items), it is tight closed in the same div that was at the beginning of this exercise. Adding a temporary border like this

| Indents ul from edge of container |

```
div#listmenu ul {margin:0 0 0 30px;
        border: 1px solid #000;}
```

displays **Figure 7.18**.

FIGURE 7.18 The bottom edge of the ul element touches the top edge and is visible to the right of the yellow li elements.

What we need to do is make the ul enclose the list items by floating it, like this

| Makes the ul wrap the li's |

```
* html div#listmenu ul {
    float:left;
}
```

which results in **Figure 7.19**.

FIGURE 7.19 Now the ul encloses the list items.

Now add a left border to take the place of the missing list item border, remove the temporary solid border, and add a blue line on just the left edge. (Note that one rather strange side effect of floating this element is that the indent from the edge of the div has doubled, and so you'll adjust for that also.) Here's the code

```
* html div#listmenu ul {

    float:left;

    border-left:1px solid #000;

    margin-left:15px;

}

* html a {display:block;}
```

Makes the ul wrap the li's

Adds the rightmost vertical line to the ul

IE doubles the given value above

Makes IE 5 and 5.5 accept the padding on the link

FIGURE 7.20 The left line now displays in Internet Explorer for Windows, but the background doesn't produce a hover effect.

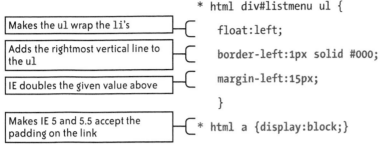

Now that the left line shows up in Internet Explorer, we need to make the hover on the list items work.

The Hover Behavior for Internet Explorer

Before CSS2, only links could provide a response to being hovered over. Using the `:hover` pseudo-class on a selector enables you to define a response when an item is rolled over; for example, here's the CSS for a div with a blue background that turns red when the div is hovered over

`div#respond {background-color:blue;}`

`div#respond:hover {background-color:red;}`

It's that easy, although Internet Explorer doesn't produce a hover effect for any selector except a, a link. Fortunately, a very smart programmer, Peter Nederlof, came up with an Internet Explorer behavior that solves this problem. The file is called csshover.htc and you can download it from www.xs4all.nl/~peterned/hovercraft.html. Here's how you add it to the CSS

`body {font:1em verdana, arial, sans-serif; behavior:url(css/ csshover.htc);}`

In this case, we created a new folder called `css` in the same folder as the files for this example and put the csshover.htc file in that new folder. If you decide to put the file in a different location, you will need to modify the URL.

With the `csshover.htc` file associated with your file in this way, Internet Explorer can respond to hovers. Now, across all of the target

A behavior is an imported file that adds functionality to a browser.

browsers, except Internet Explorer 5 for Mac, the background of the list item turns white when it is hovered over.

Our horizontal menu is complete.

Here's the complete code

```
body {font-family: verdana, arial, sans-serif; font-
weight:100%; behavior:url(css/csshover.htc);}
```

The horizontal menu starts here —⊏ `* {margin:0; padding:0;}`

```
div#listmenu {
```

Makes the div full width —⊏ `    width:100%;`

Makes the div enclose the list —⊏ `    float:left;`

Draws line on top edge of div —⊏ `    border-top:1px solid #069;`

Draws line on bottom edge of div —⊏ `    border-bottom:1px solid #069;`

```
    font-size:.8em;
```

Colors the div —⊏ `    background-color:#CCF;`

Pushes the div away from the top of the browser for clarity in this example —⊏ `    margin-top:20px;`

```
    }
```

Indents ul from edge of container —⊏ `div#listmenu ul {margin:0 0 0 30px;`

```
    }
```

```
div#listmenu li {
```

Indents ul from edge of container —⊏ `    float:left;`

Removes the bullet off list items —⊏ `    list-style-type:none;`

Sets background of the menu items —⊏ `    background-color:#FFA;`

Creates dividing lines —⊏ `    border-right:1px solid #069;`

```
    }
```

```
div#listmenu li:first-child {
```

The first vertical line on the menu —⊏ `    border-left:1px solid #069;`

```
    }
```

```
div#listmenu li:hover {
```

Sets the background of the menu items —⊏ `    background-color:#FFF;`

```
    }
```

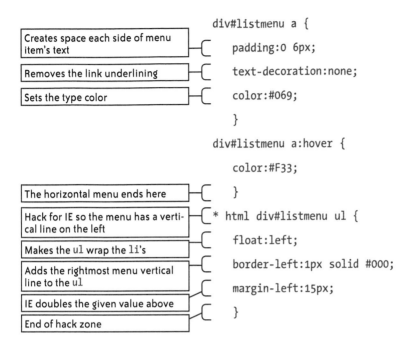

```
div#listmenu a {

    padding:0 6px;

    text-decoration:none;

    color:#069;

    }

div#listmenu a:hover {

    color:#F33;

    }

* html div#listmenu ul {

    float:left;

    border-left:1px solid #000;

    margin-left:15px;

    }
```

Creates space each side of menu item's text

Removes the link underlining

Sets the type color

The horizontal menu ends here

Hack for IE so the menu has a vertical line on the left

Makes the ul wrap the li's

Adds the rightmost menu vertical line to the ul

IE doubles the given value above

End of hack zone

Creating Drop-Down Menus

Now we need to take our horizontal list a step further and add drop-down choices. CSS-based drop-down menus aren't going to work in Internet Explorer for Mac. I will, however, show you a way you can use CSS so that your menu degrades nicely in this browser and still offers the user an acceptable navigation experience.

In the following exercise, we'll assume that the horizontal menu items each have a related page, and we'll code their responses accordingly. All you need to do is add URLs in place of the # symbols in each link's href.

Marking Up Drop-Down Menus

To mark up a drop-down menu, we need to nest a complete list within a list item of the horizontal menu. This nested list becomes the contents of that list item's drop-down menu. **Figure 7.21** shows the finished menu so you can see what you are shooting for.

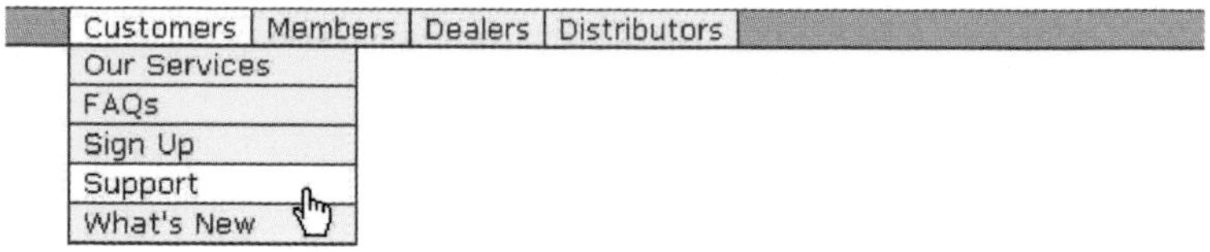

FIGURE 7.21 Here's your completed drop-down menu.

Here's the complete markup for a menu with four choices, each with a drop-down

```
<body>
<div id="listcontainer" class="clearfix">
<ul>
  <li><a href="#">Customers</a>
    <ul> <!-- drop down menu items -->
        <li><a href="#">Our Services</a></li>
        <li><a href="#">FAQs</a></li>
        <li><a href="#">Sign Up</a></li>
        <li><a href="#">Support</a></li>
    </ul>
  </li>
  <li><a href="#">Members</a>
    <ul> <!-- drop-down menu items-->
        <li><a href="#">Benefits</a></li>
        <li><a href="#">Programs</a></li>
        <li><a href="#">Renewals</a></li>
        <li><a href="#">Questions?</a></li>
    </ul>
 </li>
  <li><a href="#">Dealers</a>
    <ul> <!-- drop down menu items-->
        <li><a href="#">Join us</a></li>
        <li><a href="#">Programs</a></li>
        <li><a href="#">National Network Map</a></li>
        <li><a href="#">Support</a></li>
    </ul>
  </li>
  <li><a href="#">Distributors</a>
```

```
    <ul> <!-- drop down menu items-->
        <li><a href="#">Products</a></li>
        <li><a href="#">Dealer Finder</a></li>
        <li><a href="#">Commissions</a></li>
        <li><a href="#">Customers</a></li>
    </ul>
  </li>
</ul>
</div>
</body>
```

Here are a couple of notes about the markup:

1. None of the ul or li elements have classes or IDs—in fact, the only thing that differentiates this list from a regular nested list is the containing div, with its ID listcontainer, which causes the appropriate CSS rules to target the list.

2. This markup is the same as the previous exercise's horizontal navigation bar, but with a sublist nested inside each list item. It is vital to nest the list correctly—*you must put the entire nested list, from* ul *to* /ul, *inside of a list item, right before the list item's closing* /li, as this simple example, with the nested list highlighted, illustrates

```
<ul>

<li><a href="#">This is a top level item 1, without a
drop-down</a></li>

<li><a href="#">This is a top level item 2, with a drop-
down</a>

<ul>

<li><a href="#">This is item 1 of the drop-down</a></li>

<li><a href="#">This is item 2 of the drop-down</a>

</ul>

</li> <!--note this is the close of top-level list item
2-->

<li><a href="#">This is a top level item 3, without a
drop-down</a></li>

</ul>
```

3. href values are simply designated as #—a placeholder—in this markup. This placeholder does nothing; you need to replace each # with an appropriate URL, either relative or absolute, to point to the relevant page.

Let's start simply. Instead of working immediately with the final markup earlier in this section, start with the horizontal navigation markup, which has a sublist added to only the first li. You will add the other nested lists after you have one menu working correctly. Here's the markup

```
<body>

<div id="listcontainer" class="clearfix">

 <ul>

  <li><a href="#">Customers</a>

     <ul> <!-- drop down-down menu items -->

         <li><a href="#">Our Services</a></li>

         <li><a href="#">FAQs</a></li>

         <li><a href="#">Sign Up</a></li>

         <li><a href="#">Support</a></li>

     </ul>

 </li>

  <li><a href="#">Members</a></li>

  <li><a href="#">Dealers</a></li>

  <li><a href="#">Distributors</a></li>

 </ul>

</div>

</body>
```

Now take a look at **Figure 7.22**.

FIGURE 7.22 The submenu is not stacked like a drop-down yet, but it is inheriting the styles from the parent list, as shown when you point at a link.

We need some styles specifically for the drop-down menu to get it to stack under its parent element.

Instead of adding a class or ID to the submenu so we can target it, just write a selector that only affects a list that is within a list. For example, the selector ul li ul {…some CSS here…} only targets a ul element that is contained within the li element of a parent list—just what we want. As you can see in the following code, just three simple CSS declarations get you well on the way to the desired result

| The drop-down starts here |

```
div#listmenu ul li ul {
```

| Prevents the temp margin on the ul from inheriting here |

```
    margin:0;
```

| Sets the width of the menu; in combo with the li's 100% width, makes the menu stack |

```
    width:10em;

}

div#listmenu ul li ul li {
```

| Makes the list items fill the list container (ul) |

```
    width:100%;
```

| The drop-down menu ends here |

```
}
```

Now take a look at **Figure 7.23**.

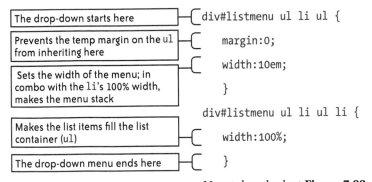

FIGURE 7.23 Although this menu needs better styling and doesn't yet open and close automatically, it is starting to look like a drop-down menu.

If we set the width of the ul of the nested list, and then force the li elements within to be 100 percent of that width, they stack nicely. Without the 100 percent width on the li, the short words, "FAQs" and "Sign Up," would be on the same line, and each li element would be a different length.

The next step is to get drop-downs correctly positioned with respect to the menu. The way to do this is to set the child element's position property to absolute and the parent's to relative. At the same time, we'll want to correctly style the drop-down's borders, so we can see that the drop-down is, in fact, accurately aligned to the menu. Here's the code

```
div#listmenu li {
```

| Causes the list to align horizontally |

```
    float:left;
```

| Positioning context for the absolutely positioned drop-down |

```
    position:relative;

    list-style-type:none;

    background-color:#FFA;

    border-right:1px solid #069;

}
```

code continues on next page

```
div#listmenu ul li ul {

    margin:0;

    position:absolute;

    width:10em;

}

div#listmenu ul li ul li {

    width:100%;

    border-left:1px solid #069;

    border-bottom:1px solid #069;

    border-right:1px solid #069;

}

div#listmenu ul li ul li:first-child {

    border-top:1px solid #069;

}
```

Positions the drop-down `ul` in relation to its relatively positioned `li` parent

Makes the list items fill the list container (`ul`)

Three sides of each drop-down item

The top edge of the drop-down

Now take a look at **Figure 7.24**.

FIGURE 7.24 With the contextual positioning set, and the borders styled, you can see that the alignment of the drop-down to the menu is almost perfect.

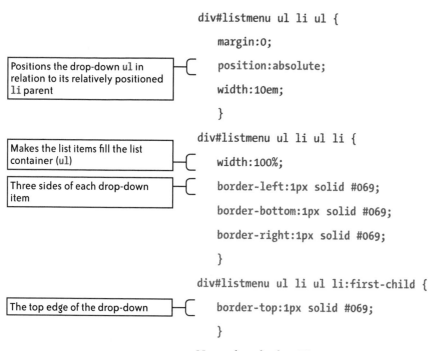

The drop-down is 1 pixel off because it aligns with the list item, not the list item's border, but because its positioning context is now its parent element (its `position` is set to `absolute`, the parent to relative), it's just a matter of defining a left offset to nudge it into the correct location. Here's what to do

```
div#listmenu ul li ul {

    margin:0;

    position:absolute;

    width:10em;

    left:-1px;

}
```

Aligns the drop-down exactly under the menu

Now look at **Figure 7.25**.

With the exception of some styling problems in Internet Explorer (a missing top line, and the inherited left `ul` border from an earlier hack) that we will fix later, the drop-down is now nicely styled, and we're ready to make it visible only when the pointer is over the appropriate choice of the menu.

In the horizontal menu, the element that changes is the one that is being hovered over, but in the case of the drop-down menu, that's not true. The drop-down should display when its parent menu (the choice on the horizontal menu) is hovered over. A brilliantly simple selector makes that happen.

First, hide the drop-down when it's not being hovered over, like this

```
body div#listcontainer ul li ul {display:none;}
```

Display is inherited, so all the list items within the `ul` disappear too. With the drop-down hidden, next make it appear when the drop-down's menu choice is hovered, like this

```
div#listcontainer ul li:hover ul {display:block;}
```

This selector states that the drop-down `ul` should display when its parent `li` is hovered over. However, we also want the menu to remain visible when we move off the parent menu choice and onto the drop-down itself. To do so, group a second selector with the `display:block` declaration like this

```
div#listcontainer ul li:hover ul, div#listcontainer ul li ul:
hover {display:block;}
```

Now the menu is displayed is when you hover over either the menu or the drop-down, and your menu springs to life (**Figure 7.26**).

Now perform the fixes for Internet Explorer, like this

| Add a top line to drop-downs in IE browsers |

| Stops the drop-down from inheriting the ul border |

```
* html  div#listmenu ul li ul {

    border-top:1px solid #069;

    border-left:0px;

}
```

Now Internet Explorer displays the drop-down as other browsers do.

One thing you'll notice is that the drop-down text doesn't highlight when you are on a drop-down list item, only when you are on the text itself. Let's deal with that next. To deal with this, you might think you would need to set the drop-down links to block, but as it turns out, you have to set the parent (the menu) links to block for all browsers at this point. Here's how it works

| List items in drop down highlight and wrapped lines indent correctly |

| Creates space each side of menu item's text |

| Removes the link underlining |

| sets the type color |

```
div#listmenu a {

    display:block;

    padding:0 6px;

    text-decoration:none;

    color:#069;

}
```

Now you'll see **Figure 7.27**.

FIGURE 7.27 Now the links highlight when the pointer moves over the list items.

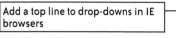

An interesting bonus is that, if a choice in the drop-down wraps to a second line, it also indents according to the padding instead of touching the edge of the list item.

So now we can remove the Internet Explorer hack from the horizontal menu exercise that set the menu links to block; it turns out we need that setting for all browsers. You'll delete this line of code

```
* html a {display:block;}
```

We now have drop-down menus built from basic list markup and without a line of JavaScript in sight.

Making Multiple Level Drop-Downs

So far we have a menu with a drop-down that allows the user to drill down to the second level of the site. With a little more effort, we can enable users to navigate directly to much lower levels of the site, like what is going on in **Figure 7.28**.

FIGURE 7.28 Pop-out menus that become visible when choices are made in the drop-down enable users to have direct access to the lower levels of a site.

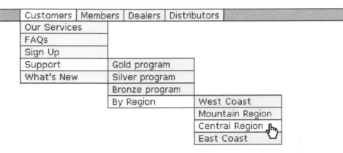

So now (in Figure 7.28) you have the horizontal menu, the drop-down, and pop-outs that offer direct access to third and fourth levels of pages. There are two quite simple steps we need to take to add these pop-outs. First, we must modify the markup to add the pop-out items within the nested lists of the drop-downs. This requires a degree of care, but if you are generating the lists according to a database structure, it's a programmer's dream; every time there is another level, we just generate another list within a list item. This format is ideally suited to basic recursive-loop programming techniques.

First, add just one pop-out by extending your markup like this

```
<div id="listmenu">

 <ul>

  <li><a href="#">Customers</a>

      <ul><!-- drop down menu items -->

        <li><a href="#">Our Services</a></li>

        <li><a href="#">FAQs</a></li>

        <li><a href="#">Sign Up</a></li>

        <li><a href="#">Support</a>

         <ul><!—pop-out menu items -->

           <li><a href="#">Gold program</a></li>
```

code continues on next page

```
                            <li><a href="#">Silver program</a></li>

                            <li><a href="#">Bronze program</a></li>

                            <li><a href="#">By Region</a></li>

                        </ul>

                        </li>

                        <li><a href="#">What's New</a></li>

                    </ul>

                </li>

                <li><a href="#">Members</a>…

                (…unchanged to end…)
```

Then add two lines to your CSS

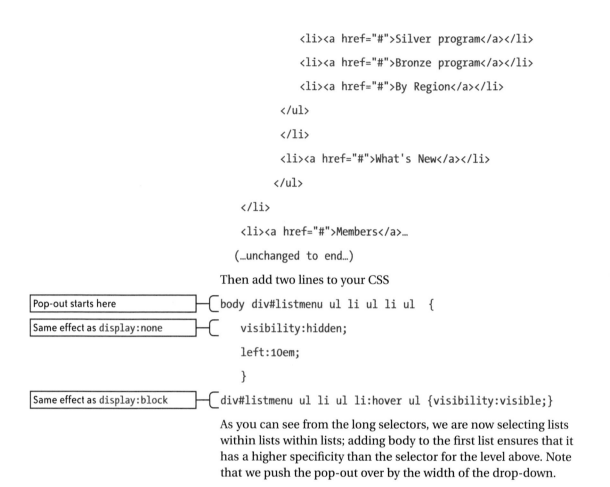

Pop-out starts here

Same effect as `display:none`

Same effect as `display:block`

```
body div#listmenu ul li ul li ul  {

    visibility:hidden;

    left:10em;

    }

div#listmenu ul li ul li:hover ul {visibility:visible;}
```

As you can see from the long selectors, we are now selecting lists within lists within lists; adding body to the first list ensures that it has a higher specificity than the selector for the level above. Note that we push the pop-out over by the width of the drop-down.

The additional markup and CSS gives you **Figure 7.29**.

FIGURE 7.29 The pop-out is functional, but it takes on the same positioning offset as the drop-down and sits below the choice instead of next to it.

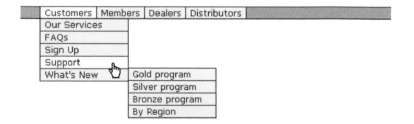

Although we got the left offset right, clearly the pop-out is much too low; it should align with the top of the drop-down choice, but it's almost aligned with the next choice in the drop-down. At the moment, it's inheriting the vertical offset that positions the drop-downs under the horizontal menu; that's why it is too low. It just takes one line of CSS to correct this

Pop-out starts here —┤

Same effect as `display:none` —┤

Same effect as `display:block` —┤

```
body div#listmenu ul li ul li ul  {

    visibility:hidden;

    top:-1px;

    left:10em;

    }
```

```
div#listmenu ul li ul li:hover ul {visibility:visible;}
```

Now it is perfectly positioned (**Figure 7.30**). (Setting `top` to `0px` instead of the `-1px` offset aligns the menu with the top of the list item rather than the top of its border.)

FIGURE 7.30 With the `top` property set, the pop-out aligns correctly with the drop-down.

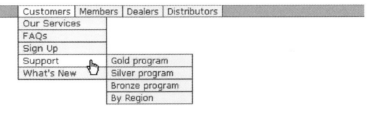

The code for the finished style sheet is over two hundred lines with the CSS and the markup. You can find it on the Stylin' *Web site (www.bbd. com/stylin).*

By nesting another list and adding two more lines of CSS

```
div#listmenu ul li ul li:hover ul li ul {visibility:hidden;}
```

```
div#listmenu ul li ul li ul li:hover ul {visibility:visible;}
```

you can support another level of menus.

Rollovers with Graphical Backgrounds

In the drop-down menu example, each menu item's background changed color when it was rolled over. We achieve this by having the element's `color` value change on `:hover`. However, sometimes, rather than wanting to change the background color, we want to have a graphic background change.

In the past, this meant you had to make different graphics for each state of the button and then use JavaScript. If you have done this before, you know how much work is involved for a relatively simple effect; if you haven't, you'll be pleased to know that you don't have to do this any more, because there is a much easier way to achieve the same effect using CSS.

Typically the markup for a graphical button is something like this

```
<div class="button">
<a class="roll" href="#">Graphics</a>
</div>
```

So that the whole of the area of the div (or whatever the container might be) responds to the rollover, you need to force the anchor link to fill it, so you need some CSS like this

```
div.button {
    width:120px;
    height:24px;
    top:0px;
    left: 0px;
    border: 1px #000 solid;
    }
a.roll {width:120px;
    height:24px;
    display:block;
    padding-top:2px;
    font: bold 10pt;
    text-align:center;
    border:1px solid red;
        }
```

Temp to check link fills div

Note that here we change the link to a block level element so that it responds to the specified dimensions instead of shrink-wrapping the text, and we temporarily add a red border so that we can see that it actually does (**Figure 7.32**).

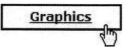

FIGURE 7.32 When the link's display property is set to block (from the default inline), it can be sized to fill the div. Now the whole div is hot, not just the text.

With the div filled by the link element, the link switches to the :hover state when the mouse enters the div.

At this point, we need to add the CSS LoVeHAte relationship for the links

```
div.button a.roll:link {color: black; text-decoration:none;}
```

```
div.button a.roll:visited {color: black; text-decoration:
none;}
```

```
div.button a.roll:hover {color:#069; text-decoration:
underline;}
```

```
div.button a.roll:active {color:#CCC;}
```

This removes the default underlining; instead, the link becomes underlined when the mouse is in the a element, which now fills the div.

The next step is to create a graphic with all four of the required states of the button on it. Minimally, this includes the :link (normal, unrolled) state and a :hover state, but you can have up to four by adding the :active (mouse button down) state and the :visited state. **Figure 7.33** shows a graphic with all four states.

FIGURE 7.33 Here's a four-state button graphic.

This graphic is 120 by 100 pixels and each button is 120 by 24 pixels. Now put this graphic into the background of our a element, like this

```
a.roll  { a.roll  {width:120px; height:20px; display:block;
padding-top:2px; font: bold 10pt; text-align:center;
```

```
background:  url("images_pres/four_state_roll_bg.gif") 0px
0px no-repeat #000;}
```

You now have what is shown in **Figure 7.34**.

FIGURE 7.34 The background image is masked by the div so only one button area shows.

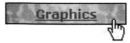

The background property is actually shorthand for all the other background properties. In one line, we specify the background's source image, its left and top location with respect to the container, its tiling repeat, and a background color of black. (The `background-color` is always behind the `background-image`, so in this case, where the graphic fills the background, the background color doesn't show).

Now we are ready for the last step—making the graphic change. The container is acting like a window through which we can see part of the larger graphic. All we have to do is move the graphic up and down behind the container and the background will appear to change. Here's the code

```
div.button a.roll:link {background-position: 0px 0px; color:
black; text-decoration:none;}
```

```
div.button a.roll:visited {background-position: 0px -25px;
color: green;}
```

```
div.button a.roll:hover {background-position: 0px -50px;
color:#069;}
```

```
div.button a.roll:active {background-position: 0px -75px;
color:white;}
```

Using the `background-position` property, we are causing the graphic to be repositioned with each change of state of the a link. One graphic, no JavaScript, no preloading of images—that's the CSS way to create graphical rollovers.

Developing Forms

Forms are one of the most interactive elements of any Web site. A Web site might provide information to your visitors, but if visitors are going to provide information in return, that's almost always going to involve a form. My focus here is to show you how you can lay out a form using CSS and a minimal amount of markup, so that you can quickly build form components.

Understanding the Form Element

When I build a form, I first create a container div for the form with the `form` element inside it, like this

```
<div id="formcontainer>

  <form method="post" action="../forms_tests/page.htm">

    <!--all form markup in here-->

  </form>

<div>
```

The container div lets me add related elements for headings and text above and below the form element and set margins around the whole thing.

It's important to understand the purpose of the form element. When the visitor presses the Submit button, the data (name/value pairs) from every input within the form element is sent to the URL defined by the action attribute of the form. The *way* in which it is passed to that target URL, either by post (not displayed in a destination page URL) or get (visible in the destination page URL), is determined by the method attribute. Each item of a form comprises of the input element (for example, a text field, a menu, etc.) and a text label to let the user know what they should do (for example, Enter your Name, Choose a Car).

My usual approach is to put the label to the left and the input to the right so the user can read what to do and then do it. In the XHTML, I handle each item the same way; I mark up the label with a label element and then follow it with the input element, like this

```
<div class="clearfix">

        <label>Enter your First Name</label>

        <input onfocus="clearText(this)" name="firstName"
type="text" size="35" value =" enter first name here" />

    </div>
```

I wrap them both in a div with the clearfix class so that no matter which of the two contained elements is the taller, the next item of the form gets pushed down below them. Then in my CSS, I float the label to the left so the two contained elements sit side by side, and then I add a border to the top of the containing div, so that, as the divs stack up, there is dividing horizontal line between each item.

Figure 7.35 shows how a form might look once you have done the markup of a few items and have made a start on the CSS.

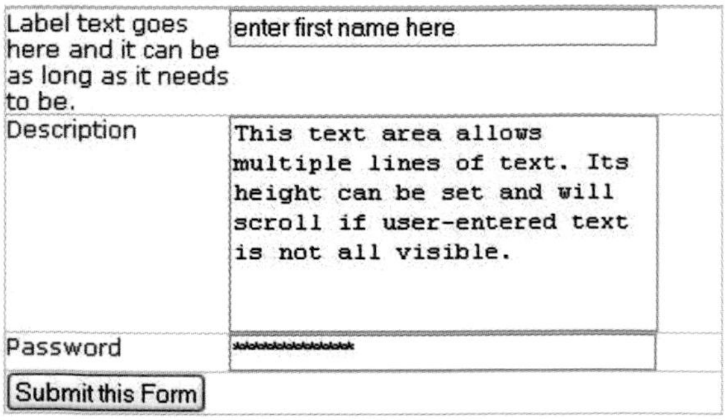

FIGURE 7.35 Here's a form with some simple styles and borders on the containing divs.

Here's the CSS that produces Figure 7.35

```
body {font-family: verdana, sans-serif; color:
#003366; font-size:1em;}

* {margin:0; padding:0;}

div#formcontainer {width:390px; margin-left:40px;
margin-top:20px}

div#formcontainer form  {border:1px solid #CCC;}

div#formcontainer div.clearfix {border-top: 1px solid
#CCC;}

div#formcontainer form label {width:120px; float:
left; font-size:.75em;}
```

Start of the form CSS

Adds the line above each section

This is the text label on the left of each input

To save space, I have not included the CSS for the clearfix *code here, although you do need it for this project. I will include it in code of the final CSS step at the end of this example.*

The following is the XHTML for Figure 7.35

```
<body>

<div id="formcontainer"><!--overall container div-->

 <form method="post" action="../forms_tests/page.htm">

 <!--SINGLE LINE TEXT FIELD-->

 <div class="clearfix">

    <label>Label text goes here and it can be as long as it
needs to be.</label>

    <input name="firstName" type="text" size="35" value ="
enter first name here" />

 </div>

 <!--MULTI-LINE TEXT FIELD-->

 <div class="clearfix">

 <label>Description</label>

    <textarea name="firstName" rows="6" cols="26">This text
area allows multiple lines of text. Its height can be set
and will scroll if user-entered text is not all visible.

 </textarea>

 </div>

 <!--PASSWORD TEXT FIELD-->

 <div class="clearfix">
```

```
<label>Password</label>

 <input name="firstName" type="password" size="35" value ="
enter it here" />

</div>

<!--SUBMIT BUTTON-->

<div class="clearfix">

<input type="submit" value="Submit this Form" />

</div>

</form>

</div><!--end of overall container div-->

</body>
```

We still have a way to go before we have a good-looking form, but you can see that the two-column effect is visible. In the first item, the label text is longer than the input element, and in the second item, the input is longer than the text, but the items are separated with a horizontal line (the top border of the `clearfix` div), so your floating and clearing is working properly.

A note on the way the width of the two columns is achieved—I set an overall width for the `formcontainer` div of 390 pixels and set the floated label element to a width of 120 pixels, leaving 270 pixels for the input elements. I don't need to size that explicitly. I arrived at these width values by setting the input text elements to 35 characters wide and then I played with the two width values until it looked right. So, if you want the label text to be wider, simply increase the label's `width` value by some amount, but don't forget to add the same amount onto the `width` of the `formcontainer` as well.

A good next step, now that we can see that the mechanics of the layout are working, is to turn off the border of the `form` element, add a little vertical space to move the items apart, and find some way to create some space between each label and its related input element (**Figure 7.36**).

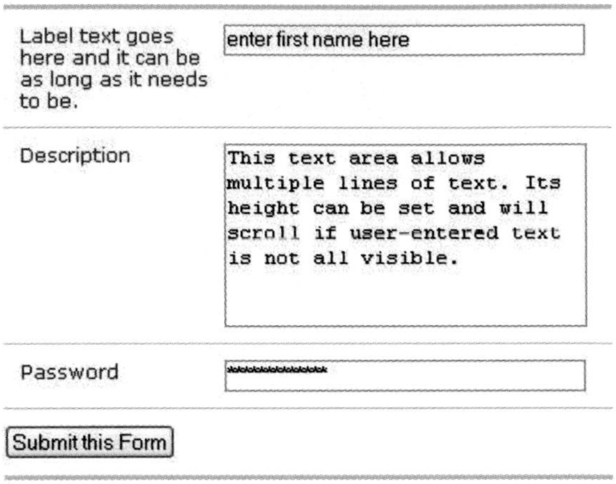

FIGURE 7.36 A few styles make these first items of your form look good.

Here's the code

```
body {font-family: verdana, sans-serif; color: #003366; font-
size:1em;}
```

Start of the form CSS

```
* {margin:0; padding:0;}
```

```
div#formcontainer {width:390px; margin-left:40px; margin-
top:20px;}
```

The top border is visually 1 px thicker because it touches the `div.clearfix` bordertop

```
div#formcontainer form  {border-top: 2px solid #CCC; border-
bottom: 3px solid #CCC;}
```

Adds the line above each section and provides vertical spacing

```
div#formcontainer div.clearfix {border-top: 1px solid #CCC;
padding:10px 0px; vertical-align:top;}
```

This is the text label on the left of each input

```
div#formcontainer form label {width:120px; float:left;font-
size:.75em; color: #003366;    margin:0 10px;}
```

As planned, I've removed the border from the form element, added the padding on the clearfix div to give some vertical spacing between the form elements and the dividing lines, and added the 10-pixel left and right margins on the label element. This added margin space creates some horizontal space on each side of the label, indenting it from the edge of the lines on the left, and making some space between it and its input element on the right.

Now it's time to move on to some more complex parts of the form where you need to have a number of select elements on the right side, not just a simple text field.

Adding Radio Buttons and Check Boxes

Other types of elements in a form include radio buttons and check boxes. Let's add some markup for a set of three radio buttons and three check boxes, like this

```
<!--RADIO BUTTONS-->
   <div class="clearfix">
      <label>Pick One</label>
      <div  class="buttongroup clearfix"><!--box for buttons
group-->
      <div class="clearfix">
<input  name="radioset" type="radio" size="35" value ="
Choice_1" checked="checked" /><label>Choice 1</label></div>
      <div class="clearfix"><input  name="radioset"
type="radio" size="35" value =" Choice_2" /><label>Choice 2</
label></div>
      <div class="clearfix"><input  name="radioset"
type="radio" size="35" value =" Choice_3" /><label>Choice 3</
label></div>
      </div><!--end of box for buttons group-->
   </div> <!--END RADIO BUTTONS-->


      <!--CHECK BOXES-->
   <div class="clearfix">
      <label>Pick One</label>
      <div class="buttongroup clearfix"><!--box for buttons
group-->
      <div class="clearfix"><input  name="boxset"
type="checkbox" size="35" value =" Choice_1" />Choice 1</div>
      <div class="clearfix"><input  name="boxset"
type="checkbox" size="35" value =" Choice_2" />Choice</div>
      <div class="clearfix"><input  name="boxset"
type="checkbox" size="35" value =" Choice_3"
checked="checked" />Choice 3</div>
   </div><!--end of box for buttons group-->
   </div> <!--END CHECK BOXES-->
```

This markup is similar to that of the text fields except that instead of a single text field that appears on the right side of our layout, we have a containing div for the group of buttons, and inside of it, we have three divs that each contain a button input element (radio or check box) and some text. If this sounds a little complex, check out **Figure 7.37** where, temporarily, the containing div for the group has a thick border and each inner div has a thin border; this figure might make things clearer.

FIGURE 7.37 Borders around the radio boxes and check boxes and their containing elements illustrate how the elements are organized.

Before I show you the CSS you need to achieve this layout, I want to share two quick observations on the markup.

First, the way that you get a group of radio buttons or a group of check boxes to behave as a group is to give them all the same name attribute. Then, for example, if you click one of the radio buttons, any other that is selected is deselected. Although each button in a group shares the same name, each button must be given a unique value so that the name/value pair (passed to the URL defined in the action attribute of the form when the form is submitted) conveys which selection (value) from the group (name) was made. Note that in the preceding markup, all the radio buttons have a common name, as do the check boxes.

Second, you can have one radio button in a group or any number of check boxes preselected when the page loads. You make this happen by adding the selected attribute and setting its value to selected. Note in the preceding markup that the first radio button and the last check box are preselected in this way.

Here's the CSS that organizes the elements in the group one above the other in the containing buttongroup div, as illustrated in Figure 7.37.

A container for a groups of buttons; suppresses the clearfix div top border on the divs around the radio buttons/check boxes

```
div#formcontainer div.buttongroup {float:left; border:0;
padding:0px;}
```

Wrapper for the INPUT and its text; margin-bottom sets the vertical distance between buttons

```
div#formcontainer div.buttongroup div {margin-bottom:5px;
font-size:.75em;}
```

Set the distance between button and its label text

```
div#formcontainer div.buttongroup input {margin-right:5px;}
```

Right after the float:left *in the markup above is* border:0. *This is here because the big container div that surrounds each section of the form has a* border-top *line to create the horizontal separators, and we use the same* clearfix *class on these inner containers. So we have to set the* border-top *of this new inner container to zero explicitly, otherwise we would have an unwanted line, defined* div.clearfix, *along the top of each containing div for our button groups also. Try removing that* border:0 *to see what I mean.*

Again, the key to the success of this rather simple CSS is the float on the containing div and its clearfix class that wraps it around the elements within. The rest of the markup is just spacing to improve the overall layout.

The last form element I'll illustrate in this form example is a pop-up menu, known as a *select*.

Creating a Form Select

Menus generated using the select tag are often used in forms for selecting State and Country names in the checkout area of e-commerce stores and in other situations where the user must choose one item from a large number of options. Unlike check boxes and radio buttons, a select is very compact because it only occupies the space of single line until the user clicks it.

The markup for a select is structured in a similar way to a list; it contains a select element with a number of option elements within it, like this

```
<!--DROP DOWN MENU-->

    <div class="clearfix">

    <label>Pick from menu and then click submit below</label>

    <select name="menuChoice">

    <option value="no_selection_made">Pick your favorite
guitar</option>

    <option value="fender">Gibson</option>

    <option value="fender">Fender</option>

    <option value="taylor">Taylor</option>

    </select>

    </div>

    </div>
```

Figure 7.38 shows you what you get.

FIGURE 7.38 A select element creates a menu within your form.

This element doesn't require any extra CSS; you can just add the markup. The same CSS that is used on the text fields works here too.

XHTML allows you to add submenus to `select` elements using the `optgroup` tag, but this is so poorly supported in the various browsers that it hardly seems worth demonstrating here.

TWO FINAL TOUCHES

The first final touch is to move the Submit button to the right; it just seems that users expect it to be there. Also, if you must add a Reset button for the form, put it to the left because this is visually perceived as being out of the way and is not as likely to be clicked accidentally. The simple way to do this is to add a special class to it and either float it to the right or add a lot of `margin-left`. The elegant way, on the other hand, is to select it using an *attribute selector* that requires no additional markup but simply allows you to write a selector that selects only an input with the `submit` attribute. It's elegant, but IDWIMIE. So in Internet Explorer, you get the button on the left; it's not a disaster.

The second final touch is to add a small JavaScript function into the head of the document that clears default text out of the fields when the user clicks in them. This allows a field to contain instructions, as stated in the `value` attribute of the `input`, for the user (such as: Enter 16 digit card number without spaces), which obligingly disappear when the user clicks in the field. As you can see, I have added the `clearText` JavaScript function in the head of the document and, on each select, where I want to use text prompts for the user, I have added the `onfocus` attribute to call that function and clear the text when the user click in (moves the keyboard focus) that text field.

After you make these changes, your final form looks like **Figure 7.39**.

A form like this can run to many lines of code, and when you have an e-commerce site form for credit card information that includes a `select` with 50 state names in it and another `select` with 300 country names, well, let's just say it doesn't get any shorter. However, as in this case, forms are usually the same elements with slight variations over and over, so although they can run into many lines, they are not too complicated to develop, review, and modify.

To see the final CSS along with the complete markup, go to the Stylin' Web site (www.bbd.com/stylin).

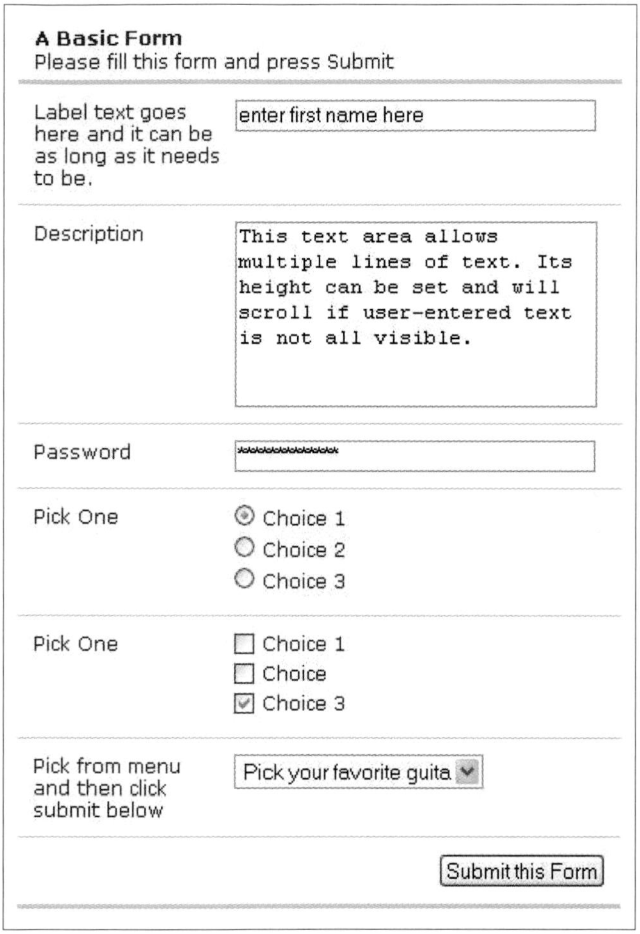

FIGURE 7.39 Here's the completed
form.

A Basic Form
Please fill this form and press Submit

Label text goes
here and it can be
as long as it needs
to be.

enter first name here

Description

This text area allows
multiple lines of text. Its
height can be set and will
scroll if user-entered text
is not all visible.

Password

****

Pick One

◉ Choice 1
○ Choice 2
○ Choice 3

Pick One

☐ Choice 1
☐ Choice
☑ Choice 3

Pick from menu
and then click
submit below

Pick your favorite guita ⌄

Submit this Form

Implementing Search

A search component, such as the one in **Figure 7.40**, can be found
on virtually every site.

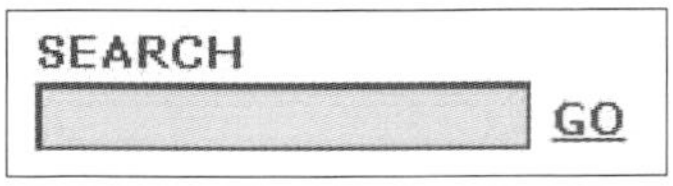

FIGURE 7.40 Here's a simple search
component.

SEARCH

GO

The markup for such a component looks like this

```
<div id="searcharea">

    <h3>SEARCH</h3>

    <form name="search" action="search.htm">

        <input name="search" size="20" />

        <a href="javascript:document.search.submit()">GO</a>

    </form>

</div><!--end searcharea-->
```

Here's the CSS:

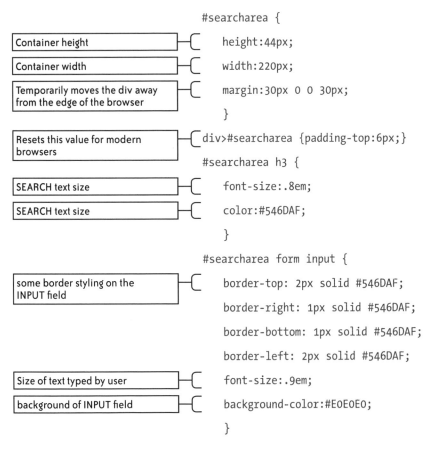

```
#searcharea {

    height:44px;

    width:220px;

    margin:30px 0 0 30px;

}

div>#searcharea {padding-top:6px;}

#searcharea h3 {

    font-size:.8em;

    color:#546DAF;

}

#searcharea form input {

    border-top: 2px solid #546DAF;

    border-right: 1px solid #546DAF;

    border-bottom: 1px solid #546DAF;

    border-left: 2px solid #546DAF;

    font-size:.9em;

    background-color:#E0E0E0;

}
```

Container height

Container width

Temporarily moves the div away from the edge of the browser

Resets this value for modern browsers

SEARCH text size

SEARCH text size

some border styling on the INPUT field

Size of text typed by user

background of INPUT field

```
#searcharea a {

    font-size:.75em;

    font-weight:bold;

    color:#546DAF;

}
```

GO link styles

The same principle applies here as for the larger form in the previous example; the input field and the Submit button are within a form element and when the form is submitted, the data is sent to the URL defined in the form's action attribute. In the previous example, we used a button to submit the form. Here we use a text link instead, using the following JavaScript in the href of the Go link

```
<a href="javascript:document.search.submit()">GO</a>
```

The submit function is built into JavaScript, so it just works with this small amount of code. To use this construction on another form, just change the word search to the name of your form; if your form is named shoppingList, then you would write

```
<a href="javascript:document.shoppingList.submit()">GO</a>
```

I also did some styling on the user input element. Most designers don't style input elements, but as long as you don't overdo it, you can give forms a unique look quite easily. I also set the font-size for the field, something many designers don't know is possible. Because this makes the size of the field itself smaller, this is a useful trick if you need to pack a form into a small area, such as a sidebar.

CHAPTER 8

Building Web Sites

How to size columns to contain graphics properly

Learn how to create a fluid header

More about how to create lists

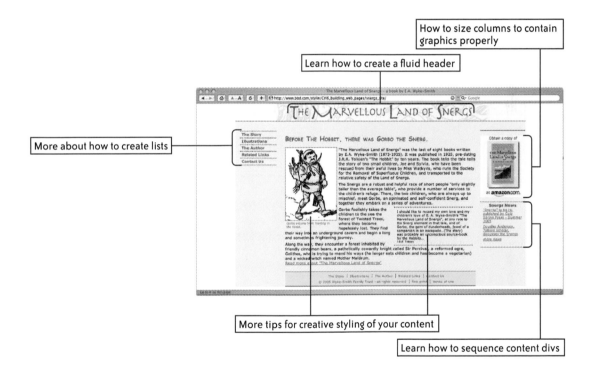

More tips for creative styling of your content

Learn how to sequence content divs

In this final chapter, you will take everything you have learned so far and create pages that will actually appear on a Web site. In doing so, not only will you come to understand the process for putting together a site, but you'll also learn two new useful techniques.

First, you'll see how reusable components, such as the page templates and the interface components you created in the previous chapters, can speed development time and save you a lot of tedious work. This way you can focus on the look, and not the technology, of your design.

Second, you'll see how to lay out a page in a "round robin" process. The first time through, you'll simply aim to get each component of the design—the header, the navigation, the content area, and so on—in place on the page with basic styling and you won't obsess too much over the details. Then you'll take a long, hard look at what you've got and go around again, with an eye to fine-tuning and unifying everything into a cohesive design.

You'll also see that this cohesiveness is most easily achieved through simplicity; for example, the design I'm going to show in this chapter uses just two fonts and six colors.

So what is this design? The site I'm going to create is for the book, *The Marvellous Land of Snergs,* a children's fantasy book written by my grandfather, E. A. Wyke-Smith, in 1925. J.R.R. Tolkien acknowledged this book as being a source of inspiration for *The Hobbit,* as well as being a book that his children loved for him to read to them. The book may shortly be republished, so I want you to create a site where visitors can learn more and link to Amazon to buy it.

Ready? Let's go!

The process I am using here is fairly informal. For real-world projects where several people are all working on a Web site, you need a much more structured development process where the project leader creates functional specifications and content matrix charts, architecture diagrams, wire-frame page layouts, design comps, and so on. The whole process can take weeks.

Getting Started With the Snergs Site

We're going to use the "Absolute Three-Column Layout with Header" template that we created in Chapter 5. It's the one with three columns, a header, and absolutely positioned side columns.

We are going to use the "Absolute Three-Column Layout with Header" template instead of the negative margins technique we learned at the end of Chapter 6 because it is the less complex and therefore easier to use for learning purposes. Those of you who feel ready may want to look at the negative margins version of this page that I've put up on the Stylin' site (www.bbd.com/stylin). See "The

You can the download the "Absolute Columns with Header" example from the Stylin' site at www.bbd.com/ stylin, which has this template set up and ready for you to use.

Be warned, if you leave the style tags around the styles in a style sheet, the style sheet will not load.

Snergs Site Created with Negative Margins" sidebar at the end of this chapter for more information.

The difference between the templates folder for each type of layout and the associated demo files used to develop these layouts is that real sites have separate XHTML and CSS files.

When you were learning how to create layouts in Chapter 5, it was convenient to have the CSS styles at the head of the page. However, such styles can only be seen by the page in which they live, which is not good for a real site where you want multiple pages to share a common set of styles.

Because of this, I have moved the styles for each template example from the `style` element in the head of the template's XHTML document into a separate CSS file in a folder named `css`. The `css` folder is located at the same level as the XHTML document, and it is linked to the XHTML page using the `link` tag.

Simply use a link tag in the head of each XHTML page to link the style sheet to the page, like so

```
<link href="css/stylesheetname.css" type="text/css"
rel="stylesheet" />
```

If you open any .css style sheet file, you will notice that the `style` tags don't get put in an external style sheet—the `link` tag tells the browser that the style sheet is pure CSS, so a style sheet simply starts with the first declaration. Note that each *Stylin'* template's style sheet has its own identifying name; I just used the placeholder `stylesheetname.css` to represent that name in the `link` tag example above.

Setting Up the Folder Structure

When you start building a Web site, you first set up a folder, usually referred to as the *local folder,* on your computer. This folder ultimately contains an exact copy of the finished Web site located in the *root folder* on your Web server (see "The Root Directory" sidebar on the next page). When you have finished your Web site, or even when it is still in development, and you are ready to upload the site to your Web server, you need to copy the contents of the local folder, but not the folder itself, into the root directory on the Web server.

Usually, you need an FTP (File Transfer Protocol) client and, to log in, the host name, user name, and password. Then you can upload your files and folders into the root folder of your site. You can obtain FTP information from your ISP (Internet Service Provider) or, if you are in a corporate environment, your network administrator.

The Root Directory

The root directory is the one to which the URL for your Web site points. A URL provides a unique address for every document on the Internet.

Every domain, such as snergs.com, is associated via the Domain Name System (DNS, a kind of phone book for the Web) with an IP address (Internet Protocol address, the unique numerical name of every server on the Internet). When you type a URL in your browser, the DNS looks up the domain name, finds the IP address of the associated server, and forwards the request to that server.

When the server receives the request for the page, it can see the domain name associated with the request and can then route the request to a specific folder on the server that relates to that domain: the root folder. If the URL contains a path directly to a specific page, that page is served to the requesting Web browser. If the requested URL is simply www. snergs.com, with no file name specified, the root folder is searched, and if it contains a page called default.html (or .htm), home.html, or index.html, that page is automatically served.

In short, the root folder is the top folder in the hierarchy of your Web site and, thanks to your ISP or network administrator, it is associated with your Web address. Learn more about the DNS system on the InterNIC site (www.internic. net/faqs/authoritative-dns.html).

As I mentioned earlier, you are going to use the Stylin' template that is a three-column layout with absolutely positioned side columns and a header. To do so, follow these steps:

1. First, download this template, called three_columns_absolute_ header, from www.bbd.com/stylin.

2. Next, create the site's local folder in a suitable place on your computer and name it snergs_site.

3. Copy the contents of the three_columns_absolute_header folder into it. If viewed in Macromedia Dreamweaver's site window, the file organization looks like **Figure 8.1**.

FIGURE 8.1 The Snergs Web site's local folder contains the template's XHTML document and a folder called css, which contains the style sheet.

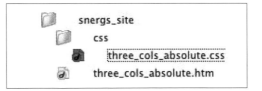

4. Clearly, you need better file names that relate to the project, so change the name of the three_cols_absolute.htm XHTML file to index.htm (see "The Root Directory" sidebar for the reason for using that name) and change the three_cols_absolute.css style sheet file name to snergs.css.

5. Because you've changed the name of the .css file, you also need to change the URL in the link tag of the .htm document so

that the renamed style sheet is once again associated with the XHTML file. The new link tag looks like this

```
<link href="css/snergs.css" rel="stylesheet" type="text/css" />
```

6. This is a good time to open the index.htm file in your browser and check to see that you successfully linked it to the style sheet. If the XHTML can't see the style sheet, you get default styled markup (**Figure 8.2**).

FIGURE 8.2 The unstyled document indicates that the link's URL to the style sheet is incorrect.

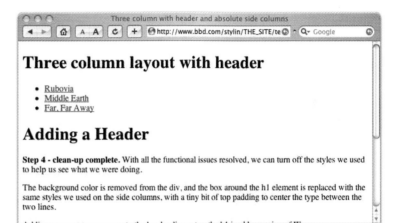

If you got the link URL correct, and the XHTML document can see the style sheet, a screen similar to **Figure 8.3** appears.

FIGURE 8.3 The styled document indicates that the link's URL to the style sheet is correct.

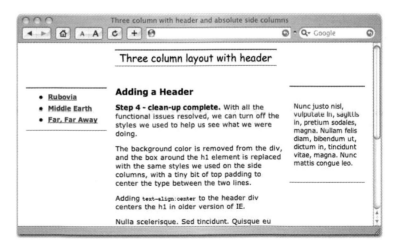

Once the style sheet is linked to the XHTML document, it's time to start developing the site from this template. Let's start at the very beginning.

Creating the Site Architecture

Even for a simple site like this one, it's worth drawing an *architecture diagram* to make you think the project through and to achieve any consensus you need from team members about the site's structure before you start creating graphics and code. An architecture diagram also helps keep you on track as you work. **Figure 8.4** shows the architectural diagram for the Snergs site.

FIGURE 8.4 In this Web site architecture diagram, each box represents a page and the lines represent links between them. Don't start coding without one!

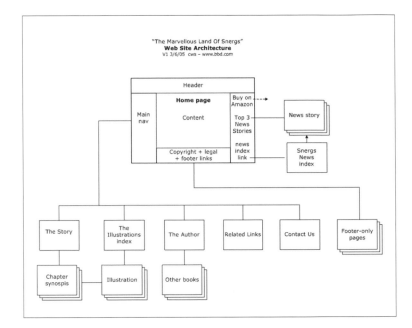

You can learn more about developing Information Architecture diagrams and download a set of Visio or .eps symbols especially for this purpose from Jesse James Garrett's site (www.jjg.net/ia/visvocab).

I also highly recommend his book, The Elements of User Experience (New Riders Press, 2002), a succinct and insightful introduction to planning and designing Web sites and online applications.

I use Microsoft Visio to create architecture diagrams, but you can also use a graphics application like Adobe Illustrator, Macromedia FreeHand, or Macromedia Fireworks. There are a some benefits to Visio, though—the connecting lines glom onto the boxes so the connections between boxes remain attached as you move them around; boxes automatically route themselves around other boxes and over other lines; and you just click in the boxes to create labels.

Some presentational aspects are suggested by Figure 8.4 (although its primary purpose is to indicate structure). For example, the plan for the home page is to have the main navigation in the left column, a promotion for the book and news links in the right column, and a footer at the bottom of the content area with links to legal and copyright information.

Modifying the Markup

Now you need to modify the template's markup to reflect the architecture of the home page.

First change the div for the links in the left column so they look like this

```
<div id="nav">

  <ul>

    <li><a href="#">The Story</a></li>

    <li><a href="#">Illustrations</a></li>

    <li><a href="#">The Author</a></li>

    <li><a href="#">Related Links</a></li>

    <li><a href="#">Contact Us</a></li>

  </ul>

</div>
```

Next, modify the right column to look like this (edited for space here):

```
<div id="rightcolumn">

<img src="images/snergs_book_promo.jpg" />

  <div id="newslinks">

<ul>

<li>Snergs to be re-published by Cold Spring Press</li>

<li>Douglas Anderson, Tolkien scholar, discusses the
Snergs</li>

<li class="morelink">more news</li>

</ul>

</div>
```

This is an image tag for a small promotional graphic that you will later link to Amazon.com

The text is taken from an article that appeared in "Instant" magazine of Edinburgh, Scotland, in April 2005, with thanks to editor Ian Sclater.

Now replace the placeholder content in the content div and add a footer div (highlighted in the code) after the content, but within the content div, like this

```
<div id="content">

    <h1>Before "The Hobbit," there was "The Marvellous Land of
    Snergs"…</h1>

    <img alt="Mother Meldrum in disguise, from the book 'The
    Marvelous Land of Snergs'" src="images/meldrum_in_disguise_
    180w.jpg" width="180" height="212"/>

    <p>"The Marvellous Land of Snergs" was the last of eight
    books written by E.A. Wyke-Smith (1873-1935). The book was
    published in 1925, pre-dating J.R.R. Tolkien's "The Hobbit"
    by ten years. The book tells the tale tells the story of
    two small children, Joe and Sylvia, who …(text removed here)
    … meet Gorbo, an opininated and self-confident Snerg, and
    together they embark on a series of adventures. </p>

    <blockquote>I should like to record my own love and my
    children's love of E. A. Wyke-Smith's "The Marvellous Land
    of Snergs," at any rate to the Snerg element in that tale,
    and of Gorbo, the gem of dunderheads, jewel of a companion
    in an escapade&#8230;(The story) was probably an unconscious
    source-book for the Hobbits&#8230;<p>J.R.R. Tolkien</p></
    blockquote>

    <p>Along the way, they encounter a forest inhabited by
    friendly cinnamon bears, a pathetically cowardly knight
    called Sir Percival, a reformed ogre, Golithos, who is trying
    to mend his ways (he longer eats children and has become
    avegetarian) and a wicked witch named Mother Meldrum. <a
    href="story.htm">Read more</a></p>

    <div id="footer">

    <ul>

        <li><a href="#">The Story</a></li>

        <li><a href="#">Illustrations</a></li>

        <li><a href="#">The Author</a></li>

        <li><a href="#">Related Links</a></li>

        <li><a href="#">Contact Us</a></li>
```

This quote is in a blockquote tag. This enables you to create what's called a pull-quote in the printing world and make a feature of this element on the page

```
    </ul>

    <ul class="fineprint">

    <li>&copy; 2005 Wyke-Smith Family Trust - all rights
reserved</li>

    <li><a href="#">fine print</a></li>

    <li><a href="#">terms of use</a></li>

    </ul>

    </div>

</div><!--end of content div-->
```

Stylin's tech editor, Shaun Inman, is leading the effort to devise a method to clear absolutely positioned elements. If you want to understand what it's like to be at the cutting edge of Web design techniques, read his blog entries on this subject and download his prototype code (www. shauninman.com/mentary/past/ absolute_clearance.php).

You may be wondering why I added the footer right before the close of the contentarea div. The reason is that although absolute positioning is a quick and robust way to develop multicolumn layouts, it is almost impossible to get elements to clear absolutely positioned elements because absolutely positioned elements are removed from the flow of the layout. What this means here is that you can't put a footer under those side columns and have the footer move down as the columns get longer, as you did with the floating columns layout in Chapter 6.

If you try it, you will find that in cases where the side columns are longer than the content area (which *can* be made to push the footer because it's not absolutely positioned), the side columns extend over the footer. That's not a pretty sight. So I'll simply add my footer information at the end of the content column and know that if the side columns have a lot of content, they may extend down beyond the footer at the bottom of the content area. At least they won't cover it up!

If you want the footer to be full width under the columns, use the negative margin template. This "absolute" layout is easier to start with for a first effort, though.

With all this markup in place, your page should now looks like **Figure 8.5**.

FIGURE 8.5 Here is the markup as displayed by the unmodified template style sheet. Note that the style sheet does not yet have any styles for the footer or the right column. The text in this figure was edited and the text size reduced using the View menu in order to simplify capturing this image.

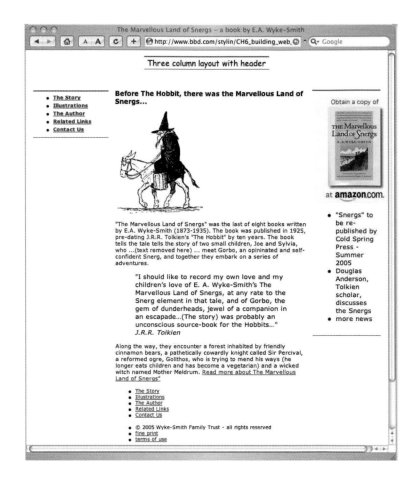

Creating the Header

You should start refining the markup by adding a graphical header. The template's header area is currently styled with some centered text. You want a graphic in the header, but because the layout is fluid (that is, changes width as the browser window is resized by the user), you need to take an extra step to make the graphic appear to fill the entire width no matter what that is.

Refer back to the box model diagram at the start of Chapter 4, which clearly shows that an element's background image overlays its background color—that's the key to success here. The idea is to create a graphic that is centered in the header, and to have each end of that graphic fade into the background color that it overlays. Normally, if the browser is wider than the graphic, the background color is visible at each end. By fading the ends of the graphic into the background color, you can't see where one starts and the other begins.

Figure 8.6 shows the header graphic while it is under construction in Macromedia Fireworks. In this figure, I'm overlaying small rectangles at each end (note the blue dots that show one rectangle's selection). These small rectangles are filled with a side-to-side blend, which progresses from the header div's background color (the hexadecimal color #FFFFCC) to no color at all (transparent). When overlaid on the graphic, these little rectangles make the ends of the graphic fade to the background color.

FIGURE 8.6 Making the sides of the image blend to the background color.

Now, when you add this graphic into the header div

```
<div id="header">

<img src="images/snergs_header.gif" alt="The Marvellous Land
of Snergs" width="776" height="100"/>

</div>
```

and, in the style sheet, set the background of the div to the same color and height

Styles for the header; text-align centers the graphic

```
div#header {height:60px; background-color:#FFC; text-align:
center;}
```

the graphic simply seems to fade into an endlessly wide background as the user resizes the browser (see **Figure 8.7**).

FIGURE 8.7 The header graphic's "soft" edges makes it appear to fill any width of browser.

Now let's move on to the left navigation.

Creating the Left Navigation

For the left navigation column, start with the file called list_unor-dered_12.htm from the Chapter 5 examples.

Copy the styles from list_unordered_12.htm into the end of the style sheet, right after the div#footer style. Now your style sheet should look something like this

…(other styles)

div#rightcolumn p {font-size:.75em;}

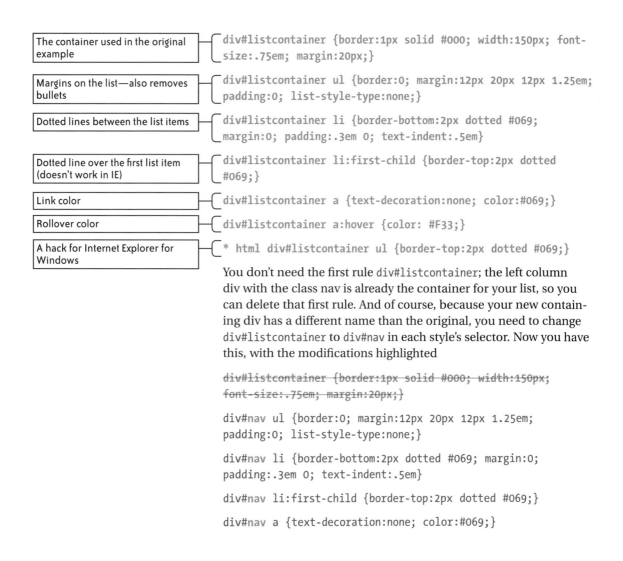

The container used in the original example	div#listcontainer {border:1px solid #000; width:150px; font-size:.75em; margin:20px;}
Margins on the list—also removes bullets	div#listcontainer ul {border:0; margin:12px 20px 12px 1.25em; padding:0; list-style-type:none;}
Dotted lines between the list items	div#listcontainer li {border-bottom:2px dotted #069; margin:0; padding:.3em 0; text-indent:.5em}
Dotted line over the first list item (doesn't work in IE)	div#listcontainer li:first-child {border-top:2px dotted #069;}
Link color	div#listcontainer a {text-decoration:none; color:#069;}
Rollover color	div#listcontainer a:hover {color: #F33;}
A hack for Internet Explorer for Windows	* html div#listcontainer ul {border-top:2px dotted #069;}

You don't need the first rule div#listcontainer; the left column div with the class nav is already the container for your list, so you can delete that first rule. And of course, because your new contain-ing div has a different name than the original, you need to change div#listcontainer to div#nav in each style's selector. Now you have this, with the modifications highlighted

div#listcontainer {border:1px solid #000; width:150px; font-size:.75em; margin:20px;}

div#nav ul {border:0; margin:12px 20px 12px 1.25em; padding:0; list-style-type:none;}

div#nav li {border-bottom:2px dotted #069; margin:0; padding:.3em 0; text-indent:.5em}

div#nav li:first-child {border-top:2px dotted #069;}

div#nav a {text-decoration:none; color:#069;}

```
div#nav a:hover {color: #F33    ;}
```

A hack for Internet Explorer for
Windows only ——

```
* html div#nav ul {border-top:2px dotted #069;}
```

Now our left navigation looks like the list template from which you "stole" the styles (**Figure 8.8**).

FIGURE 8.8 Now the links are styled again but need some positional adjustment in this context.

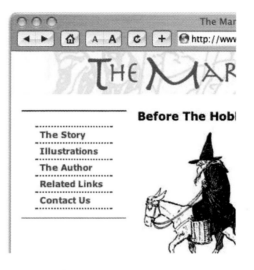

Let's do a few improvements to complete this navigation area. We no longer need the horizontal lines at the top and bottom of the left nav element now that we have the dotted line styles for the ul and li elements of the list, so remove them

```
div#nav {position:absolute; left:0px; top:60px; width:150px;
padding:.5em 0 0 0; margin:22px 0 0 15px; border-top:2px
solid #069; border-bottom:1px solid #069;}
```

Also we can change the color of the dotted lines to a more appropriate color

```
div#nav ul {border:0; margin:12px 20px 12px 1.25em;
padding:0; list-style-type:none;}
```

```
div#nav li {border-bottom:2px dotted #960; margin:0;
padding:.3em 0; text-indent:.5em}
```

```
div#nav li:first-child {border-top:2px dotted #960;}
```

```
div#nav a {text-decoration:none; color: #960;}
```

```
div#nav a:hover {color: #F33;}
```

A hack for Internet Explorer for
Windows only ——

```
* html div#nav ul {border-top:2px dotted #960;}
```

Finally, let's change the color of the link and its rollover color

```
div#nav a {text-decoration:none; color: #C60;}
```

```
div#nav a:hover {color: #960;}
```

which results in **Figure 8.9**.

FIGURE 8.9 The left column is now
styled.

Now let's develop the right column.

Styling the Right Column

This column certainly needs some work. First off, the markup is not complete.

The promo graphic should link to the book on Amazon.com. A quick search reveals that the book's URL is www.amazon.com/exec/obidos/ASIN/1882968042/qid=1110169295/sr=2-1/ref=pd_bbs_b_2_1/103-3869840-5485440.

Let's add that to the promo image

```
<div id="rightcolumn">

<a href="http://www.amazon.com/exec/obidos/ASIN/1882968042/
qid=1110169295/sr=2-1/ref=pd_bbs_b_2_1/103-3869840-5485440">

<img src="images/snergs_book_promo.jpg" /></a>

  <div id="newslinks">

  <ul>

  <li>"Snergs" to be re-published by Cold Spring Press -
Summer 2005</li>…
```

If you are working in Internet Explorer for Windows, you will see that adding the link that makes the image clickable has an unwanted side effect; there is now a blue border around the image (**Figure 8.10**).

FIGURE 8.10 Internet Explorer for Windows adds a blue border around an image when you enclose the `image` tag in a `link` tag to make it clickable.

Presumably the developers at Microsoft think users need a visual cue that an image is clickable, but I think this graphic speaks for itself. Certainly, if I wanted a border for this graphic, it wouldn't be pure blue. Let's just get rid of it, like this

```
div#rightcolumn img {border:none;}
```

Now the blue border is gone.

The bigger problem, also apparent in Figure 8.10, is that the right column isn't wide enough to accommodate the graphic. You can see how the content area text is overlapping it.

The graphic is 156 pixels wide and 211 pixels high. It's good practice to add the dimension to any image in the markup because it helps the browser render the page faster. Because I did not do that in the original markup, I need to fix this oversight next. More importantly, we need to adjust some of the template's dimensions to accommodate this graphic.

A quick check of the style sheet reveals that this column is only 125 pixels wide

```
div#rightcolumn {position:absolute; width:125px; top:60px;
right:0px;  margin:20px 15px 0 0; padding:1em  .5em; border-
top:2px solid #069; border-bottom:1px solid #069;}
```

That's also rather narrow for the news headlines that we want to add here; the line length will be very short, so, between this and the graphic issue, we need to make this column wider.

The obvious first step is to set the right column's 125 pixels (high-lighted in the code on the previous page) to 156 pixels—the width of the graphic. Although this makes the column wider, text from the content area still overlaps it.

FIGURE 8.11 Widening the column gives the graphic more space, but the center column's right margin isn't wide enough and therefore it overlaps.

The layout requires the center column to have left and right margins with areas wide or wider than the left and right columns, respectively, to prevent the content area from intruding into the columns. This is exactly the problem you see in Figure 8.11. We need to increase the right margin on the center column as well as clean up some of the right column styles; for example, removing the margins from the right column will make it flush with the right edge of the browser, and removing its left/right padding will make the graphic fill the width of the column. The overall objective is to make the column accommodate that 156-pixel-wide graphic perfectly (instead of trimming the graphic to fit, always the other option), so, first, take care of the center column

```
div#content {margin:20px 156px 0 165px; padding: 0 1em;}
```

then the right column

```
div#rightcolumn {position:absolute; width:156px; top:60px;
right:0px;    margin:20px 15px 0 0; padding:1em 0; border-
top:2px solid #069; border-bottom:1px solid #069;}
```

and then don't forget to add the image dimensions and a missing `alt` attribute to the markup

```
<img src="images/snergs_book_promo.jpg" width="156"
height="211" alt="Buy 'The Marvellous Land of Snergs' at
Amazon.com" /></a>
```

Take a look with the border of the center column temporarily turned on to check exactly how the two columns relate (see **Figures 8.12a** and **8.12b**). The top border of the right column is already visible (the code is not shown for the temporary thin black border on the content area—you know how to do that by now).

FIGURES 8.12A AND 8.12B Internet Explorer for Windows is shown on the left and Safari is shown on the right. Both show very similar results in the relationship between the center and right column. Note that a thin black border is temporarily turned on in the center column to show how nicely it aligns with the right column.

OK, that looks good, so let's move on to styling the news links in the right column.

Styling the News Links

The first step in styling the news links is to remove the bullets from the list and make the type size smaller

```
div#rightcolumn div#newslinks ul {list-style-type:none; font-size:.7em;}
```

Unstyled lists achieve their layouts differently depending on the browser—some use padding and some use margins—so it's important to set both on a `ul` element to override the defaults

```
div#rightcolumn div#newslinks ul {list-style-type:none; font-size:.7em; margin-left:0; padding-left: 10px;}
```

This gets us to **Figure 8.13.**

FIGURE 8.13 The list needs `link` tags to be added to make the list items clickable.

Now let's finish the markup on the links

```
<ul>

  <li><a href="#">"Snergs" to be re-published by Cold Spring Press - Summer 2005</a></li>

  <li><a href="#">Douglas Anderson, Tolkien scholar, discusses the Snergs</a> </li>

  <li class="morelink"><a href="#">more news</a></li>

  </ul>
```

and give them some styles

```
div#rightcolumn a {color: #C60; text-decoration:underline}
```

```
div#rightcolumn a:hover {color: #960; text-decoration: none;}
```

```
div#rightcolumn li.morelink {font-style:italic;}
```

Next, we need to add markup for a heading for these news items

```
<div id="newslinks">

  <h3>Snergs News</h3>

  <ul>

  <li><a href="#">"Snergs" to be re-published…
```

and then style that heading and reduce the default top margin on the ul element below it to close the gap between the heading and the list

```
div#rightcolumn div#newslinks ul {list-style-type:none; font-
size:.7em; margin-left:0; padding-left: 10px; margin-top:0;}
```

```
div#rightcolumn h3 {text-align:center; font-size:.8em;
color:#960; margin-bottom:0px; padding-top:3px; border-
top:2px dotted #960;}
```

Note that I added a dotted line above the heading by styling its border-top and added a few pixels of padding-top to create a bit of breathing space between the line and the heading (**Figure 8.14**).

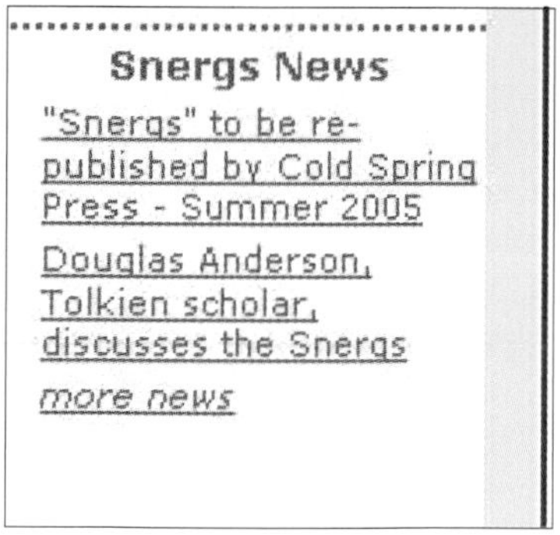

FIGURE 8.14 The news links look much better, but I don't like the way the right side of the links touch the edge of the browser.

Finally, notice that the way the right side of the news links touches the browser's edge isn't very appealing, so let's set the right margin on the ul element to fix that. Because you are now adding a third margin style, you should consolidate them into a single shorthand style

```
div#rightcolumn div#newslinks ul {list-style-type:none; font-size:.7em; padding-left: 10px; margin:0 6px 0 0;}
```

Now it's time to turn off the temporary border on the center column that's been a useful reference during these last steps; then take a look at the finished right column (**Figure 8.15**).

FIGURE 8.15 Here's the finished right column.

Creating the Content Area

Now let's move on to the content area.

We'll deal with the headline last, once the rest of the page is done. Start by wrapping the text around the picture of Mother Meldrum, the old witch disguised as a peddler (**Figure 8.16**). (I'll add back some text I removed earlier also.)

```
div#content img {float:left; border: 1px solid #096; margin:0
4px 4px 0;}
```

FIGURE 8.16 Floating the image causes the text to wrap around it.

Because the image is primarily white on a white page, you can see that I added a border and small right and bottom margins to ensure that the text will not touch it.

CREATING A CAPTION FOR THE MAIN IMAGE

Now add a caption for the picture of the witch. The easiest way to do this is to add the caption text in a paragraph directly after the image in the markup and wrap both the image and the paragraph in a div

```
<div id="mainimage">

  <img alt="Mother Meldrum in disguise, from the book 'The
Marvellous Land of Snergs'" src="images/meldrum_in_disguise_
180w.jpg" width="180" height="212"/>

  <p class="caption">Mother Meldum disguised as a peddler</p>

</div>
```

Next you need to float the div; the paragraph is a block level element, so it automatically appears under the picture. Let's change the styles by moving the float and the margins from the image on to your new div and styling the new paragraph

```
div#content div#mainimage {width:180px; float:left; margin:0
4px 4px 0;}
```

```
div#content div#mainimage img {float:left; border: 1px solid
#960; margin:0 4px 4px 0;}
```

```
div#content div#mainimage p {font-size:.65em; margin:0px
5px;}
```

Next, style the blockquote. The blockquote tag is specifically designed for material that is quoted, so it's the right element to use for this Tolkien quote.

You don't need to put quote marks around text in a blockquote. No tag specifically for attributing the quote exists, and very few tags validate when you use them within a blockquote. That's why you need to put Tolkien's name in a p tag.

You want the blockquote to float to the right and have the main body text wrap around it. (I added back the text I temporarily removed now, so you can clearly see this.)

Figure 8.17 and the code here show the styling for the blockquote

```
div#content blockquote {width: 250px; float:right; font-
size:.7em; border-top: 3px dotted #960; border-bottom:2px
dotted #960; margin:0 10px; padding: 6px 10px;}
```

```
div#content blockquote p {margin:0;font-style:italic}
```

I won't get into all the issues surrounding the use of blockquotes here; there is a good article at the "Web authoring and surfing" on the free information site IT and communication by Jukka "Yucca" Korpela (www.cs.tut.fi/~jkorpela/html/ bq.html).

FIGURE 8.17 The blockquote floats to the right, with small margins to create space around it and a small amount of padding to hold the text away from the edge of the blockquote container.

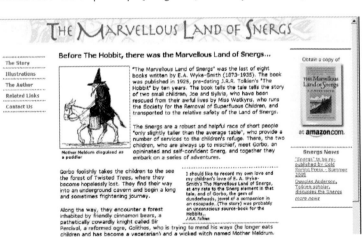

The most important steps are setting the blockquote's width and its float. Other new styles include dotted lines running across the top and bottom of the quote, a margin you can use to create some space on each side of the quote, and padding you can use to bring the text in from the edge, making the lines extended beyond the text on each side. Take the margin off the paragraph with the attribution to tuck it up under the quote.

Then all that's left to do in the content area, besides adding the footer, is to style the link at the end of the text (and we'll also add the quote mark that is missing from the markup at the beginning of the book's title in that link!) (see **Figure 8.18**).

```
div#content a {color:#C60; text-decoration:underline;}

div#content a:hover {color: #960; text-decoration:none;}
```

FIGURE 8.18 The link is now underlined in its regular "unrolled" state.

knight called Sir Percival, a reformed ogre, Golithos, who eats children and has become a vegetarian) and a wicked Read more about "The Marvellous Land of Snergs"

FIGURE 8.19 When the link is rolled, it changes color and the underlining is removed.

knight called Sir Percival, a reformed ogre, Golithos, wh eats children and has become a vegetarian) and a wick Read more about "The Marvellous Land of Snergs"

Styling the Footer

We can quickly lay out the footer with the footer styles we developed in Chapter 5. To do so, download the file called footer_template from the Components folder on the Stylin' site (www.bbd.com/stylin), open the file, and copy the following (heavily commented!) styles into the style sheet

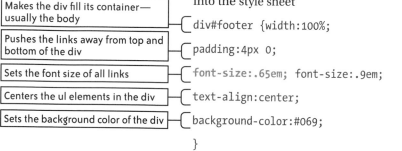

Makes the div fill its container—usually the body	`div#footer {width:100%;`
Pushes the links away from top and bottom of the div	`padding:4px 0;`
Sets the font size of all links	`font-size:.65em; font-size:.9em;`
Centers the ul elements in the div	`text-align:center;`
Sets the background color of the div	`background-color:#069;`
	`}`

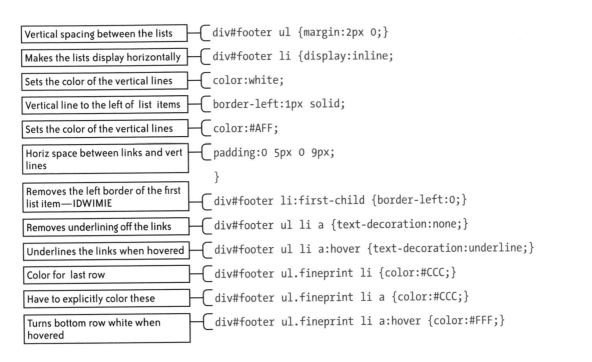

Vertical spacing between the lists	`div#footer ul {margin:2px 0;}`
Makes the lists display horizontally	`div#footer li {display:inline;`
Sets the color of the vertical lines	`color:white;`
Vertical line to the left of list items	`border-left:1px solid;`
Sets the color of the vertical lines	`color:#AFF;`
Horiz space between links and vert lines	`padding:0 5px 0 9px;` `}`
Removes the left border of the first list item—IDWIMIE	`div#footer li:first-child {border-left:0;}`
Removes underlining off the links	`div#footer ul li a {text-decoration:none;}`
Underlines the links when hovered	`div#footer ul li a:hover {text-decoration:underline;}`
Color for last row	`div#footer ul.fineprint li {color:#CCC;}`
Have to explicitly color these	`div#footer ul.fineprint li a {color:#CCC;}`
Turns bottom row white when hovered	`div#footer ul.fineprint li a:hover {color:#FFF;}`

FIGURE 8.20 The footer needs some adjustment to the colors, but the layout is good for the first time. Note that because a specific link rollover color is not yet defined in the footer styles, it is inherited from the containing content div.

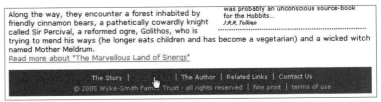

Along the way, they encounter a forest inhabited by friendly cinnamon bears, a pathetically cowardly knight called Sir Percival, a reformed ogre, Golithos, who is trying to mend his ways (he longer eats children and has become a vegetarian) and a wicked witch named Mother Meldrum.
Read more about "The Marvellous Land of Snergs"

was probably an unconscious source-book for the Hobbits...
J.R.R. Tolkien

The Story | | The Author | Related Links | Contact Us
© 2005 Wyke-Smith Family Trust - all rights reserved | fine print | terms of use

With the modification of the one style noted (which was made because we have a reduced "master" font size inherited from the body tag, and further inheritance of 0.65 of an em makes the type unreadably small), the first preview is a pretty good start.

Here's a great example of how taking the time to archive components can really speed up development. This footer probably took at least an hour to write and fine-tune the first time, but because we are reusing a suitable set of styles, and because the markup is always a basic list format, it now only takes a few minutes to create a suitable footer.

We now need to work on the background and type colors. First, let's pick a background color that's more in keeping with the overall design—the green from the header graphic. We'll style the links and the little dividers between them with the same colors we used for the other links (**Figure 8.21**).

```
div#footer li {display:inline; color:white; border-left:1px
solid; color:#C60; padding:0 5px 0 9px; }

 div#footer li:first-child {border-left:0;}

div#footer ul li a {text-decoration:none; color:C60;}

div#footer ul li a:hover {text-decoration:underline;
color:#960;}

 div#footer ul.fineprint li {color:#C60;}

div#footer ul.fineprint li a {color:#C60;}

div#footer ul.fineprint li a:hover {color:#960;}
```

FIGURE 8.21 Here is the styled footer with the new background and link colors.

Figure 8.22 shows where you are at this point.

FIGURE 8.22 The big styling tasks are done. It's cleanup time.

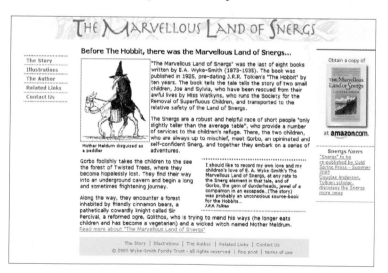

Cleanup Time

With the main elements styled, it's time to provide the finishing touches. The header and the page color are too similar; as a result, it's a good idea to either insert a dividing line or change the background color of the page. The same could be said for the footer. There is too much space around the navigation on the left side; let's look at closing that up. The right column still has blue lines at the top and bottom—you need to either change or lose them—and the news items are too close together. There are two minor markup changes we need to make: we need to place quotes around the book title in the block quote and add a period at the end of the picture caption.

You can imagine what the markup changes look like, but it's worth looking closer at the other issues. Let's start with the left column (**Figure 8.23**)

```
div#nav {position:absolute; left:0px; top:60px; width:150px;

padding:.5em 0 0 0; margin:22px 0 0 0;}

div#nav ul {border:0; margin:12px 1.25em 12px 1.25em;
padding:0; list-style-type:none; font-weight:bold; font-
size:.75em;}

div#content {margin:20px 156px 0 150px; padding: 0 1em;}
```

FIGURE 8.23 With the margins adjusted, the navigation element is centered in the left column and the center column's margin is closer to the left column.

Now we need to clean up on the right side by recoloring those top and bottom lines of the content

```
div#rightcolumn {position:absolute; width:156px; top:60px;
right:0px;

    margin:20px 0 0 0; padding:1em  0; border-top:2px
solid #069; border-bottom:1px solid #069000;}
```

and by adding some lines to define the header and footer to give them a little more definition

```
div#header {height:60px; background-color:#FFC; text-align:
center; border-bottom: 1px #960 solid;}
```

```
div#footer {width:100%; padding:4px 0; font-size:.9em; text-
align:center; background-color:#DEE7B6; border-top:1px solid
#960; border-bottom:2px solid #960;}
```

When thinking about styling the headline, you might realize its text redundant; right now, the title of the book appears three times at the top of the page. Let's do something a little more creative with the headline, and as a tie-in, change the picture to represent the hero of the story. First, go over the markup

```
<div id="content">

  <h1>Before The Hobbit, there was Gorbo the Snerg.</h1>

  <div id="mainimage">

   <img alt="Gorbo the Snerg, from the book 'The Marvellous
Land of Snergs'" src="images/gorbo_180w.jpg" width="180"
height="248" />  <p class="caption">Gorbo returns from
hunting in the forest.</p></div>

  <p>"The Marvellous Land of Snergs" was the last of eight
books written by E.A.

   Wyke-Smith (1873-1935)…(etc.)
```

Next, style the headline

```
div#content h1{font-size:1.4em; font-variant:small-caps;
margin-top:2em; font-family:'comic sans MS', verdana, sans-
serif;}
```

Note the use of font-variant to style the type into large and small capital letters (remember Chapter 3?), but, of course, IDWIMIE; in this case, Internet Explorer just displays regular type. Let's also increase the image's right margin to move the text further away from the right edge of the picture

```
div#content div#mainimage {width:180px; float:left; margin:0
8px 4px 0;}
```

OK, now take a look at **Figure 8.24** to see what this looks like.

As you can see, a few things aren't very appealing. For instance, the caption under the photo is lost in all the surrounding type, and news items are all scrunched together (except in Internet Explorer for Windows). And that orange headline is . . . well, let's just say it's too strong. The orange headline is the visual entry point for reading, so you need it to attract, not jar. Also, there's a little too much space between the main paragraphs. Let's fix these things.

First, the picture caption could actually benefit from the "pop" of the headline's orange color because it's so small

```
div#content div#mainimage p {font-size:.65em; margin:0px 5px;
color:#C60;}
```

The headline, currently in that same color, is too eye-catching, so switch to a darker option

```
div#content h1{font-size:1.4em; font-variant:small-caps;
margin-top:2em; font-family:'comic sans MS', verdana, sans-
serif; color: #960;}
```

Next, fix the spacing problem between the news headlines on the right. The solution is simple. Because that distance was never specified, there is no li selector. So al you need to do is write one and set the top margin to zero and the bottom one to half the line height. Remember, vertical margins collapse, so you only need to spec one of them in this kind of situation; you can kill the other so that you know which one is controlling the spacing.

```
div#rightcolumn div#newslinks li {margin-top:0; margin-
bottom:.5em;}
```

Last but not least, tighten up the space between the paragraphs. This involves the same question you asked yourself in the previous example, is it the top margin or the bottom margin that dominates in the collapse? Who cares? Just set one to zero and spec the other

```
div#content p {font-size:.8em; margin-top:0; margin-
bottom:.5em;
```

Try this technique when you have paragraphs that appear one after the other; it lets you take absolute control over the distance between them. These little touches add up and take your layout into a professional-looking world with minimal effort. For instance, I strive to create a "flirtation" between every character, word, paragraph, and element, and the sum of all these details yields in an overall harmony to even the simplest design.

Now you want to align the top of the right column with the left

```
div#nav {position:absolute; left:0px; top:60px; width:150px;

padding:0; margin:22px 0 15px 0;}div#rightcolumn {position:
absolute; width:156px; top:60px; right:0px; margin:32px
0 0 0; padding:1em  0; border-top:2px solid #960; border-
bottom:1px solid #960;}
```

Now, as you can see in **Figure 8.25**, the appearance is quite consistent between Internet Explorer and other more compliant browsers.

FIGURE 8.25 Here's the improved styling as displayed in Firefox.

FIGURE 8.26 Here's the improved styling as displayed in Internet Explorer.

You still have one final step to take, a technical one. The problem with fluid layouts is that the user can crush them down to nothing or stretch them out so wide that its impossible for the reader's eye to scan accurately from the end of one line to the start of the next (**Figure 8.27**).

FIGURE 8.27 When the user makes the browser very narrow, the center content becomes crushed and the right column overlays it. Not pretty, but fixable.

I've seen data that shows that up to 10 percent of users have JavaScript turned off in their browsers, so keep this in mind when the quality of your user's experience depends on whether he or she can use JavaScript. In this case, the user is still be able to use the site success-fully if the JavaScript doesn't load; but the experience is simply better if it does.

Constraining Min and Max Widths

To prevent these problems, you need to constrain the maximum and minimum widths of the layout. There, CSS had two properties—`min-width` and `max-width`—both specifically for this kind of use, but IDWIMIE. Internet Explorer does implement these properties, so you need to use the `minmax.js` JavaScript function so Internet Explorer can respond to them.

Add a JavaScript folder in your local folder and put the `minmax.js` script into it. Then link the script to the document by adding a script tag in the head of the document.

```
<script type="text/javascript" src="javascript/minmax.js"></
script>
```

Put a div that acts as a wrapper around all of the markup; this ele-ment will have the max and min widths applied to it. This div func-tions as a box around your layout that can only get so wide or so narrow, and everything else is inside it. Modify the markup like this

```
<body>

    <div id="container">

        ...all other the markup in here...

    </div>

</body>
```

Now style the container div like this:

```
div#container {position:relative; min-width:800px; max-
width:1000px; margin-left:auto; margin-right:auto;
background-color:#ECf2C9}
```

Most importantly, you have to set its positioning to `relative`. Now this wrapper div is the closest relatively positioned parent, making it function as the positioning context for the sidebars instead of the body. Without this declaration, the side columns continue to align with the edges of the `body` tag (for example, the edge of the browser window) instead of aligning with the edges of the container div. (Try temporarily removing this declaration to see the result for yourself.)

Once I had this container in place, I couldn't resist coloring its back-ground. As you see in **Figure 8.28**, this is one of those last-minute touches that really unifies the entire layout.

The max-width and min-width declarations set the limits of width for the layout. The auto margins make the mazimized layout center in the browser window when the window reaches the defined max-width. As an added bonus, you now have a div whose area exactly matches the overall dimensions of the layout, so you can color it to provide the design with a background color.

Also, you can't resist, at this late stage, adding a little space above the footer to separate it from the body copy

div#footer {width:100% (etc…) margin-top:1.5em;}

which balances the space at the top.

Now you have a layout that's ready for primetime (**Figure 8.28**).

FIGURE 8.28 Now, after the layout reaches its maximum width, it centers itself in the browser window.

That's it. Your page is finished.

In Closing . . .

As I said at the beginning of this book, technical skills are the underpinnings of creative expression, whether you are a musician, a dancer, or a Web site designer. I hope you found this book to be helpful in building your own technical skills and that you are perhaps even more inspired to pursue your own creative vision. I have filled its pages with the most useful stuff I could think of that you might need to understand and use CSS. This information is a blend of the results of long hours of trying to make things work they way I wanted them, and the encapsulation of the ideas, examples, and advice that so many brilliant and generous people in the Web community have posted for the rest of us to use. Now it's your turn to start stylin'!

The Snergs Site Created with Negative Margins

And for a final parting shot, here's the Snergs page laid out in with negative margins (**Figure 8.29**):

FIGURE 8.29 Here's the Snergs site created with the same styles as in the negative margins template.

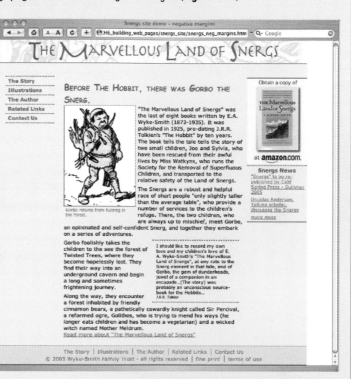

This site looks virtually identical to the version we laid out in this chapter, but if you download the snergs_negative_ margins.htm file from the *Stylin'* site, you will see that the markup is very different. Because we are using a floated columns layout, instead of an absolutely positioned one, we can extend the footer full width as there is no danger of the side columns extending over it if their content becomes very long; the longest column determines the position of the footer with this template, whichever that might be.

CSS Properties and Values

In this appendix, you'll find a listing of all CSS properties and values. The table was reproduced with permission from W3 Schools, an award-winning and free e-learning site for Web developers (www. w3schools.com). This table can be found on the W3 Schools site where every section has links to examples and detailed explanations of each property.

BACKGROUND

PROPERTY	DESCRIPTION	VALUES	NN	IE	W3C
background	A shorthand property for setting all background properties in one declaration	background-color background-image background-repeat background-attachment background-position	6.0	4.0	CSS1
background-attachment	Sets whether a background image is fixed or scrolls with the rest of the page	scroll fixed	6.0	4.0	CSS1
background-color	Sets the background color of an element	color-rgb color-hex color-name transparent	4.0	4.0	CSS1
background-image	Sets an image as the background	url none	4.0	4.0	CSS1
background-position	Sets the starting position of a background image	top left top center top right center left center center center right bottom left bottom center bottom right x-% y-% x-pos y-pos	6.0	4.0	CSS1
background-repeat	Sets if/how a background image will be repeated	repeat repeat-x repeat-y no-repeat	4.0	4.0	CSS1

Key to tables:

• NN: Netscape

• IE: Internet Explorer

• W3C: Web Standard

* All values shown in italic indicate a type of value that can be used. For example color-rgb would indicate that you can specify any RGB color. Values shown in regular type are literals and can be used as is. For example, the word "thin" can actually be used as a value in your CSS code.

BORDER

PROPERTY	DESCRIPTION	VALUES	NN	IE	W3C
border	A shorthand property for setting all of the properties for the four borders in one declaration	border-width border-style border-color	4.0	4.0	CSS1
border-bottom	A shorthand property for setting all of the properties for the bottom border in one declaration	border-bottom-width border-style border-color	6.0	4.0	CSS1
border-bottom-color	Sets the color of the bottom border	border-color	6.0	4.0	CSS2
border-bottom-style	Sets the style of the bottom border	border-style	6.0	4.0	CSS2
border-bottom-width	Sets the width of the bottom border	thin medium thick length	4.0	4.0	CSS1
border-color	Sets the color of the four borders, can have from one to four colors	color	6.0	4.0	CSS1
border-left	A shorthand property for setting all of the properties for the left border in one declaration	border-left-width border-style border-color	6.0	4.0	CSS1
border-left-color	Sets the color of the left border	border-color	6.0	4.0	CSS2
border-left-style	Sets the style of the left border	border-style	6.0	4.0	CSS2
border-left-width	Sets the width of the left border	thin medium thick length	4.0	4.0	CSS1
border-right	A shorthand property for setting all of the properties for the right border in one declaration	border-right-width border-style border-color	6.0	4.0	CSS1
border-right-color	Sets the color of the right border	border-color	6.0	4.0	CSS2
border-right-style	Sets the style of the right border	border-style	6.0	4.0	CSS2
border-right-width	Sets the width of the right border	thin medium thick length	4.0	4.0	CSS1
border-style	Sets the style of the four borders, can have from one to four styles	none hidden dotted dashed solid double groove ridge inset outset	6.0	4.0	CSS1

BORDER

PROPERTY	DESCRIPTION	VALUES	NN	IE	W3C
border-top	A shorthand property for setting all of the properties for the top border in one declaration	border-top-width border-style border-color	6.0	4.0	CSS1
border-top-color	Sets the color of the top border	border-color	6.0	4.0	CSS2
border-top-style	Sets the style of the top border	border-style	6.0	4.0	CSS2
border-top-width	Sets the width of the top border	thin medium thick length	4.0	4.0	CSS1
border-width	A shorthand property for setting the width of the four borders in one declaration, can have from one to four values	thin medium thick length	4.0	4.0	CSS1
border-top	A shorthand property for setting all of the properties for the top border in one declaration	border-top-width border-style border-color	6.0	4.0	CSS1
border-top-color	Sets the color of the top border	border-color	6.0	4.0	CSS2
border-top-style	Sets the style of the top border	border-style	6.0	4.0	CSS2
border-top-width	Sets the width of the top border	thin medium thick length	4.0	4.0	CSS1
border-width	A shorthand property for setting the width of the four borders in one declaration, can have from one to four values	thin medium thick length	4.0	4.0	CSS1
border-top	A shorthand property for setting all of the properties for the top border in one declaration	border-top-width border-style border-color	6.0	4.0	CSS1
border-top-color	Sets the color of the top border	border-color	6.0	4.0	CSS2
border-top-style	Sets the style of the top border	border-style	6.0	4.0	CSS2
border-top-width	Sets the width of the top border	thin medium thick length	4.0	4.0	CSS1
border-width	A shorthand property for setting the width of the four borders in one declaration, can have from one to four values	thin medium thick length	4.0	4.0	CSS1

CLASSIFICATION

PROPERTY	DESCRIPTION	VALUES	NN	IE	W3C
clear	Sets the sides of an element where other floating elements are not allowed	left right both none	4.0	4.0	CSS1
cursor	Specifies the type of cursor to be displayed	url auto crosshair default pointer move e-resize ne-resize nw-resize n-resize se-resize sw-resize s-resize w-resize text wait help	6.0	4.0	CSS2
display	Sets how/if an element is displayed	none inline block list-item run-in compact marker table inline-table table-row-group table-header-group table-footer-group table-row table-column-group table-column table-cell table-caption	4.0	4.0	CSS1
float	Sets where an image or a text will appear in another element	left right none	4.0	4.0	CSS1
position	Places an element in a static, relative, absolute or fixed position	static relative absolute fixed	4.0	4.0	CSS2

DIMENSION

PROPERTY	DESCRIPTION	VALUES	NN	IE	W3C
visibility	Sets if an element should be visible or invisible	visible hidden collapse	6.0	4.0	CSS2
height	Sets the height of an element	auto length %	6.0	4.0	CSS1
line-height	Sets the distance between lines	normal number length %	4.0	4.0	CSS1
max-height	Sets the maximum height of an element	none length %			CSS2
max-width	Sets the maximum width of an element	none length %			CSS2
min-height	Sets the minimum height of an element	length %			CSS2
min-width	Sets the minimum width of an element	length %			CSS2
width	Sets the width of an element	auto % length	4.0	4.0	CSS1

FONT

PROPERTY	DESCRIPTION	VALUES	NN	IE	W3C
font	A shorthand property for setting all of the properties for a font in one declaration	font-style font-variant font-weight font-size/line-height font-family caption icon menu message-box small-caption status-bar	4.0	4.0	CSS1
font-family	A prioritized list of font family names and/or generic family names for an element	family-name generic-family	4.0	3.0	CSS1

FONT

PROPERTY	DESCRIPTION	VALUES	NN	IE	W3C
font-size	Sets the size of a font	xx-small x-small small medium large x-large xx-large smaller larger length %	4.0	3.0	CSS1
font-size-adjust	Specifies an aspect value for an element that will preserve the x-height of the first-choice font	none number			CSS2
font-stretch	Condenses or expands the current font-family	normal wider narrower ultra-condensed extra-condensed condensed semi-condensed semi-expanded expanded extra-expanded ultra-expanded			CSS2
font-style	Sets the style of the font	normal italic oblique	4.0	4.0	CSS1
font-variant	Displays text in a small-caps font or a normal font	normal small-caps	6.0	4.0	CSS1
font-weight	Sets the weight of a font	normal bold bolder lighter 100 200 300 400 500 600 700 800 900	4.0	4.0	CSS1

GENERATED CONTENT

PROPERTY	DESCRIPTION	VALUES	NN	IE	W3C
content	Generates content in a document. Used with the :before and :after pseudo-elements	string url counter(name) counter(name, list-style-type) counters(name, string) counters(name, string, list-style-type) attr(X) open-quote close-quote no-open-quote no-close-quote			CSS2
counter-increment	Sets how much the counter increments on each occurrence of a selector	none identifier number			CSS2
counter-reset	Sets the value the counter is set to on each occurrence of a selector	none identifier number			CSS2
quotes	Sets the type of quotation marks	none string string			CSS2

LIST AND MARKER

PROPERTY	DESCRIPTION	VALUES	NN	IE	W3C
list-style	A shorthand property for setting all of the properties for a list in one declaration	list-style-type list-style-position list-style-image	6.0	4.0	CSS1
list-style-image	Sets an image as the list-item marker	none url	6.0	4.0	CSS1
list-style-position	Sets where the list-item marker is placed in the list	inside outside	6.0	4.0	CSS1

TITLE

PROPERTY	DESCRIPTION	VALUES	NN	IE	W3C
list-style-type	Sets the type of the list-item marker	none disc circle square decimal decimal-leading-zero lower-roman upper-roman lower-alpha upper-alpha lower-greek lower-latin upper-latin hebrew armenian georgian cjk-ideographic hiragana katakana hiragana-iroha katakana-iroha	4.0	4.0	CSS1
marker-offset		auto length			CSS2

MARGIN

PROPERTY	DESCRIPTION	VALUES	NN	IE	W3C
margin	A shorthand property for setting the margin properties in one declaration	margin-top margin-right margin-bottom margin-left	4.0	4.0	CSS1
margin-bottom	Sets the bottom margin of an element	auto length %	4.0	4.0	CSS1
margin-left	Sets the left margin of an element	auto length %	4.0	3.0	CSS1
margin-right	Sets the right margin of an element	auto length %	4.0	3.0	CSS1
margin-top	Sets the top margin of an element	auto length %	4.0	3.0	CSS1

OUTLINES

PROPERTY	DESCRIPTION	VALUES	NN	IE	W3C
outline	A shorthand property for setting all the outline properties in one declaration	outline-color outline-style outline-width			CSS2
outline-color	Sets the color of the outline around an element	color invert			CSS2
outline-style	Sets the style of the outline around an element	none dotted dashed solid double groove ridge inset outset			CSS2
outline-width	Sets the width of the outline around an element	thin medium thick length			CSS2

PADDING

PROPERTY	DESCRIPTION	VALUES	NN	IE	W3C
padding	A shorthand property for setting all of the padding properties in one declaration	padding-top padding-right padding-bottom padding-left	4.0	4.0	CSS1
padding-bottom	Sets the bottom padding of an element	length %	4.0	4.0	CSS1
padding-left	Sets the left padding of an element	length %	4.0	4.0	CSS1
padding-right	Sets the right padding of an element	length %	4.0	4.0	CSS1
padding-top	Sets the top padding of an element	length %	4.0	4.0	CSS1

POSITIONING

PROPERTY	DESCRIPTION	VALUES	NN	IE	W3C
bottom	Sets how far the bottom edge of an element is above/below the bottom edge of the parent element	auto % length	6.0	5.0	CSS2
clip	Sets the shape of an element. The element is clipped into this shape, and displayed	shape auto	6.0	4.0	CSS2

POSITIONING

PROPERTY	DESCRIPTION	VALUES	NN	IE	W3C
left	Sets how far the left edge of an element is to the right/left of the left edge of the parent element	auto % length	4.0	4.0	CSS2
overflow	Sets what happens if the content of an element overflow its area	visible hidden scroll auto	6.0	4.0	CSS2
right	Sets how far the right edge of an element is to the left/right of the right edge of the parent element	auto % length		5.0	CSS2
top	Sets how far the top edge of an element is above/below the top edge of the parent element	auto % length	4.0	4.0	CSS2
vertical-align	Sets the vertical alignment of an element	baseline sub super top text-top middle bottom text-bottom length %	4.0	4.0	CSS1
z-index	Sets the stack order of an element	auto number	6.0	4.0	CSS2

PROPERTY

PROPERTY	DESCRIPTION	VALUES	NN	IE	W3C
border-collapse	Sets the border model of a table	collapse separate		5.0	CSS2
border-spacing	Sets the distance between the borders of adjacent cells (only for the "separated borders" model)	length length			CSS2
caption-side	Sets the position of the caption according to the table	top bottom left right			CSS2
empty-cells	Sets whether cells with no visible content should have borders or not (only for the "separated borders" model)	show hide	6.2		CSS2
table-layout	Sets the algorithm used to lay out the table	auto fixed		5.0	CSS2

TEXT

PROPERTY	DESCRIPTION	VALUES	NN	IE	W3C
color	Sets the color of a text	color	4.0	3.0	CSS1
direction	Sets the text direction	ltr rtl			CSS2
letter-spacing	Increase or decrease the space between characters	normal length	6.0	4.0	CSS1
text-align	Aligns the text in an element	left right center justify	4.0	4.0	CSS1
text-decoration	Adds decoration to text	none underline overline line-through blink	4.0	4.0	CSS1
text-indent	Indents the first line of text in an element	length %	4.0	4.0	CSS1
text-shadow		none color length			
text-transform	Controls the letters in an element	none capitalize uppercase lowercase	4.0	4.0	CSS1
unicode-bidi		normal embed bidi-override		5.0	CSS2
white-space	Sets how white space inside an element is handled	normal pre nowrap	4.0	5.5	CSS1
word-spacing	Increase or decrease the space between words	normal length	6.0	6.0	CSS1

Index

SYMBOLS

* (asterisk), universal selector, 47
: (colon), pseudo-classes, 51
(hash symbol), IDs, 46

A

absolute method, sizing fonts, 76
absolute positioning, 114–115
absolute values, declarations, 61
acronyms, markup basics, 23
active links, anchor link pseudo-class, 50
:after pseudo-class, 53
Alsett, Tony, 144
Alsett Clearing method, three-column page layout, 144–147
alt tags, 49
anchor links, pseudo-classes, 50–51
Arial Black font, common to Mac and Windows, 72
Arial font, common to Mac and Windows, 72
Arial Narrow font, common to Mac and Windows, 72
asterisk (*), universal selector, 47
attributes
    defining, 15
    selector, 48–49
    XHTML rules, 15
authors, style sheet, 56
auto margins, 157–158

B

background-attachment property, 255
background-color property, 255
background-image property, 151–153, 255
background-position property, 255
background property, 255
background-repeat property, 151–153, 255
backgrounds, 150
    adding graphics, 150
    basics, 151–153
    drop-down lists rollovers, 205–208
    full-length columns, 153–154
        adding to layout, 160–162
        faux-column technique, 154–160
Backslash-Comment hack, 185
:before pseudo-class, 53
block level tags, XHTML rules, 14

blockquote tag, 228
body tags, markup basics, 20
border-bottom-color property, 256
border-bottom property, 256
border-bottom-style property, 256
border-bottom-width property, 256
border-collapse property, 264
border-color property, 256
border-left-color property, 256
border-left property, 256
border-left-style property, 256
border-left-width property, 256
border property, 256
border-right-color property, 256
border-right property, 256
border-right-style property, 256
border-right-width property, 256
border-spacing property, 264
border-style property, 256
border-top-color property, 257
border-top property, 257
border-top-style property, 257
border-top-width property, 257
border-width property, 257
bottom property, 263
Bowman, Doug, faux-column technique, 154
box model, 102–103
    border, 103–105
    collapsing margins, 108–109
    margins, 106–107
    padding, 106
    width, 109–111
browsers
    default styles, 17
    default style sheets, 55

C

captions, three-column layouts, 241–243
caption-side property, 264
cascade
    rules, 57–59
    style sources, 55–56
Cascading Style Sheets. See CSS
Caslon, Steve, 170
CDATA tags, 32
center value, text-align property, 92
centimeters, absolute values, 61

Century Gothic font, common to Mac and Windows, 72
check boxes, forms, 213–215
Clagnut Web site, 77
classes
    versus IDs, 46–47
    naming, 21
    pseudo-classes
        anchor links, 50–51
        condition application, 52
    targeting tags, 41
        contextual class selectors, 43–45
        simple use, 42
classification properties, 258
clearfix code, 210
clear property, 118–121, 258
clip property, 263
collapsing margins, box model, 108–109
collections, fonts, 68, 69–70
colon (:), pseudo-classes, 51
colors
    inheritance, 54
    name values, 64
    properties, 265
        box border, 103
    value declarations, 60, 63–64
    web-safety, 64
columns
    full-length
        adding to layout, 160–162
        faux-column technique, 154–160
        page layouts, 153–162
    three-column layouts, 130–134
        Alsett Clearing method, 144–147
        floating footer, 139–144
        header, 135–139
        Web site creation, 227–253
    two-column layouts, 126–130
Comic Sans MS font, common to Mac and Windows, 72
commands, View menu, Text Size, 82
comments, 20
components, interface
    drop-down menus, 186–208
    forms, 208–217
    links, 184–185
    lists, 174–183
    search, 217–219
content, 5
    declaring type, XHTML rules, 13
    properties, 261
    property, 261
    three-column layouts, 241–243
contextual selectors, targeting tags, 37–40
The Counter.com Web site, 156

counter-increment property, 261
counter-reset property, 261
Courier New font, common to Mac and Windows, 72
CSS2, 4
CSS3, 4
CSS (Cascading Style Sheets), 5
    basics
        cascade, 55–59
        embedded styles, 32–33
        inheritance, 54–55
        inline styles, 30–32
        linked styles, 33–34
        pseudo-classes, 50–52
        pseudo-elements, 53
        targeting tags, 36–50
    declarations, 60
        color values, 63–64
        numerical values, 61–62
        writing rules, 35–36
    defining, 34
    rules
        structure, 35
        writing, 35–36
CSS-Discuss Web site, 77
cursive fonts, 70
cursor property, 258

D

declarations, 60
    color values, 63–64
    numerical values, 61–62
    writing CSS rules, 35–36
definition lists, 174
deprecated tags, 11
dimension properties, 259
direction property, 265
display property, 122, 258
Dive Into Mark Web site, 12
div tags, markup basics, 20–22
DOCTYPEs, XHTML
    compliance rules, 12
    markup basics, 17–18
documents
    font styling, 74
    hierarchy
        inheritance, 54–55
        targeting tags, 36–50
        XHTML, 25–27
    presentation, 5
    structure, 5
document type definition (DTD), 10

drop-down menus
    creating, 195–202
    horizontal navigation element, 186–193
    Internet Explorer hover behavior, 193–195
    multiple levels, 203–205
DTD (document type definition), 10

E

elements
    positioning
        box model, 102–109
        clear property, 119–121
        display property, 122
        float property, 117–118
        position property, 112–116
        widths, 109–111
    pseudo-elements, 53
embedded styles, 32–33
    font families, 74–75
empty-cells property, 264
em values
    declarations, 61
    font sizes, 62
encoding entities, XHTML rules, 16
entities, encoding, XHTML rules, 16
eXtensible HyperText Markup Language. See XHTML
ex values, declarations, 61

F

faces, fonts, 68
families, fonts, 68, 72–74
    embedded styles, 74–75
    generic font families, 71
    setting for entire page, 75–76
fantasy fonts, 70
faux-column technique, 154–160
Firefox
    font-weight property, 85
    generic font families, 71
:first pseudo-class, 53
fixed positioning, 115–116
floating footers, three-column layouts, 139–144, 243–245
float property, 117–118, 258
fluid layouts, converting from fixed-width, 162–167
font-family properties, 73, 259
font property, 85–86, 259

fonts, 68
    collections, 69–70
    common to Mac and Windows, 72
    em value, 62
    families, 72–74
        embedded styles, 74–75
        setting for entire page, 75–76
    generic font families, 71
    inherited styles in nested tags, 81–82
    properties, 259–260
        font shorthand, 85–86
        font-style, 83–84
        font-variant, 85
        font-weight, 84–85
    sizing, 76–81
    styling markup, 97–99
font-size-adjust property, 260
font-size property, 86, 260
font-stretch property, 260
font-style property, 83–84, 260
font-variant property, 85, 260
font-weight property, 84–85, 260
footers, three-column layouts, 139–144, 243–245
forms
    check boxes, 213–215
    creating select element, 215–217
    element, 208–213
    radio buttons, 213–215
frameset DOCTYPEs, 12
Franklin Gothic font, common to Mac and Windows, 72
full-length columns, page layouts, 153–154
    adding to layout, 160–162
    faux-column technique, 154–160

G

Garrett, Jesse James, x
generic font families, 71
Georgia font, common to Mac and Windows, 72
graphics
    adding, 150
    backgrounds, 150–153
    drop-down menu rollovers, 205–208

H

hacks, 4, 185
hash symbol (#), IDs, 46
headers, three-column layouts, 135–139, 230–231
head tags, markup basics, 18

height property, 259
hexadecimal values, colors, 63
home pages
  architecture, 226
  folder structure, 223–225
  three-column layouts, 227–230
    constraining minimum and maximum widths,
      251–253
    content area, 241–243
    finishing touches, 246–250
    footer, 243–245
    header, 230–231
    left navigation column, 232–234
    news links, 238–240
    right column styling, 234–237
horizontal navigation elements, drop-down menus,
  186–193
hover links, anchor link pseudo-class, 50
:hover pseudo-class, 193
HTML (HyperText Markup Language), 7
  development
    changed original purpose, 7–8
    content non-standard compliant sites, 8–9
    future presentation, 9–10
HTML Tidy, conversion to XHTML, 16
hyperlinks, markup basics, 23

I

IDs
  versus classes, 46–47
  naming, 21
  targeting tags, 46
IDWIMIE (It Doesn't Work In Microsoft Internet Explorer), 4
images
  adding, 150
  backgrounds, 150–153
img tag, markup basics, 21
Impact font, common to Mac and Windows, 72
inches, absolute values, 61
Infohound Web site, 16
inheritance, 54–55
  font styles in nested tags, 81–82
  text-indent property values, 89
inline styles, 30–32
inline tags, XHTML rules, 14
Inman, Shaun, 229
interface components
  drop-down menus
    creating, 195–202
    horizontal navigation element, 186–193
    Internet Explorer hover behavior, 193–195
    multiple levels, 203–208

forms
  check boxes, 213–215
  creating select element, 215–217
  form element, 208–213
  radio buttons, 213–215
  links, 184–185
  lists, 174–183
  search, 217–219
Internet Explorer
  auto margins, 157
  bulleted lists, 178
  floating elements, 170
  generic font families, 71
  hacks, 185
  hover behavior, 193–195
  Web standards, 4
It Doesn't Work In Microsoft Internet Explorer (IDWIMIE), 4

J - K

Jak Psat Web site, 93
justify value, text-align property, 92

keywords method, sizing fonts, 76

L

:lang pseudo-class, 53
layouts, 149–150
  backgrounds, 150–153
  converting to fluid layout, 162–167
  full-length columns, 153–154
    adding to layout, 160–162
    faux-column technique, 154–160
  negative margins, 167–171
  three-column, 130–134
    Alsett Clearing method, 144–147
    floating footer, 139–144
    header, 135–139
  two-column, 126–130
leading, 62, 92
left navigation columns, three-column layouts, 232–234
left property, 264
left value, text-align property, 92
letter-spacing property, 90, 265
line-height property, 92–93, 259
linked styles, 33–34
links
  anchor link pseudo-class, 50
  interface components, 184–185
  tags, 19–20, 238
  three-column layouts, 238–240

A List Apart Web site, 76
lists
    interface components, 174–183
    markup basics, 22–23
    properties, 261
list-style-image property, 261
list-style-position property, 175, 261
list-style property, 261
list-style-type property, 175, 262
local styles, 30–32

M

Mac, font-weight property, 85
margin-bottom property, 262
margin-left property, 262
margin property, 262
margin-right property, 262
margins
    auto, 157–158
    box model, 106–107
    negative, 167–171
    properties, 262
margin-top property, 262
marker-offset property, 262
marker properties, 261
markup
    styling with font and text, 97–99
    XHTML
        basics, 17–24
        rules, 11–16
The Marvellous Land of Snergs, 222
max-height property, 259
max-width property, 259
menus
    drop-down
        creating, 195–202
        horizontal navigation element, 186–193
        Internet Explorer hover behavior, 193–195
        multiple levels, 203–208
    lists
        interface components, 174–183
        markup basics, 22–23
meta head tags, markup basics, 19
metatags, 18
Meyer, Eric
    Cascading Style Sheets 2.0, 118
    Web site, 55
Microsoft Web standards, 4
millimeters, absolute values, 61
min-height property, 259

min-width property, 259
monospace fonts, 70
Monotype font, common to Mac and Windows, 72

N

namespaces, 18
navigation
    drop-down menus
        creating, 195–202
        horizontal navigation element, 186–193
        Internet Explorer hover behavior, 193–195
        multiple levels, 203–208
    horizontal navigation element, 186–193
    links
        anchor link pseudo-class, 50
        interface components, 184–185
    lists
        interface components, 174–183
        markup basics, 22–23
negative margins, 167–171, 253
nested lists, 174
nested tags
    inherited font styles, 81–82
    XHTML rules, 13–14
Nolan, Michael, x
normal value, 84
numerical values, declarations, 60–62

O

ordered lists, 174
outline-color property, 263
outline property, 263
outlines, properties, 263
outline-style property, 263
outline-width property, 263
overflow property, 264

P

padding
    box model, 106
    properties, 263
padding-bottom property, 263
padding-left property, 263
padding property, 263
padding-right property, 263
padding-top property, 263

page layouts, 149–150
  architecture, 226
  backgrounds, 150–153
  converting to fluid layout, 162–167
  folder structure, 223–225
  full-length columns, 153–154
    adding to layout, 160–162
    faux-column technique, 154–160
  negative margins, 167–171
  three-column, 130–134, 227–230
    Alsett Clearing method, 144–147
    constraining minimum and maximum widths, 251–253
    content area, 241–243
    finishing touches, 246–250
    floating footer, 139–144
    footer, 243–245
    header, 135–139, 230–231
    left navigation column, 232–234
    news links, 238–240
    right column styling, 234–237
  two-column, 126–130
Palatino font, common to Mac and Windows, 72
percentages RGB values, colors, 63
percentage values, declarations, 61
picas, absolute values, 61
pixels, absolute values, 61
points, absolute values, 61
pop-out menus, 203–208
positioning
  context, 114, 116
  elements
    box model, 102–109
    clear property, 119–121
    display property, 122
    float property, 117–118
    position property, 112–116
    widths, 109–111
  properties, 263–264
    absolute, 114–115
    fixed, 115–116
    positioning context, 114, 116
    relative, 113
    static, 112
Position is Everything Web site, 121, 170
position property, 258
presentation, documents, 5
properties, 35
  background, 255
  background-image, 151–153
  background-repeat, 151–153
  border, 256–257
  classification, 258
  content, 261

  declarations, 60
  dimension, 259
  fonts, 68, 259–260
    font shorthand, 85–86
    font-style, 83–84
    font-variant, 85
    font-weight, 84–85
  list, 261
  margins, 262
  outlines, 263
  padding, 263
  positioning, 263–264
    absolute, 114–115
    context, 114, 116
    fixed, 115–116
    relative, 113
    static, 112
  text, 68, 86, 265
    letter-spacing, 90
    line-height, 92–93
    text-align, 92
    text-decoration, 91
    text-indent, 88–89
    text-transform, 94
    vertical-align, 93, 95–96
    word-spacing, 91
  text-align, 157
  title, 262
proportional sizing, fonts, 77
pseudo-classes
  anchor links, 50–51
  condition application, 52
pseudo-elements, 53

Q - R

Quirks mode, 12
quoted attributes, case sensitivity, 15
quotes property, 261

radio buttons, forms, 213–215
Reich, Dan, x
relative method, sizing fonts, 76
relative positioning, 113
relative sizing, fonts, 77
relative values, declarations, 61
right property, 264
:right pseudo-class, 53
right value, text-align property, 92
robust fluid layouts, 162–167
rules, CSS
  structure, 35
  writing, 35–36

S

Safari
    bulleted lists, 178
    font-weight property, 85
    generic font families, 71
sans-serif fonts, 69
    spacing, 70
Schlater, Ian, 228
search component, 217–219
select element, forms, 215–217
selectors, 35
    pseudo-classes, 51
    targeting tags, 36
        adjacent sibling selector, 48
        attribute selectors, 48–49
        child selectors, 40–41
        classes, 41–47
        contextual selectors, 37–40
        IDs, 46–47
        universal selector, 47
    writing CSS rules, 36
serif fonts, 69–70
shorthand styling
    background property, 255
    border property, 256–257
    box borders, 105
    font property, 259
    margin property, 262
    outline property, 263
    padding property, 263
sibling selectors, 48
sites, three-column layouts, 227–230
    constraining minimum and maximum widths, 251–253
    content area, 241–243
    finishing touches, 246–250
    footer, 243–245
    header, 230–231
    left navigation column, 232–234
    news links, 238–240
    right column styling, 234–237
sizing fonts, 76–81
Snergs site, three-column layouts, 227–230
    constraining minimum and maximum widths, 251–253
    content area, 241–243
    finishing touches, 246–250
    footer, 243–245
    header, 230–231
    left navigation column, 232–234
    news links, 238–240
    right column styling, 234–237

span tags, 37
SpiderPro Web site, 10
standards
    markup validation, 11
    Web standards, 4–6
standards-based coding, benefits, 6
Star hack, 185
static positioning, 112
strict DOCTYPEs, 12
structure, documents, 5
styles
    box border properties, 103
    document fonts, 74
    embedded, 32–33
    inline, 30–32
    linked, 33–34
    lists. See lists
    sheets, 10
        cascade, 56
        defining, 34
    tags, markup basics, 18
styles tag, 32
Stylin' with CSS Web site, xi
Symbol font, common to Mac and Windows, 72

T

table-layout property, 264
tables, valign attribute, 93
tags
    case sensitivity, XHTML rules, 14
    closing, XHTML rules, 13
    targeting, 36
        adjacent sibling selector, 48
        attribute selectors, 48–49
        child selectors, 40–41
        classes, 41–47
        contextual selectors, 37–40
        IDs, 46–47
        universal selector, 47
    XHTML (eXtensible HyperText Markup Language), 5
Tahoma font, common to Mac and Windows, 72
targeting tags, 36
    adjacent sibling selector, 48
    attribute selectors, 48–49
    child selectors, 40–41
    classes, 41, 46–47
        contextual class selectors, 43–45
        simple use, 42
    contextual selectors, 37–40
    IDs, 46–47
    universal selector, 47

text, 68
  float property, 117–118
  inheritance, 54
  properties, 86, 265
    letter-spacing, 90
    line-height, 92–93
    text-align, 92
    text-decoration, 91
    text-indent, 88–89
    text-transform, 94
    vertical-align, 93, 95–96
    word-spacing, 91
  snake, 87
  styling markup, 97–99
text-align property, 92, 157, 265
text-decoration property, 91, 265
text-indent property, 88–89, 181, 265
  value inheritance, 89
text-shadow property, 265
Text Size command (View menu), 82
text-transform property, 94, 265
three-column layouts, 130–134
  Alsett Clearing method, 144–147
  floating footer, 139–144
  header, 135–139
  Web site creation, 227–230
    constraining minimum and maximum widths, 251–253
    content area, 241–243
    finishing touches, 246–250
    footer, 243–245
    header, 230–231
    left navigation column, 232–234
    news links, 238–240
    right column styling, 234–237
tiling, 151
Times New Roman font, common to Mac and Windows, 72
title properties, 262
title tags, markup basics, 18–19
Tolkien, J.R.R., 222
top property, 264
transitional DOCTYPEs, 12
Trebuchet MS font, common to Mac and Windows, 72
two-column layouts, 126–130
type
  fonts
    collections, 69–70
    families, 72–76
    generic font families, 71
    inherited styles in nested tags, 81–82
    properties, 83–96
    sizing, 76–81
    styling markup, 97–99

text
  properties, 86–96
  styling markup, 97–99

U

unicode-bidi property, 265
universal selectors, 47
unordered lists, 174
users, style sheet, 56

V

validation, XHTML, 11
valign attribute, tables, 93
values, 35
  declarations, 60
Verdana font, common to Mac and Windows, 72
vertical-align property, 93, 95–96, 264
vertical margins, 108
View menu commands, Text Size, 82
visibility property, 259
visited links, anchor link pseudo-class, 50

W

W3C (World Wide Web Consortium), 4
  cascade information, 57
  markup validator Web site, 11
  Web site
    box model, 102
    cascade information, 57
    markup validator, 11
Web
  sans-serif fonts, 69
  standards, 4–6, 11
Web Design Group Web site, 16
Webdings font, common to Mac and Windows, 72
Web sites, 222–223
  architecture, 226
  Clagnut, 77
  The Counter.com, 156
  CSS-Discuss, 77
  Dive Into Mark, 12
  folder structure, 223–225
  Infohound, 16
  Jak Psat, 93
  A List Apart, 76
  Meyer, Eric, 55
  Position is Everything, 121, 170
  SpiderPro, 10

Stylin' with CSS, xi
three-column layouts, 227–230
    constraining minimum and maximum widths,
       251–253
    content area, 241–243
    finishing touches, 246–250
    footer, 243–245
    header, 230–231
    left navigation column, 232–234
    news links, 238–240
    right column styling, 234–237
W3C (World Wide Web Consortium)
    box model, 102
    cascade information, 57
    markup validator, 11
    Web Design Group, 16
    W3 Schools, 255
white-space property, 265
widths
    box border properties, 103
    box model, 109–111
    property, 259
    three-column layouts, 251–253
Windows, font-weight property, 85
word-spacing property, 91, 265
word values, declarations, 60
World Wide Web Consortium. See W3C
W3 Schools Web site, 255
Wyke-Smith, E. A., The Marvellous Land of Snergs, 222

X – Y – Z

XHTML (eXtensible HyperText Markup Language), 5
    defining, 10
    document hierarchy, 25–27
    element, 5
    HTML development
        changed original purpose, 7–8
        content non-standard compliant sites, 8–9
        future presentation, 9–10
    markup
        basics, 17–24
        rules, 11–16
    sample document, 3
    standards-based coding, benefits, 6
XML, 10
    CDATA tags, 32
    namespaces, XHTML rules, 13

Zeldman, Jeffrey
    classitis, 47
    sizing fonts, 76
z-index property, 264

Visit Peachpit on the Web at www.peachpit.com

- Read the latest articles and download timesaving tipsheets from best-selling authors such as Scott Kelby, Robin Williams, Lynda Weinman, Ted Landau, and more!

- Join the Peachpit Club and save 25% off all your online purchases at peachpit.com every time you shop—plus enjoy free UPS ground shipping within the United States.

- Search through our entire collection of new and upcoming titles by author, ISBN, title, or topic. There's no easier way to find just the book you need.

- Sign up for newsletters offering special Peachpit savings and new book announcements so you're always the first to know about our newest books and killer deals.

- Did you know that Peachpit also publishes books by Apple, New Riders, Adobe Press, Macromedia Press, palmOne Press, and TechTV press? Swing by the Peachpit family section of the site and learn about all our partners and series.

- Got a great idea for a book? Check out our About section to find out how to submit a proposal. You could write our next best-seller!

You'll find all this and more at www.peachpit.com. Stop by and take a look today!